Masculinity in the
Interracial Buddy Film

Masculinity in the Interracial Buddy Film

MELVIN DONALSON

McFarland & Company, Inc., Publishers
Jefferson, North Carolina, and London

With love and appreciation, this book
is for the men who have influenced my manhood:
my father, Wilbert,
my brother, Brian,
my son, Derek,
and my buddy-brothers,
John Jenkins, Marcus Bruce,
James Tobey, Wilfred "Pepie" Samuels,
Bill Edwards, Reggie McDowell,
Fred Lamster, Harold Perkins,
Joseph DaLuz, John Marcelino,
Michael Whitted, David Massey,
Rodney Hooks, Dave Kee,
Bill Paden, Steve Jones

LIBRARY OF CONGRESS CATALOGUING-IN-PUBLICATION DATA

Donalson, Melvin Burke, 1952–
    Masculinity in the interracial buddy film / Melvin Donalson.
        p.   cm.
    Includes bibliographical references and index.

    ISBN 0-7864-2301-3 (softcover : 50# alkaline paper) ∞

    1. Masculinity in motion pictures.   2. Male friendship in
    motion pictures.   3. Race relations in motion pictures.   I. Title.
    PN1995.9.M46D66 2006
    791.43'653 — dc22   2005031068

British Library cataloguing data are available

On the cover: Mel Gibson and Danny Glover in the 1987
Lethal Weapon (Photofest)

Manufactured in the United States of America

McFarland & Company, Inc., Publishers
    Box 611, Jefferson, North Carolina 28640
    www.mcfarlandpub.com

Contents

Acknowledgments

In order to complete a book of this scope, an extensive amount of energy, time, and sacrifice is required. While pressing toward the mark, I received a great deal of support and encouragement along the way.

First of all, I must thank my wife, Beverly, for the never-ending help she provided. More than anyone else, she listened to my ideas and plans for this book, and gave me the most valuable feedback that shaped the content and structure of the manuscript. I am sustained by her thoughtfulness, concern, and love.

Secondly, I have to thank my friend and former student, Aaron Harris. He assisted me with my research, and often took much of his personal time to locate and obtain materials for me. I enjoyed our dinner discussions, and I cherish our common passion for film.

Next, I want to express my gratitude to my colleagues in the English Department at California State University, Los Angeles. Many of them offered useful perspectives about the topic and consistent good wishes: Alfred Bendixen, Mary Bush, Michael Calabrese, Hema Chari, John Cleman, Christopher Herr, Andrew Shin, and the Katherine Carter Fund.

I received considerable assistance from librarians and staff at the Motion Picture Academy's Margaret Herrick Library. I thank them for their knowledgeable and efficient help, especially Eddie Baker and Sandra Archer.

I spent many hours at the Book Castle in Burbank, California, obtaining film stills. I am also extremely grateful for the patience and help given by Pete Bateman at the Larry Edmunds Bookstore in Hollywood, California.

Preface

In 1999, I had the good fortune to be invited to be a columnist for a new magazine that targeted men of color as its national audience. The column was named "Family Rites," and I was excited about writing regular pieces that reflected upon both the memorable and the forgettable about various family relationships. Unfortunately, my tenure with the magazine was short-lived, and after a year the magazine itself faded from the shelves.

However, one essay that I wrote, entitled "My Father's Son," continues to bring me some of the warmest and sincerest compliments ever given about my writing. The piece was republished recently in a book titled *Chicken Soup for the African American Soul* (2004). Interestingly enough, even among my scholarly colleagues, the title of that popular book is better known than the scholarly and literary periodicals that have published my poetry, fiction, and creative nonfiction.

It was that essay that provided me the opportunity to comment on my relationship with my father and my teenage son, and at its core, examined the ways in which "manhood" was manifested within my family. Since that time I have been drawn back to this construct of manhood, and through the classes I've taught in popular culture, ethnic literature, and film studies, my choices for materials and prompts for paper assignments and discussions have returned to this area. For me, this is an ongoing endeavor, just as manhood is a continual process. As I wrote in "My Father's Son" about the "nature of manhood": "It is not someplace that one arrives at like a scheduled train stop on a cross-country holiday. Manhood, like a river, runs true — moving toward its own end, taking its shape and form from the terrain it touches. Like a river, manhood has its recognizable traits — responsibility, commitment, integrity, compassion — but also possesses its own individual qualities."

At the same time that I was working as a columnist, I was enjoying the reception given to my short film, *A Room Without Doors*, at a number of film festivals. The short film was the result of a full-length screenplay that had been optioned, but died in development. In an effort to keep the project alive, I resurrected the central story and moved it into a shorter visual format. The focus of the film was the relationship between an African American father and his son, emphasizing the positive affection and durability of that relationship. With so many negative images of black men sweeping through the media, I wanted to present the fact that many black men, like my father, were committed, responsible, reliable, and inspiring.

My essay and film were personal expressions, but they appeared during a decade that had begun to place the various dimensions of masculinity and manhood in the national spotlight. With Masculinities Studies gaining significance and authenticity in academia, university presses, and popular culture, the discussions about men, both profound and trendy, became part of the public discourse. Likewise, with the increased visibility of men of color in national politics, business, education, publications, films, and television, the complexity of being male in American society became vital. Connected to perspectives and ideas from feminist theory, queer theory, and cultural criticism, the dynamics about masculine identity and behavior received an extensive examination.

My hope is that *Masculinity in the Interracial Buddy Film* will augment the dialogues and debates about the topic, offering information and viewpoints that are crucial to discussions and reflections. This book's study ends in 2003, but hopefully the contents will encourage contemporary and future examinations of the intersection of gender, race, and cinema. Ideally, I hope that all men will actively scrutinize the many lessons taught about being a man via personal relationships, cultural associations, religious doctrines, popular culture, and the dominating social and political order. More importantly, I hope that all men will claim attributes of manhood that affirm their individual souls and spirits.

Introduction: The Intersection of Gender, Race, and Cinematic Genres

American cinema provides such an abundance of messages and notions that audiences take its power for granted. There is, at best, an aesthetical debate about distinguishing Hollywood films from independent films as a way of assessing the former as escapist and the latter as polemical and experimental. Yet scholars and critics continue to caution viewers that the label "Hollywood" doesn't prevent the film's content from issuing significant direct and coded ideas that permeate the viewers' attitudes, emotions, and political postures. Numerous American films have underscored themes and issues about gender, while others have accentuated race and culture. However, in the interracial buddy film, an engaging convergence of these areas serves to validate society's most enduring perspectives about manhood and to optimize its interracial congruence. Often, these perspectives are rigid and unbending, but on occasion, particularly in contemporary films, discernible ripples in the presentation of gender and racial dynamics might occur, reflecting the trends of the given time period.

Gender and Sexuality

Since the 1970s, examinations of gender identification and human sexuality have incorporated interdisciplinary approaches and four interrelated, critical strategies—feminism, masculinity studies, gay and lesbian studies, and queer theory. The driving objective has been to utilize various disciplines and critical approaches to enable a comprehension of the reasons for and nature of the prevailing precepts about gender and sexuality. As scholar Deborah Blum notes, "Sex differences [biologically] are always generalizations: they refer to a behavior, with some evolutionary rationale behind it. They never define, entirely, an individual."[1] Expanding upon that position, sociologist Michael Kimmel concludes: "Men and women are different because we are taught to be different.... We acquire the traits, behaviors, and attitudes that our culture defines as 'masculine' or 'feminine.'"[2] The correlation between one's nature and one's nurturing continues to inflame the debate concerning the determining source of human attitudes and behavior.

Masculinity and manhood, often used synonymously, still intrigue those who attempt to analyze gender configurations. In spite of an individual's autonomy, the existence of broader standards and precepts about masculinity that shape and influence men collectively is undeniable. Scholar Cooper Thompson frames those learned cultural traits in this manner: "Traditional definitions of masculinity include attributes such as independence, pride, resiliency, self-control, and physical strength.... But masculinity goes beyond these qualities to stress competitiveness, toughness, aggressiveness, and power."[3] The attributes of masculinity, which become embedded "norms," are readily observed, though not consistently expressed, by all males at all times. Moreover, on occasion, the anointed aspects of masculinity may vary and be deceptive. As author Lee Clark Mitchell states, the "alchemy for 'making the man' is more complex, dependent on an intricate mixture of bodily and behavioral traits."[4]

Moving outside of those limiting aspects of manhood can be devastating. In some cases the experiences can be brutalizing. In her essay on homophobia, author Carmen Vazquez recounts incidents where heterosexuals were physically attacked simply because they appeared to be gay or lesbian as defined by gender stereotypes. She states that "economic and ideological underpinnings of enforced heterosexism and sexism or any other form of systematic oppression are formidable foes.... [O]ur sacrifices to conformity rarely guarantee ... privilege or protection."[5]

In the contemporary reading of masculinity, the norms articulated have been maintained even while enduring efforts at transformation. Academic and popular studies, as alluded to in chapter five, have examined the relevance of those beliefs, and as indicated in chapter six, certain trendy concepts such as "metrosexual" have entered the public discourse on masculinity, suggesting revisions of the prevailing attributes. However, a fundamental truth serves as the cornerstone to any academic or popular debate about the nature of manhood: the gender doctrines that support the ongoing political-economic system will be maintained, despite any analysis, debate, or trendiness that confronts it. Consequently, the norms at any particular time will be inextricably linked to the dominant power structure, and until that system is replaced, the recognizable attributes mentioned above, in their various manifestations, will remain vital.

American cinema, whether viewed as an art form or a commercial endeavor, becomes an expressive form that emanates from the society of socialized gender within a patriarchal power structure. Therefore, the stories, images, and icons of masculinity will extend themselves from that source, whether camouflaged with labels of "entertainment" or coded in terms such as "film genre" or "film cycles." The best viewers can do is to make powerful political-economic decisions to avoid specific films due to their content, or at the very least, to position themselves as critical thinkers who analyze the intercalated messages and meanings of the viewing experience.

Race, Ethnicity, and Culture

In its progression from a colonial landmark to an independent country, America has wrestled with the many issues related to race and ethnicity. Over generations, the America of the imagination — decorated with concepts such as democracy, freedom, and equality — has collided with the America of actuality, which has perpetuated practices and institutions such as slavery, manifest destiny, reservations, xenophobia, relocation camps, and segregation. The question to be asked about American cinema has never been whether race would be an on-screen element — an already established political-economic fact behind the camera — but rather in what ways race and ethnicity would find depiction. Black scholar W. E. B. DuBois's announcement that "the problem of the twentieth century is the problem of the color line" was a statement of astute comprehension about American society based upon its racial history.[6]

Following the fictional framework of literature, cinema merely visualized the racial representation already made popular in written expression, as well as the popular performance tradition of the minstrel show. That representation affirmed the popular ideas about white superiority and "colored" inferiority as a working model of race relations. As critic Stuart Hall writes, "America has always had a series of ethnicities, and consequently, the construction of ethnic hierarchies has always defined its cultural politics."[7] The appearances of *The Birth of a Nation* (1915) — based upon a novel — as the first feature film, and *The Jazz Singer* (1927) — reflecting the minstrel show — as the first successful synchronized sound film, emphasized the manner in which cinema complemented renditions of race already present in the literature and popular entertainment of the day. American cinema has merely upheld the acceptable and practiced racial machinations, while defending itself against generations of criticism and objections.

Both academic and popular studies have attempted to illuminate and condemn the flaws and distortions of race, ethnicity, and culture in cinema. *Slow Fade to Black* (1977), by Thomas Cripps; *Framing Blackness: The African American Image in Film* (1993), by Ed Guerrero; *Redefining Black Film* (1993), by Mark A. Reid; *Toms, Coons, Mulattoes, Mammies, and Bucks* (2001), by Donald Bogle; and others have evaluated the impact of black screen depictions. *The Only Good Indian: The Hollywood Gospel* (1979), by Ralph E. Friar; *Hollywood's Indian: The Portrayal of the Native American in Films* (1998), by Peter C. Rollins and John E. O'Connor; *Celluloid Indians: Native Americans and Film* (1999), by Jacquelyn Kilpatrick; and others have examined Hollywood's portrayals of indigenous cultures. *Hispanic Hollywood: The Latins in Motion Pictures* (1993), by George Hadley-Garcia; *Latino Images in Film: Stereotypes, Subversion, and Resistance* (2002), by Charles Ramirez Berg; *Heroes, Lovers, and Others: The Story of Latinos in Hollywood* (2004), by Clara E. Rodriguez; and others have assessed the complex grouping referred to as Latinos. *Romance and the "Yellow Peril": Race, Sex, and Discursive Strategies in Hollywood Fiction* (1994), by Gina Marchetti; *Out of the Shadows: Asian American Cinema* (2001), edited by Roger Garcia; *Identities in Motion: Asian American Film and Video* (2002), by Peter X. Feng; and others have investigated the dimensions of Asian American images.

In a similar manner, valuable studies that inspect the ramifications and relevancy of specific cultural expressions, symbols, and icons within American society have often intersected with matters of race and ethnicity. Among the many notable texts are Vito Russo's *The Celluloid Closet: Homosexuality in the Movies* (1987); Alexander Doty's *Making Things Perfectly Queer: Interpreting Mass Culture* (1993); Tricia Rose's *Black Noise: Rap Music and Black Culture in Contemporary America* (1994); Richard Dyer's *White* (1997); David Ehrenstein's *Open Secret: Gay Hollywood, 1928–2000* (2000); Boze Hadleigh's *The Lavender Screen: The Gay and Lesbian Films: Their Stars, Makers, Characters and Critics* (2001); and Bakari Kitwana's *Hip Hop Generation: Young Blacks and the Crisis in African American Culture* (2002).

The above-mentioned works, among others, reflect the significance of race, ethnicity, and culture in cinema — not only for those who might be members of a recognized group but to the general impact on society at large. In a society that owes its existence to diverse groupings of people, an extensive and fair investigation of those people is a reasonable and crucial objective. Race, ethnicity, and culture *do* matter, and cinema, in its collective genres, cannot be immune to the academic and popular dialogues about its contribution to meanings and messages.

Film Genres

In a critical discussion of cinema, at some point the concept of genre enters the discourse. Film scholar Steve Neale asserts that in "the late 1960s and early 1970s" this critical discussion of genre became significant to "theorists, critics, and teachers of film" who sought "to complement, temper or displace altogether the dominant critical approach used hitherto—auteurism."[8] Auteurism proclaims the film's director is, in spite of the contributions of the dozens of collaborators, the key individual whose vision, decision making, and personality dictated and shaped the content and style of a given film; over the years, this analytical approach found both supporters and detractors, as it lionized a selective list of directors. Rather than praising the filmmaker, genre criticism places the focus back upon the film and its resulting connection to audiences. Viewers become an essential component in the process of qualifying the success or failure of the film by its type or kind. Film critic Wes D. Gehring notes that the "significance of genre stories ... long predates the *Poetics* [of Aristotle], and might just be addressed by repeating a question which frequently surfaces in genre study: Why does an audience member keep returning to a favored story type (genre) which a formulaic structure often makes predictable?"[9] Indeed, the familiar fictional narrative connects with deeply ingrained desires for people to reflect and meditate on the fundamental nature of their individual existence and their social relationships.

So, what exactly is film genre? What are the ingredients that distinguish a western, musical, horror, war, gangster, or science fiction movie, to name specific groups? Critic Tom Ryall suggests that "[g]enre may be defined as patterns/forms/styles/structures which transcend individual films, and which supervise both their construction by the film maker, and their reading by an audience."[10] Film genre, consequently, identifies those films that belong to a body of sameness in story elements, images, and film aesthetics. And serious genre critics and theorists would quickly asseverate the distinction between film genre and film cycles (films of similarity made in a limited set of years) and film trends (varying aspects within a film that represent expressions of popular culture). Yet, any definition of film genre evokes questions and counterarguments about identifying a set of consistent elements that never vary from one film to another. Author Jeanine Basinger emphasizes the point when she observes that "[g]enre, as related to the movies, is a tricky term to define. Although models of genre exist in literature and art, film genre as pursued by a large business system and the collaborative filmmaking process ... becomes an ever-changing and evolving concept."[11] Augmenting that viewpoint with a comment about contemporary society, scholar S. Craig Watkins observes that in "a cultural milieu marked by pastiche, ambiguity and boundary crossing, genre lines are often blurred, disrupted and/or recombined, thus making 'genre' a difficult term to sustain analytically."[12]

With these considerations recognized, two significant questions for this study would be the following: Is there a distinctive "buddy film" genre, and how is the "interracial buddy film" linked to the "buddy film"? Although it is tempting to call the buddy film a genre because of its demonstrated durability from the silent era to the present — similar to a western or horror film — the major prohibitive factor is that buddy films lack an essential, connecting, and replicated foundation identified in film genre by critic Stuart M. Kaminsky. Kaminsky writes: "Genre in film, if it is to have meaning, must have a limited scope, a limited definition. The films must have clearly defined constants so that the traditions and forms within them can be clearly seen and not diluted into abstraction."[13] The possession of "clearly defined constants" undermines the approach to the buddy film as a distinctive genre since the buddy film can be configured to delineate opposing themes, divergent cinematic styles, contradictory story structures, and shifting cinematic aesthetics. Without question, buddy films have similarities, but they are not restricted to those similarities since dynamics of age, class, race, gender, and/or culture can dislocate those likenesses. There is no persistent cinematic syntax that makes a buddy film, and consequently the buddy "pattern," "formula," "category," "motif," "scenario," "riff," or "paradigm" serves more appropriately as an identifying term. At the same time, this pattern transcends one specific type of film and is utilized in different film genres for the purpose of visualizing abstractions and politically charged concepts, such as the "interracial buddy pattern."

The Interracial Buddy Pattern

With the long decades of black depiction being relegated to racial stereotypes, male relationships across racial lines have been problematic in American cinema. With race, ethnicity, or culture as visible qualifiers, the challenge of men forming constructive and lasting connections despite the baggage of racial history has been quite formidable. The reciprocity between society's racial policies and Hollywood's depiction has been undeniable, as the industry repelled ongoing pressures to modify its approaches.

The prevailing aspects of masculinity on screen have been considerably more conventional and steady than the presentation of interracial male relationships. From the early decades of the studio system, Indian, black, Asian, and Latino male characters have been foils of symbolic value to white male protagonists, with very rare exceptions. Throughout the twentieth century, men of color in Hollywood features—with black men being the most prevalent—have been juxtaposed with white male characters to accentuate and enhance the latter; in short, the characters of color have been rendered to make white males appear more courageous, tolerant, heroic, intelligent, etc., in the narrative. At the very least, characters of color have served as emotional caretakers for whites, even to the point of denying their own interests and welfare. This delineation often resulted in a racial hierarchy that assigned positive and laudable qualities to white characters by virtue of race. Again, this construction was not created by the cinema, but merely a reflection of a similar process existing in literature, as in Daniel Defoe's *Robinson Crusoe* (1719); Mark Twain's *Adventures of Huckleberry Finn* (1885); John Steinbeck's *Of Mice and Men* (1937); and Ernest Hemingway's *Islands in the Stream* (1970), just to name four works. Throughout the golden years of Hollywood, films such as *Judge Priest* (1934), *Man About Town* (1939), and *Body and Soul* (1947) incorporated interracial male connections in a manner that would encourage the audience's pathos and concern with the white protagonist. In a significant way, the war film *Home of the Brave* (1949) attempted to move away from that model, presaging the modern civil rights era that transformed those racial polarities into a possible compatibility. Two notable films illustrating that point were the western *Broken Arrow* (1950) and the drama *The Defiant Ones* (1959), both of which reflected males reaching toward shared values and tolerance across racial lines. With the emphasis on ethnic distinctions in the late 1960s and early 1970s—specifically with the violence, sexuality, and political aggressiveness in the "blaxploitation" film cycle—men of color received extreme screen makeovers that often propelled them into superhero status, in contrast to the parade of white male villains. With few exceptions, such as *The Last Detail* (1973) and *The Wilby Conspiracy* (1974), early in the decade, feature films reversed the nuances of good and evil, replacing a previous set of polarities with another. But by the mid–'70s, that phase was truncated by the box-office preference for "crossover" stars who would appeal to audiences across racial and cultural divides when paired with one another, primarily in comedies and action films. In a profitable manner, films such as *Silver Streak* (1976) and *Rocky* (1979) led the way for the interracial buddy pattern to become a staple in American cinema into the 1980s; then, in the 1990s—with the multicultural movement, masculinity studies, and queer theorists—the pattern increased in regularity and in its inclusion of various ethnic male pairings.

So what are some of the perceptible ingredients that comprise the interracial buddy film? What gives the pattern its own succinct referencing and structure? The following four areas frame the authentic interracial buddy paradigm as replicated in Hollywood features:

1. The relationship between the interracial male characters serves as the story's center or a focused plot point in the film. Usually antagonistic at the beginning, the development of the relationship and its consequential existence by the film's end are crucial to the story line.

2. The emotional, personal, and professional lives of the interracial males are intertwined, often in regard to life-changing and/or life-and-death issues, dilemmas, and situations. In particular, this interconnection provides the foundation for trust and a confessional comfort between the males.

3. The two males must be heterosexual. This commandment ensures that same-sex romantic or physically intimate behavior does not prompt the closeness of the male characters. At the same time, this element allows for the conformity with the dominant notions of masculinity that traditionally indict homosexuality as synonymous with weakness and moral perversion, which are two unacceptable attributes of male heroism on screen.

4. The relationship between the males is not limited to a casual friendship. Indeed, the two males achieve a union that acknowledges personal sharing and sacrifice for one another—personal demands that go beyond the conveniences of a friendship. Ideally, they reach what scholars Robert A. Strikwerda and Larry May refer to as "comradeship," which is a unique bonding, "a form that may pass for intimacy" framed by "loyalty" and "mutual vulnerability."[14] This closeness can be expressed in action, verbal banter, physical touching, and shared space, but never in regard to any sexually fulfilling expression.

Some of the films alluded to in this study do not achieve the above four attributes for the entirety of a given film. Instead, traces of the interracial buddy pattern are used to achieve some other primary objective, allowing the film to merely "echo" or reflect the pattern. These "echo" films are not completely dismissible, because through their very existence, they make reference to the authentic pattern, drawing upon its narrative power. Further, the "echo" film exists as a marketing tool to lure audiences by promising the familiar pattern; this strategy demonstrates the extent of the popularity and profitability of the interracial buddy paradigm in the American cinematic tradition.

However, the majority of the films assessed in the following pages contain these four elements, some emphasized more than others. Those authentic interracial buddyships occur in various genres, and they serve not only the thematic demands of an individual film but also the broader ideological needs for American society:

First of all, since feature films function as a keeper of America's collective conscience — the repository for fears, guilt, and hopes — the interracial buddy film creates a world where that conscience can find a peaceful balance, that is to say where conflicts can find resolutions.

Second, the interracial buddy film suggests that democracy and equal treatment have been obtained because if it exists on the big screen, it must exist in the world of those who watch. The tacit popular-culture maxim, both powerful and flawed, seems to be: *If something is expressed and/or performed in a medium, then it must be true in reality.*

Third, the interracial buddy film serves as an argument that the American capitalistic system nurtures humanity and tolerance.

Fourth, the interracial buddy film confirms that men of all races share positions in the dominant power scheme, which intrinsically promotes principles of heterosexuality and sexism.

The four notions mentioned above divert attention from existing evidence that asserts the problematic nature of America's race relations and the deleterious effects of gender bias. Negating, or at the very lease altering, the history, sociology, politics, and economics of race relations in America, the interracial buddy film skews the real and the ideal, proposing to audiences that by consuming racial egalitarianism on the screen, they have participated sufficiently in responding to the complex racial issues prevalent in society. Consequently, too many viewers are encouraged to remain passive in the social and political arena because they have been active consumers at the box office. At the same time, the interracial buddy film invites viewers to accept traditional tenets of masculinity, with all of their defects, as the superior platform for behavior and ethos. Likewise, for men of color, the messages provided state that acceptance into the dominant male culture depends upon maintaining and replicating the demeanor and attitudes of the dominant group that has oppressed them.

Masculinity in the Interracial Buddy Film examines the manner in which Hollywood films have incorporated and presented the diverse racial backgrounds of men in simplistic and innocuous models. Further, it explores the connection of those cinematic relationship patterns to the larger political designs within society. Finally, it assesses the aspects of masculinity and notions of manhood that permeate those male screen characters, noting the inextricable links to areas of heterosexism and male hegemony.

1

Old Times There Are Not Forgotten: 1930s–1940s

When *The Birth of a Nation* found an audience in 1915, it signaled the beginning of feature films as storytelling medium that coalesced both the technical achievements in form and the political messages in the content. As one scholar notes: "The cinema of [director D.W.] Griffith . . . actively narrates events, shaping the audience's perception of them.... *The Birth*, which sustains an intricate narrative for three hours of screen, held audiences spellbound.... Its success transformed the nature of American Film production and exhibition."[1] The many films that followed *The Birth of a Nation* may not have accomplished a similar level of filmmaking techniques, but too many of them replicated the racial images and masculine notions of that work. The film itself did not create those images and notions, but borrowed from the literary tradition and the popular minstrel show tradition.

As the studio system developed in the '20s, it continued those images and notions, capturing a wide audience with the fascination of synchronized sound and maintaining an audience with a star system and distinctive film genres. Feature films, under the assumption of being only entertainment, nurtured established racial characterizations and conventional codes of masculinity, with a particularly fondness for the antebellum setting and Old South sentiments found in *The Birth of a Nation*. Scholar-critic Ed Guerrero concludes: "This tendency towards denial and escapism in times of crisis accounted for plantation melodrama's national popularity, which resulted in the production and exhibition of more than seventy-five features about the South between 1929 and 1941."[2] These melodramas functioned as a safe harbor for the romanticized perspectives that framed discernible polarities between the nature of white men and black men during the early part of the twentieth century.

At the same time, complementing the plantation setting, the urban milieu offered up its version of romanticized perspectives in numerous films. One could argue that *The Jazz Singer* (1927), credited as the first feature to successfully present synchronized sound, was the significant bearer of a black male icon to the city setting via the blackface performance of the star Al Jolson. Certainly, the urban black male as servant, chauffeur, chef, bootblack, and entertainer flourished over the years. As cultural critic Donald Bogle observes, the "black servants of the Hollywood films of the 1930s met the demands of their times.... With their incredible antics, their unbelievable dialects, and their amazing absurdities, the black servants provided a downhearted Depression age with buoyancy and jocularity ... always around when the boss needed them ... always ready to lend a helping hand.... It was many a down-and-out movie hero or heroine who realized his Negro servant was his only friend."[3] The limitations of these characterizations served cultural and political agendas effectively, ever widening the gap that already existed along racial and gender lines.

Whether in the rural setting or in an urban space, between 1915 and 1948, Hollywood fashioned an impervious set of types that assumed the actual natures of both black and white males with deleterious results for both. Additionally, with the emphasis on black and white males, there were salient omissions of other men of color from the screen, with few exceptions, as in the western genre or the Charlie Chan series of the '30s and '40s. Subsequently, the interracial buddy film found little vitality during the first three decades of the studio system. Instead, across racial lines there emerged popular duos, white male stars and supporting black actors, or symbolic relationships between black-white males that usually facilitated the redemption and/or moral awareness of the white protagonist.

In 1934, one of the most popular American humorists, Will Rogers, had two films appear that highlighted his brand of average–Joe observations and attitudes about life. Unfortunately, included in that humor were elements of racial arrogance that many whites supported at that time. In *David Harum* (1934) and *Judge Priest* (1934), Rogers portrayed the title protagonists whose masculinity found embellishment through buffoonified black male characters, portrayed in both films by black performer Lincoln "Stepin Fetchit" Perry. In the same manner that Rogers enjoyed an immense popularity for his stylized homespun wisdom, Stepin Fetchit "was the best known and most successful black actor working in Hollywood."[4] During the 1930s Rogers and Fetchit made four films together, two of which were directed by noted filmmaker John Ford.[5]

Set in the 1890s in rural New York, *David Harum* follows the titular bank owner through a variety of episodes that revolve around his people-oriented banking procedures, family counseling, and horse-trading. Harum takes life with considerable ease, offering his assistance to family, friends, and bank patrons. Although rich, Harum is not elitist and aloof, nor is he driven by profits and exploitation. Instead, he supports his single sister and protects widows in need. His one vice revolves around the enjoyment he gets from horse-trading, particularly with one church deacon (Charles Middleton). A man of ethics, success, and wisdom, Harum remains sensitive to the plight of others, serving as a model of the good-hearted, magnanimous white male.

However, Harum's masculinity becomes qualified by race, when with one horse trade, he also receives Swifty (Fetchit), a slow-talking, lazy, dimwitted black man who also answers to "boy" when spoken to by Harum and other whites. Owning Swifty after winning a deal, Harum allows the black man to attend to his horse and to accompany him on various errands, which Swifty completes without any reference to his own personal needs or familial relationships.

In contrast to Harum, Swifty possesses few qualities that make him an admirable man, beginning with the assigned aspect of being a perpetual boy. With an obvious stupidity that borders on being a disability, Swifty serves as fodder for laughter. For example, in his one featured scene inside of his blighted shanty home, Swifty — in his slow, almost unintelligible drawl — mumbles about his tired feet as he soaks them in a wash tub positioned near a wooden stove. A black woman appears— possibly his wife or sister — who chastises him for using the kettle of hot water she prepared for washing the dishes. Assuring her that he was "killing two birds with one stone," Swifty bends over to lift the dinner dishes from the same wash tub in which he soaks his feet.

After such a scene, an audience has little doubt about Swifty's silliness and ineptitude. Like a minstrel show reflection, Swifty exists in the realm of the ridiculous, while David Harum represents the idealized, benevolent white male. Although Harum and Swifty both reside within a romanticized vision of the filmmakers, the dichotomy shaped between black and white males finds valorization in the big-screen visuals. The two male images add to the historical dialogue about the qualitative value of race differences. One *Variety* review hailed the film for "some dandy laughs, some of them provided by the lazy-gaited Stepin Fetchit,"[6] while another observation from the *Hollywood Reporter* asserted that the film "is almost too much of the same old thing. It is just too homely and wholesome and quaint, and it is also frightfully slow."[7] Still, somewhere in the middle was

David Harum (Will Rogers, left) and the deacon (Charles Middleton, middle) contemplate the trading value of Swifty (Stephin Fetchit) in *David Harum*. Courtesy of the Academy of Motion Picture Arts and Sciences.

another review that declared: "Possibly the pleasantest thing about the production is the fact that it includes Stepin Fetchit.... Again, too lazy to use words when he talks, his amazing rapid incoherence is still, particularly against the background of Will Rogers' careful drawl, almost frightfully funny."[8]

With the Rogers-Fetchit team winning popularity, *Judge Priest* allowed them to reprise their roles. In this vehicle, Rogers portrays a circuit court judge in Kentucky during the 1890s. In addition to showcasing Rogers' style of humor, this movie intentionally celebrates the Confederacy and the antebellum South. In that adoration, the white males who fought in the Confederate army, even if they were criminals, were worthy of heroic stature, while black men were childish, incompetent dependents of white society.

In the opening scene, Judge Priest rules at his bench, listening to the charges of chicken stealing and a call for six months on the chain gang.

The accused black man, Jeff Poindexter (Fetchit), sleeps during the legal proceedings, until awakened by Judge Priest's admonition: "Hey, boy, wake up. If anybody sleeps in this courtroom, it's gonna be me.... Come here, boy."

Jeff obeys, and manages to avoid a guilty verdict because he shares with the judge his secret bait for catching fish. In the following scene, Judge Priest and Jeff are shown walking a wooded path together, both carrying their homemade fishing poles over their shoulders discussing their fishing strategy. As the two are shown walking side by side, engaged in their angler's conversation, there appears to be the early indication of a growing friendship. However, this seeming equality between the two men ends with the scene as the remainder of the story embraces the old racial and gender stereotypes.

Once again, Rogers plays a character that resembles David Harum; the difference is in the manner in which Judge Priest extols the virtues of the Old South. Priest, along with his white male associates, spends much of the film preparing for the Confederate Reunion Festival, where old soldiers can gather to discuss and reminisce about the Civil War. The major disturbance that interrupts the plans extends from a white worker named Bob Gillis (David Landau) who is wrongly charged with knife-attacking three local men. After the praise given by Priest and the local minister — who is also an ex–Confederate soldier — Gillis, an ex-con who volunteered and fought heroically for the Confederate cause, wins his freedom from a jury of his peers.

While all these events occur, the black people in the story spend most of their time cleaning, washing, cooking, and singing various ditties, including "Dixie" and "My Old Kentucky Home," usually led by Aunt Dilsey (Hattie McDaniel). On his part, Jeff remains the fishing sidekick to Judge Priest, but he also serves as a personal attendant: Jeff plays the harmonica for the Judge; helps chase croquet balls for the Judge; and runs errands for the Judge. While performing this last task, one of the more noteworthy scenes occurs, as Judge Priest inquires whether Jeff can play "Dixie" on the harmonica. When Jeff hears that he would be compensated by gaining the Judge's old coonskin coat, Jeff admits that for that eye-catching coat he'd be willing to play "Marching through Georgia." Judge Priest reminds him that such a song that refers to the South losing a battle in the war might get Jeff lynched, adding: "If I catch you playing 'Marching through Georgia,' I'll join the lynching." Here, lynching is viewed as a reasonable punishment for disrespecting the Confederate memory, presenting such a vicious act as acceptable punishment.

But Jeff, waiting outside the open window of the courthouse, comes through for the Judge in loyal fashion when the latter gives a signal for the song "Dixie" to be played while Reverend Brand (Henry B. Walthall) tells the heroic story about Gillis. Jeff, in his coonskin coat and top hat leads a group of black men who suddenly appear in an inspiring instrumental version of the song; their performance leads to the movie's big finale of a parade through the town's streets, led by the white Confederate soldiers, marching to the melody of "Dixie."

In a mixed critique of the film, a *Variety* review declared: "Rogers gives one of the best performances of his career," adding that "[m]ost of the comedy, however, is contributed by Rogers and Stepin Fetchit, a natural foil to the Rogers character. Other efforts at local color through the use of Negroes are less effective."[9] In juxtaposition to the Will Rogers image on screen, the Stepin Fetchit image crystallized the peculiar perception that white America wanted to nourish about black masculinity during the 1930s. The confused, inarticulate, and childish nature in the characterization reduced a black male to a non-threatening entity who was satisfied with his condition and controllable through any gesture, benevolent or otherwise, extended by whites. His mere presence lifted the status of Will Rogers to a superior level, preventing any perceptible equality between the black and white male.

From all indications, the framework and content of *The County Chairman* (1935) and *Steamboat Round the Bend* (1935) merely augmented the established paradigm of white male–black male relations established in the above films. Of the two, the latter received more attention due to its direction by John Ford. Ford, who began "his career as an extra in the Ku Klux Klan sequences on *The Birth of a Nation*," seemed comfortable with the Southern settings.[10] The movie showcased Rogers as a Mississippi River steamboat captain committed to exonerating his nephew who's been charged with murder, but even with Fetchit portraying the sidekick, Jonah, the vehicle "lack[ed] comedy relief—it [was] somber all the way through."[11]

Although Stepin Fetchit surfaced as the most popular black male icon in the decade, he was not the only actor receiving roles to support white leading males. Black performers Mantan Moreland, Bill Robinson, and Willie Best were familiar faces as well on the big screen in various comedies, historical movies, and dramas. But another contemporary black performer, Eddie "Rochester" Anderson, attained his most popular roles in his pairing with white comedian Jack Benny in numerous films, on radio, and then on television.

Due to the radio exposure, Jack Benny and Rochester were an even more popular movie team than the Rogers-Fetchit duo. Set in the contemporary scene, the four feature films they did together — *Man About Town* (1939), *Buck Benny Rides Again* (1940), *Love Thy Neighbor* (1940), and *The Meanest Man in the World* (1943) — provided a more palatable racial relationship that wasn't smothered under the legacy of 19th century American conventions. Additionally, both Benny and Rochester assumed characters who were entertainers, so the show biz environment placed them into a similar milieu and shared understanding of each other's stage aspirations. With those similarities recognized, however, the lines were clearly drawn in regards to the position of power in their union. Benny was the boss, with the power to fire and dismiss Rochester at any time. Benny controlled the economic strings while manipulating the social reins that forced Rochester in one direction or another regarding his lifestyle. Despite the good-natured teasing between the two *and* despite Rochester's signature talk-back attitude, in reality, Benny's characters were always the employers, while Rochester's characters worked as the butler, servant, loyal confidant, and humorous sidekick. The friendship was evident, as "trust" was a component — though often tenuous — of their bond, but there remained a defined, separate status when the two were alone and particularly when they were in the public space.

Man About Town takes place in London, as Bob Temple (Benny) is organizing a stage revue and trying to win the heart of his show's leading lady, Diane (Dorothy Lamour). In his efforts to make Diane jealous, Temple pretends to be having an affair with high society's Lady Arlington (Binnie Barnes), which results in an angry and homicidal Sir Arlington (Edward Arnold). Throughout the story, Rochester functions as a butler; a conspirator in Temple's efforts to win Diane's affection; and a member of the stage revue where he does both singing and dance numbers. As Temple's domestic, Rochester refers to him with the words "boss," "Mr. Temple," and "sir." In numerous sight gags, Rochester completes the conventional eye rolling and ethnic mumbling to various incidents. Temple, on his part, expects such references and behavior, as he invites a chorus girl to dinner in his room, saying "my man will serve you." If there is a progressive point here, it is that Rochester is called a "man," but "serving" whites still remains his duty.

In *Buck Benny Rides Again*, the Benny-Rochester relationship remains the same. In this vehicle, Benny, who plays himself, takes his New York act to the West, and once again, he becomes enamored with a leading lady, Joan (Ellen Drew), attempting to win her affection by showing how tough he can behave in a cowboy fashion. The film's press booklet underscored Benny's masculinity by pretentiously describing the story as "the magnificent saga of a city boy who goes west to prove to his lady love that he's really a virile, two-fisted, rootin,' tootin' son of the wide open spaces."[12] The "West" serves as the signifier for the rites of masculinity that are equated with a physical performance that will win the woman as love interest or trophy. Even in the comic framework, the conventional codes of maleness attain reification.

Of related interest in this installment, Rochester meets a young black maid, Josephine (Theresa Harris), with whom he flirts, boasting of his travels to London, Paris, and Hawaii, presumably with his "boss." The studio press release even notes this element of the film stating: "Romantic Rochester gets a dancing partner ... and performs a bit of choreography after the fashion established so successfully by Astaire and Rogers. Theresa Harris, as attractive as Rochester is funny, is the dusky honey."[13] On the one hand, the statement references the black couple to the white couple via dancing, which will serve as the sexual metaphor in the film, but the label of the "dusky honey" clarifies the racial identity of the actress. Importantly, through Rochester's connection with Josephine, he affirms his heterosexuality with his boss, as well as his irresistible charm. Both Benny and Rochester become motivated by the possibility of love and reciprocated affection from women who appear to be waiting for the two men to come along.

But consistent with the pattern established in the previous film, *Buck Benny Rides Again* conspicuously maintains the power line between the white and black males, as reflected throughout the dialogue. For example, as Benny plans to go out for the evening, he orders: "Rochester, get my car!" Rochester responds with his typical expressions of "boss" and "yes, sir." Their shared behavior as heterosexual males functions to substantiate the preferred roles of aggressive predators after the objects of their affections, even as the racial line of demarcation authenticates the system of control.

In the third movie, *Love Thy Neighbor*, an on-screen resentment between Benny and fellow comedian Fred Allen serves as the center of the story's plot as both men, playing themselves, must deal with the accidental and intentional presence of the other. Complicating this ongoing feud in *Love Thy Neighbor* is the appearance of Allen's niece, Mary (Mary Martin), who captures Benny's romantic eye and who struggles to bring a peaceful coexistence between the two comedians. Josephine (Harris) appears again as she and Rochester continue their romance, attending a New Year's masquerade party as Romeo and Juliet. But later in the movie, played for humor, the innocence of their union shows another aspect. With the goal of taking her money, Rochester teaches Josephine how to shoot craps; feigning naiveté, she slyly substitutes his dice with her own loaded

In *Buck Benny Rides Again*, Eddie "Rochester" Anderson, left, and Jack Benny keep a close watch on one another. Courtesy of the Academy of Motion Picture Arts and Sciences.

pair, winning several hundred dollars. To his surprising loss, Rochester states: "I'll be old Black Joe before I earn that much from Mr. Benny." In this sequence, not only does Rochester's plan to take advantage of Josephine backfire, but his confirmation of his racial identity connects to a pejorative image of stereotypical black character.

With their heterosexual relationships secured and their typical male connection in place, Benny and Rochester represent the perimeters of black-white compatibility. In a revealing dialogue, the suggestion of racial respect is alluded to, but at the same time, the indictment of the black man's behavior is accentuated:

> Benny: "You were more than just a servant to me. I had you in my will."
> Rochester: "I didn't find it there."
> Benny: "No wonder the seal was broken."

Here, the white man is magnanimous enough to leave money for his black employee, but that same employee was devious enough to sift through the personal will. Although the setup for a joke, still the generous nature of the white man becomes emboldened by the sneakiness of the man of color.

As Hollywood production increased in the 1940s, the association between white and black males continued with two dramas that included black male characters as supportive but inextricable connections to the white male protagonists. In *Casablanca* (1942), the Second World War emerges as the backdrop for the film's celebrated love story, as well as the spine for the stoic and sacrificial masculinity exhibited by the central character, Rick (Humphrey Bogart). As one scholar observes, Bogart's character "expressed the kind of reluctant heroism that both women and men found palpably masculine," adding that "Bogart strikes a balance between self-made wealth and power and aristocratic virtue."[14]

The ever-popular *Casablanca* contributed to transforming the extreme caricatures found in earlier white and black male images of Will Rogers and Stepin Fetchit into more complex, heroic possibilities. Just as Rick's mysterious past in America and abbreviated romance in Paris framed his motivation and detachment, those attributes suggested that a white male protagonist could be multifaceted in his nature. And though in the character Sam (Dooley Wilson) the black male as entertainer surfaces once more, the bond between Sam and Rick possesses more depth in its integral weaving into the story of the ill-fated, wartime lovers Rick and Ilsa (Ingrid Bergman). Sam, a black man without any acknowledged family, remains a stalwart companion to Rick from New York to Paris and North Africa. The reasons as to why Sam maintains such loyalty to his white friend remain unclear, but there is, in both characters' demeanors, the sense that he has the freedom to leave at any time. Certainly, Sam refers to his companion as "Mr. Rick," but unlike Rochester's, Sam's entertaining functions as his livelihood and self-enjoyment rather than being an extension of his domestic duties.

At the same time, Rick's contained emotions and affected indifference stem from his sense of betrayal by Ilsa, and his ensuing stoic masculinity doesn't validate itself by exploiting Sam's presence. Rick doesn't behave in a condescending manner toward Sam, nor does he believe that Sam is his property. In the last act of the film when Rick sells his café to Ferrari (Sidney Greenstreet), he negotiates a profit-sharing deal for Sam. In fact, Rick's concern for Sam's welfare stems from the longevity of their relationship. Even more than his dubious connection to the city's self-serving Police Captain Louis Renault (Claude Rains), Rick has trusted Sam with the details of his personal emotions, in both sober and drunken moments.

Years later, *Body and Soul* (1947) incorporated professional boxing to show the pitfalls of pride, while emphasizing the limitations of male phys-

Remaining a committed buddy, Sam (Dooley Wilson, left) comforts Rick (Humphrey Bogart) in *Casablanca*.

ical prowess. In the post–*Rocky* (1976) and *Raging Bull* (1980) era, it's difficult to discuss a movie that includes boxing without comparing it to those Academy Award–winning films. But previous films such as *Body and Soul* and *Champion* (1949) succeeded in incorporating boxing for both its literal and symbolic value while exploring social and moral questions.

In *Body and Soul*, Charley Davis (John Garfield), possessed with natural pugilistic skills, uses professional boxing to seize a new materialistic life for his mother and girlfriend, Peg (Lili Palmer), while allowing his spiritual and moral fibers to sever themselves from his decision making. The character that helps Charley gain a clear view of the exploitive side of his professional dealings with an unscrupulous promoter becomes Ben (Canada Lee), the black former champ whose mental balance and physical health are sold out for profits. Ben, aware of boxing's potential dangers to Charley's soul, berates him for placing money before integrity. Although Ben and Charley share a short amount of screen time, the former's effect upon the latter becomes transformational. Ben represents the best and worst in the fight game, as his masculinity is rooted within his body's achievement as the former champ and his dignity as he stands up to the taunting of a ruthless boxing promoter.

Both *Casablanca* and *Body and Soul* are not bona fide buddy films, but the link between the black and white males demonstrated the development of images since the early '30s. As such, those two films presaged the dramatization of white/black male characters that surfaced in the four "problem" films of 1949. Those movies, including *Pinky, Lost Boundaries, Intruder in the Dust*, and *Home of the Brave*, explore the status of blacks in America in that period between World War II and the modern civil rights movement. One of those films—*Home of the Brave*—assesses the nature of manhood under the pressures of combat and life-and-death situations. The use of the high school friendship between a pair of white and black soldiers underscores the deeply entrenched racism that challenge genuine affection and the potency of that racism into adulthood.

Based upon a Broadway play that "depicted anti-semitism," the screen version of *Home of the Brave* "dramatized anti-black hatred" as it followed the dangerous mission by a five-man patrol to an occupied Pacific island to survey the grounds for map making purposes.[15] With segregation in the military and the larger society in the '40s, the presence of a black soldier named Moss (James Edwards) ignites the racist attitudes of the other white soldiers. The buddy element enters the film when Moss discovers that Finch (Lloyd Bridges), a close friend from school, is one of the men in the squad.

The story, told in flashbacks, revolves around Moss, who suffers from paralysis and amnesia as the film opens. Believing that Moss's condition is psychologically and emotionally based, the military psychiatrist Doctor (Jeff Corey) uses hypnosis to uncover the layers of the soldier's disorder. In one flashback, Moss and Finch's friendship emerges as the two are teammates on the basketball team and as Finch attempts to convince Moss to attend a graduation party with white classmates. In their bonding, the two have a comfortable interaction where teasing and encouragement strengthen their attachment. One such indicator stems from their dialogue, laced with a shared call-and-response expression of "charming" followed by "delightful." Yet Moss knows that all whites are not as open as Finch, a perspective that the latter has difficulty comprehending. Years later, their accidental meeting as soldiers rekindles their friendship as they talk affectionately about the past and speculate about their futures, with Finch suggesting the two open a restaurant-bar together after the war.

But the buddies are still in two wars— one in the Pacific and the other within their country's racist provisions. The underscoring of this latter point emerges through the comments and behavior of Corporal TJ Everett (Steve Brodie), a white bigot who unleashes an ongoing stream of prejudicial perspectives. In his defense of Moss, Finch continually confronts TJ, moving closer to a physical fight, which eventually erupts. At one point, TJ, while eating fried chicken prepared by Moss, reflects aloud: "Wonderful cooks, the colored ... great entertainers, too. I had a janitor once who was the greatest natural comedian I ever saw." Then, with an affected "darky" vernacular, he adds that the janitor stated: "Boss, I ain't lazy. I'm jest tired ... so tired!" But Finch's disdain of TJ mirrors the position of Mingo (Frank Lovejoy), the most experienced man on the mission, who asserts: "I have no more use for a bad black man as I do for a bad white man."

The strong buddyhood between Moss and Finch eventually buckles beneath the strain of combat. While frantically searching the jungle for the misplaced map case as the enemy advances, Finch calls Moss "a yellow-

Finch (Lloyd Bridges, center) brags the praises of his best friend, Moss (James Edwards, left) to his commanding officer, Major Robinson (Douglas Dick) in *Home of the Brave.* Courtesy of the Academy of Motion Picture Arts and Sciences.

bellied nigger," an expression earlier used by TJ. Although Finch cuts off the last word and tries to correct himself with the word "nitwit," the damage has already been done. The ensuing capture, torture, and killing of Finch by the enemy leads to Moss's breakdown, as he attempts to handle the conflicting anger (against his white friend) and love (despite his friend's whiteness).

The film presents Moss and Finch as sympathetic characters, as both men deal with a world of messages outside of themselves. Moss, in one of the many effective scenes, articulates the traumatic childhood of enduring name-calling and beatings by whites, confessing to the others: "You're alone. You're strange! You're something different! You make us different!"

Moss, having internalized the negativity attributed to his blackness, negotiates life in self-hatred and anger. On his part, Finch, exposed to the attitudes and privilege given to his race, has learned a perspective that is hidden deeply within him, so deep that even he remains unaware until faced with danger and stress. For these interracial buddies, their genuine affection cannot eradicate the lessons of race that have shaped them as individuals and friends. Although their union functioned as a barrier against prejudice in their adolescence, as adults the racist seeds still sprout as ugly blossoms when least expected.

In one review, the film was applauded as "a powerful drama ... brilliantly directed and expertly performed by a very capable although relatively unknown cast."[16] For its time, the movie certainly encouraged viewers to consider the manner in which external forces attribute to the self esteem and perspectives on manhood. One of TJ's repeated statements asserted that black men didn't have the courage to meet the challenge of combat, which resulted in their segregation in the military. Distorted and illogical, TJ's interpretation of Moss, and thereby all black men, accused the victim for his own victimization, suggesting a lack of manliness as defined by serving in the military. In another review, the critic praised the performances of the buddies, observing: "In the role of the Negro soldier, James Edwards does a finely tempered job, revealing the man's inner torments from behind a frame of stoic dignity," while adding that "Lloyd Bridges is equally competent as his hail-fellow, good–Joe pal who tries to assuage his friend's anguish without any possible success."[17]

Home of the Brave appeared at the end of two decades of a studio system that framed its business aspirations within the dominant suppositions of the day regarding race and gender. In the context of its time period, the film was an important step toward visualizing more three-dimensional perspectives of men in social and political settings. In contrast to *David*

Harum, Home of the Brave positioned itself at the opposing end of a depiction scale with regard to the manner in which race and masculinity intersected. Although far removed from the methods by which American cinema would eventually explore race and gender, it nonetheless announced the possibilities for future male characterizations.

2

The Content of Their
Characters: 1950s–1960s

One of the milestones of the 20th century was the Civil Rights movement in America. From the early abolitionists of the 1830s to the efforts of black activist A. Phillip Randolph — who called for a march on Washington in 1941 to "demand jobs in war industries and equality in the armed forces"[1] — the modern day civil rights movement is associated with the changes in the legal and educational institutions that eventually led to the passing of the Civil Rights Act of 1964 and then the Voting Rights Act of 1965. During an era that witnessed struggle, commitment, killings, and triumph, the United States appeared to be painfully maturing into a nation that supported equal opportunities for the majority of its people.

By 1950 Hollywood was also undergoing some changes, as the studio system that had dominated since the 1920s was being challenged by independent filmmakers vying for control of their creativity and profits. Linked to those independent efforts was the manner in which television evolved as a formidable competitor to the big screen's rule over entertainment. Audiences had more choices about the manner in which they spent their leisure time and money. As one scholar notes: "In the post-studio period ... [t]he studios themselves are no longer self-contained factories but part of large, often multinational corporations that have nothing to do with filmmaking.... [A] film can now be organized by an agent, a director, or a star, who will then hire a producer."[2] The changes in Hollywood filmmaking were significant and extensive, as were some of the changes in the depiction of male relationships across racial lines.

One of the noteworthy movies appearing in 1950 was also the first significant buddy film of the decade — the western *Broken Arrow*. Historically in American cinema, the depiction of the Indian suffered from broad strokes that often emphasized wild savagery. Distant, stoic, and without depth, the Indian was the prevailing nemesis standing in the way of decent white settlers looking for freedom and the opportunity to bring civilization to the frontier. Sometimes exotic, the Indian was an impenetrable obstacle blocking the good intentions of white settlers, miners, and modern technology, such as railroads and the telegraph.

In a laudable effort, the film *Broken Arrow* challenged the standard visualization of Indian cultures while offering "pleas for non-violent racial tolerance."[3] The story follows Tom Jeffords (James Stewart) whose voiceover explains that after ten years of a bloody war between the Apache and whites, he finds himself experiencing several incidents that lead to his efforts to strike a peace between the warring factions. As Jeffords realizes that Indian mothers cry for their children, just as whites; as he witnesses the Apaches keeping their word not to kill him; as he verbally defends Indians in front of whites; and as he clearly sees the military plan to destroy the Apache nation, he learns the Apache language and traditions from an Indian scout in order to approach Cochise (Jeff Chandler), the chief of the various Apache tribes.

With the beginning of the film centering on Jeffords and his efforts, the movie seems it might simply follow a familiar path of deifying the white male protagonist. However, once Cochise enters the film, his stature as a character ranks on an equal level with Jeffords. With the audience informed by the voiceover that the Indian characters and Jeffords would be speaking English rather than their native tongue, Cochise defends his actions, culture, and determination in an articulation that commands attention but doesn't bring a supercilious aspect to the character. Indeed, the ongoing allure of the film is the manner in which Jeffords and Cochise move from respectful but cautious attitudes to extending themselves as friends over the yearlong time frame of the film. In an early dialogue, Cochise explains to Jeffords: "We fight for our land against Americans [whites] who try to take it.... [Y]ou were not asked to come here.... [Y]ou people do not want peace." And significant to the story's element, there are several scenes where the responsibility for breaking the peace begins with whites.

Both Jeffords and Cochise are warriors who can skillfully fight, showing their traditional masculine trait for aggressive behavior and physical prowess. But both men understand that though fighting and killing have been necessities, they don't have to continue as a way of life. The two characters acknowledge cultural differences between whites and Apaches but believe that each can learn about and accept the other. This acknowledgment leads to their common belief in honor and how that signifies a man's character. Just as Jeffords defends Cochise's spoken promises to the whites, the latter stands by Jeffords's words of peace to his fellow warriors. Yet the same integrity fails to surface in the white rancher Ben Slade (Will Geer) and the Apache leader Geronimo (Jay Silverheels), as those two characters, in their addiction to war, undermine efforts at peace both verbally and in their actions.

The bond between Jeffords and Cochise takes on an additional dimension, as both men have an affinity for family. Although Cochise does not indicate a spouse or children, he comprehends the love relationship that develops between Jeffords and the young Indian woman Sonseeahray, which is translated as Morningstar (Debra Paget). After Cochise describes the host of problems and hateful environments the couple would face in both the white and Indian societies, he, in respect for their affection, explains to Jeffords the steps that must be taken to compete for and attain the right to marry an Indian woman. Jeffords acquiesces and follows the Apache requirements as Cochise serves as the negotiator of the union with Morningstar's family. In the story's final segment, after the marriage, Jeffords is wounded and Morningstar killed in an ambush led by Ben Slade and his men. However, Cochise refuses to permit Jeffords to act on his anger and feelings of revenge, as he scolds: "You're a child that you thought peace would come so easily.... Hear me now, this [the ambush] was not done by the military. As I have beared the murder of my people, so you will bear the murder of your wife." Cochise functions as the voice of reason and peace, while he comforts as a friend to give meaning to Jeffords's grief.

Although correctly criticized because it "feature[s] white actors playing the lead Indian roles ... Jeff Chandler and Debra Paget,"[4] *Broken Arrow* still demonstrates the possibilities for revisionist films that would follow, such as *Little Big Man* (1970) and *Dances with Wolves* (1990). Jeffords and Cochise represent the best of those desirable traits found in men who aspire to construct communities of tolerance and cross-cultural intimacies.

Broken Arrow reached theaters in 1950; that year also marked the appearance on the big screen of Sidney Poitier, the black actor who would become an icon for integration over the next seventeen years. Fortunately for the black male image, the "problem" films of 1949 facilitated the arrival of Sidney Poitier in *No Way Out* (1950), a dramatic film that had Poitier portraying a doctor and a family man. Within the twenty-seven films in which Poitier appeared between 1950 and 1967, a number of them deliberately explored the manner in which interracial cooperation and understanding were achievable elements within American society. In various roles showing racial, class and familial issues, Poitier personified the attributes deemed noble and exceptional for black male characters, and by implication, the black community. Collectively, the plurality of his characters, as in *The Blackboard Jungle* (1955), *Edge of the City* (1957), *Pressure Point* (1962), and *The Bedford Incident* (1965), to name some films, displayed humanity, integrity, and willingness to extend a hand of friendship across racial lines, confirming the potential for interracial connections.

In his autobiography, Poitier reflects philosophically about his career at that time. He writes: "This was still the 1950s America, however, an America in which a career like this had never been dreamed of for an outsider of color; it had never happened before in the history of the movie business—a black leading man.... I saw the truth clear as could be. The explanation for my career was that I was instrumental for those few filmmakers who had a social conscience."[5] Mentioning names such as Stanley Kramer and David Susskind, the actor acknowledges that history, creativity, politics, and access to the Hollywood system all intersected in a given set of years to give him the opportunity to transform the black male image and by association the representation of all African Americans.

In particular, there were four films between 1950 and 1967 that showcased characters portrayed by Poitier who developed connections that went beyond friendship and much deeper into a bonding that was life-altering for the characters. In these interracial buddy vehicles, black and white males encountered experiences that underscored their shared masculinity and their interlinking with one another.

One of the best films of the era brought together some memorable acting and visual symbolism without losing itself in melodrama. *The Defiant Ones* (1959), which has inspired many copycat movies since its appearance, still works effectively by a contemporary standards. Two prisoners—Joker Jackson (Tony Curtis) and Noah Cullen (Poitier)—are chained together when their transport vehicle has an accident in the rainy weather. Desperate to find freedom, the men fight one another verbally and physically, even while searching for a way to break their common chain. Eventually, they stumble across a farm where a white woman (Cara Williams) raises her son alone. Consequently, Joker must decide between a new life with the woman or saving the life of Cullen who has been deliberately given the wrong direction into a quicksand-laden swamp.

With solid acting and a thoughtful script, the film goes beyond the obvious message of chaining together men of different races by exploring the motivation behind each man's desperation. On the one hand, Joker and

In *The Defiant Ones*, Joker (Tony Curtis, left) weighs the choice between his buddy, Cullen (Sidney Poitier, center), and his love interest, the "Woman" (Cara Williams).

Cullen represent in a general way their respective races, but as individuals, they surface as average men trapped by circumstances they didn't create. As such, there are both innocent and guilty of law-breaking at the same time. Significantly, as restricting as the chain that binds them is the burden of racist thoughts and experiences that seek to destroy their souls. In order to survive, they must break the social and psychological fetters of racism that obscure their humanity before their can break the actual chain that will lead them to physical freedom. At one confrontational moment, Cullen exclaims: "Joker, don't call me boy.... You breathe it [racism] in when you're born, and you spit it out from then on." Joker defends his racist epithets and attitudes by telling Cullen: "That's the way it is, and you're stuck with it, because I didn't make any of the rules." Like naturalistic characters destined and shaped by their environments, both Joker and Cullen refuse to see beyond the surface of the other man, maintaining the conventional notions given to them by the larger society.

But the need for survival erases all the social prescriptions, leaving them to understand their interdependence, particularly as they attempt to cross a rushing river; to climb up the slippery slopes of a clay pit; to steal food via the rooftop of a general store; and to hop a speeding train at the film's finale. In their thwarted efforts to rob the general store, they find themselves faced with a mob preparing to lynch them for striking down a white citizen. In an effort to save himself, Joker emphasizes that he's "a white man," which falls empty to the mob's thirst for blood. Joker comprehends that with ignorance driving the mob, even race falls short, as both he and Cullen are viewed as the same. The same ignorance that spirits the mob is the same blindness that nurtures racism. Joker and Cullen's salvation comes in the form of Big Sam (Lon Chaney) who stands up defiantly to the mob, secretly releasing the two, as his own prison scars become evident.

Another corresponding experience that both men undergo revolves around women. Cullen, whose wife is never seen on-screen, confesses to Joker that she never understood how he felt inside, and the way in which a racist society suppressed his efforts to be a man, i.e., a provider for his family and an independent farmer/businessman. Later, after the farm woman informs Joker that she's directed Cullen to a sure death, Joker erupts in anger, as the woman pleads that she did it for him. Joker responds: "You don't know me. You don't know anything about me." Joker, an obvious heterosexual from his flirting and embracing, craves the woman's companionship but fails to connect with her as he does Cullen. Joker chooses a fugitive existence with Cullen rather than the possible freedom with the woman for whom he lusts. Joker and Cullen have discovered in one another an ability to speak innermost feelings without expectations that chide their sense of masculinity. In the final moments, the two even joke about their learned caring for one another, as Joker teases: "You're gonna make someone a fine old lady one day." Cullen returns: "Ain't it the truth." By making a joke of their lives without women and the failure of relationships with the opposite sex, the aspect of homoeroticism that might have surfaced from their earlier touching and emotional sharing is put to rest. Because they can laugh at traits that might be assumed to be feminine, they attest to the gender orientation that confirms them as "normal" males.

Just as *The Defiant Ones* is the ideal movie for the age of civil rights, it also demonstrates the ideal interracial buddy film that encompasses the pattern of transforming hatred to respect and racial difference to racial blindness, while allowing for caring and trust within the confines of a heterosexual framework. The interracial buddy films that followed its framework, particularly *Fled* (1996) with Laurence Fishburne and Stephen Baldwin, never quite achieve the quality of script and political relevance.

Two additional Poitier films require attention, though their overall pattern is not the conventional buddyship as developed in *The Defiant Ones*. Instead, they are films that utilized social institutions—the military (*All the Young Men*) and law enforcement (*In the Heat of the Night*)—to comment on the manner in which men were conditioned to hate across racial lines.

The war drama *All the Young Men* (1960) could be viewed as a film that attempts to pick up where *Home of the Brave* (1949) left off. In the summer of 1948 with Executive Order 9981, President Harry Truman pronounced that there would be "equality of treatment and opportunity" in the United States military, ushering in the racial desegregation of the armed forces.[6] Consequently, the Korean War served as testing ground for the historical policy, and *All the Young Men* explores the issue in a movie containing graphic war scenes for its time.

When a group of marines is ambushed while on a mission to secure a strategically located farmhouse, a dying lieutenant turns over the command to Sergeant Towler (Poitier), a black soldier with book knowledge, rather than Sergeant Kincaid (Alan Ladd), a white soldier with field experience. Towler, now in charge of nine white soldiers and with the responsibility to complete the mission, assumes a problematic position knowing that North Korean soldiers, who outnumber them, are advancing toward the same location.

The backdrop of the icy, snowy hills symbolizes the attitudes that the white men possess, though one soldier, Bracken (Paul Richards), expresses his displeasure aloud. He insists early on to the others: "They're [blacks] just not able to do it [command]. They're not born to do it." Towler and Bracken's verbal confrontation leads to a physical fight when Towler prevents the latter from sexually assaulting a Korean woman living at the farmhouse.

With a much more personal stake in being passed over for command, Kincaid fans the flames of prejudice by questioning and second-guessing Tolwer's orders. In one scene, Kincaid berates Towler in front of the other men by concluding: "One black man with an axe to grind. We don't pull out, and you'll be a hero. You might even get the Navy Cross. And when all your people hear what you've done, they'll build a statue for you in the cotton fields." Feeling humiliated by not being in charge, Kincaid uses race as the weapon to undermine the black man's competent leadership.

Interestingly, a dramatic turn occurs following the smashing of Kincaid's leg beneath an enemy tank. When the medic named Wade (Glenn Corbett) is compelled to amputate Kincaid's leg to save his life, the only soldier with compatible blood for transfusion is Towler. In a symbolic moment in the film, Bracken, the racist, must hold together the intravenous tubes that carry the black man's blood into the dying white man.

By the final battle scene, the white men have been transformed, and as they follow orders from and fight beside their black leader, the film reaches its ultimate statement. When Towler carries a recuperating Kincaid over his shoulder through the enemy bombs attacking the farmhouse, the black and white soldiers make one last stand together from a foxhole. Committed to dying together, the two are saved as American planes fly over and deliver an attack against the advancing enemy.

All the Young Men openly treats the problems of the enemy within — racism — and its potentially deleterious effect on individuals and an entire community of men. Lifting Towler to a heroic status assures the white viewers that the same courage under fire could benefit a peaceful co-existence at home. Although melodramatic at places, the movie proclaims that the racial problem rests with the narrow-minded whites, not inherently with a psychological disorder in African Americans.

The Korean War drama *All the Young Men* presents men in racial conflict: Sergeant Kincaid (Alan Ladd, left), Sergeant Towler (Sidney Poitier, center), and Private Bracken (Paul Richards).

Seven years later, a similar dissection of the problem at home serves as the focus of the award-winning film *In the Heat of the Night*. In the southern setting of Sparta, Mississippi, a small-town Sheriff Gillespie (Rod Steiger) must confront his own racial biases when a black city detective named Virgil Tibbs (Poitier) uses reasoning and intelligence to solve a murder. With Tibbs being "portrayed in an asexual guise,"[7] the character suffers from the same kind of one-dimensional treatment as Sergeant Towler in *All the Young Men*. With Tibbs set up on a heroic pedestal, the racial sins of Gillespie and his fellow white men in the town are laid bare for their tragic history and oppressive present.

The progress from the racist past to the future is measured in the scene where Tibbs and Gillespie travel to the agricultural estate of white land baron Mr. Endicott (Larry Gates). Subtly investigating the elder Endicott while in his greenhouse, Tibbs defers to the man's racist analogy of dependent flowers and the child-like dependence of blacks upon whites. However, when Endicott slaps Tibbs for insolence, Tibbs without hesitation strikes him back, stunning both Endicott and Gillespie. In Tibbs's action, as well as his intelligence, he announces his equality of manhood. His defiance of the old South (Endicott) and his defiance of the conventional laws (Gillespie) echo the burgeoning black pride and determinism in society. However, Tibbs's middle-class values and his willingness to work the case with Gilliespie — after vehement support by the murder victim's wife, Mrs. Colbert (Lee Grant) — indicate that Tibbs still believes in the system. Consequently, as the movie moves into its last act, Tibbs and Gillespie have discovered a common ground rooted in their allegiance to the law, their common belief in justice, and their ability to surpass the barriers of racism.

The attention received by *In the Heat of the Night*, both through its box-office success and its winning of five Academy Awards, suggests that, in addition to its acting and creative elements, the film resonated with viewers and their integrationist mood, confirmed by the passing of the Civil Rights Act and the Voting Rights Act in 1964 and 1965, respectively. Yet some voices responded in an impatient manner to what was perceived as the saintly, sterile black males portrayed by Poitier when dealing with whites.[8] From a more cautionary perspective, scholars Hernan Vera and Andrew M. Gordon claim: "*In the Heat of the Night* proposes another false dichotomy typical of Hollywood film: white racism is a disease confined to the South, and all Northerners are liberal.... Such portrayals allow white Northerners to congratulate themselves on their open mindedness in comparison to these benighted Southern rednecks."[9]

With a demonstrative shift of tone and environment, the drama *Paris*

In a clash with racist traditions, Detective Virgil Tibbs (Sidney Poitier, center) challenges plantation owner Mr. Endicott (Larry Gates, left) and Sheriff Gillespie (Rod Steiger) in the drama *In the Heat of the Night*.

Blues (1961) utilizes music — specifically jazz — and the romance genre to present a more authentic interracial buddy duo of the '60s. Living in the title city, Ram Bowen (Paul Newman), a white trombonist, and Eddie Cook (Sidney Poitier), a black saxophonist, are already popular fixtures on the music scene as the film opens, their accomplishments as jazz musicians well-known through both their club gigs and records. These two men have an established bond through the significance of music and the city. Functioning here as characters themselves, the "music" and the "city" influence Bowen and Cook as each finds passion in the former and freedom in the latter. Yet, unlike the "rat pack" films where the black buddy's ethnic identity is erased for his acceptance, in *Paris Blues*, racial identity is acknowledged and racial difference isn't qualified in polarities of superior-inferior. This point emerges during the opening credits, as the camera scans the small Paris café where Bowen and Cook play with their band on stage. The café patrons are black and white; homosexual and straight; interracial and intraracial; old and young. Their differences don't disappear, but the differences do not become an issue of conflict. Bowen

and Cook function as a microcosm of that café audience, as their friendship possesses enduring, patient, and affectionate aspects to it.

As single males in Paris and as musicians who play all night — gathering sleep and rest during the daylight hours—both Bowen and Cook
live in the moment. Their lives, centered in music, are devoid of long-
range plans and extensive responsibilities beyond their personal concerns.
And despite their closeness and shared lives, the men's sexual orientation
is never a question as Bowen's French girlfriend, Marie (Barbara Laage),
conducts an ongoing, loosely structured romance with him. Then, with
the arrival of Lily (Joanne Woodward) and Connie (Diahann Carroll), two
teachers on a two-week vacation, both men confront the effects of romance
on their music, viewpoints, and decisions.

When Bowen first meets the two at the train station, he initially flirts
with Connie —further emphasizing the interracial theme depicted in the
opening café sequence. Yet, as the evening develops, he finds himself drawn
to Lily's assertive and confident manner, as Cook and Connie pair off in
a quick physical attraction. As with most romance films, there's much
excitement and joy that the couples experience over the following twelve
days, while dealing with the truths of conflicting desires. Bowen admits
his love for Lily, but he broods over his wish to be known as an accomplished composer as well as a jazz musician. Cook admits his love for Connie, but he can't envision returning to live in the racial segregation of the
United States, the place that Connie claims as home for both of them. With
both couples, there is engaging dialogue as they unpeel the layers of surface banter to deal with more complex issues hiding beneath.

For example, Cook and Connie have moved back and forth in their
discussions about racial politics in America. After Cook returns a stray ball
to a young French boy, the latter calls him "Monsieur Noir." Connie asserts
that Cook would not accept being called "black" in America, but he allows
it in Paris. Cook asserts that he is indeed "a black man," but that the meaning is different in Paris than in the United States. He clarifies: "Here,
nobody says Eddie Cook, Negro musician. They say musician, period....
I don't have to prove anything else, like because I'm Negro I'm different
... because I'm Negro, I'm not different. I'm different, I'm not different!
Who cares? Look, I don't have to prove either case.... For me, Paris is just
fine!"

A gender-linked aspect of the Bowen-Cook buddyship is that
although they both acknowledge each other's romantic interest, they avoid
discussing their love interests directly. Instead, they allow a cushion of
silence about their love lives, even as they openly express their passion
for the music. This passion shines in the film's most energetic and

accomplished musical sequences, where dialogue becomes unnecessary. While Bowen and Cook play at the café, jazz great Wild Man Moore (Louis Armstrong) enters the club with his band, and an improvisational party erupts. As Wild Man delivers a musical challenge with his trumpet, Bowen and Cook respond with solos on their respective instruments. The two display orgasmic expressions on their faces as they jam, while the club patrons go into a frenzy.

Bowen and Cook carry the moniker of "artists" as they experience a bond based upon their distinct personalities. They arrange compositions together, they argue, they trust, and they protect one another. *Paris Blues* offers an exemplary buddy duo, where music and creativity take the place of the violence and action that structures most interracial buddy relationships, lifting the male bonding beyond mere physical expression.

The buddy films of Sidney Poitier during the civil rights era have been enduring works of cinematic and political value. However, one of the most popular buddyships at the time found an audience in the western genre and among the media of radio, film, and television — namely the Lone Ranger and Tonto. As a radio program the series began airing in 1933, and then it "became a long running television show (ABC-TV, 1949–57, plus an even longer life in syndication)."[10] The interracial heroes stormed the big screen in two features films: *The Lone Ranger* (1956) and *The Lone Ranger and the Lost City of Gold* (1958). Perhaps the longevity of the series contributed to the enormous popularity, but certainly during the 1950s, the clear, simple ethics and enduring friendship of the duo fit easily into small- and big-screen entertainment that confirmed conventional values while providing sufficient escapism.

As established in the 1949 television episode, *The Lone Ranger*'s story unfolded with a dying Texas Ranger who barely survived an ambush by the villainous Cavendish gang and his subsequent nurturing to health by Tonto (Jay Silverheels), the peripatetic Indian who found him. Calling the white man "Kemo Sabe," i.e., "trusty scout,"[11] Tonto supported the Ranger's commitment to fighting for frontier justice and his decision to wear a mask to remain anonymous. Using silver bullets to wound but never to kill, and riding his signature white horse, Silver, the Lone Ranger (Clayton Moore) was never really alone as Tonto, riding his pinto Scout, remained a trusted and loyal partner regardless of circumstances that placed them both in dangerous situations for which they reaped no financial or social rewards.

The first film, *The Lone Ranger*, placed the well-known duo in an adventure in which they prevented "a [white] rancher's plot to destroy an Indian reservation."[12] With more interest, the second feature, *The Lone*

Ranger and the Lost City of Gold, connected directly to the themes of racial tolerance and cultural pride, thus reflecting the civil rights issues in the larger society. In a rather complicated plot, the Lone Ranger (Moore) and Tonto (Silverheels) help an Indian tribe living near a mission to solve numerous murders instigated by a group of masked men. Eventually, the duo discern that the murders, connected to obtaining information about the location of a gold mine on the Indian grounds, were carried out by a conspiracy between several upstanding white citizens in the town. As a parallel story, the town's young physician, Dr. Rolfe (Dean Fredericks), who is actually Indian, has been "passing" in order to obtain a reputation and resources to help his local tribe.

The conspicuous brand of partnership between the Lone Ranger and Tonto is reinforced in this story. First of all, Tonto remains steadfast in protecting the Ranger's true identity and in upholding the codes that motivate the Ranger's action. Both men are without women, children, and family members; their symbolic marriage to the law bonds their vision of the world. For the two, there is no gray area that's defensible when it comes to their principles of what's right and wrong. At the same time, they share a philosophy of justice that renders them deep insight into human behavior. For instance, after Tonto is beaten in town by angry white assailants as the sheriff watches approvingly, Tonto later remarks to the Ranger and others: "Bruises on body go away, but sheriff has sickness that can't be fixed with medicine." The Ranger and Tonto comprehend the many forms of evil, and their tacit wisdom manifests itself as assertive, but respectful, behavior to protect and serve.

Although their buddyship serves as a hallmark for white–Indian connections, upon closer inspection, there is still a perceptible difference that falls along racial lines— specifically, a hierarchy of control. Similar to what was exhibited in earlier decades via the Jack Benny–Rochester union, this hierarchy revolves around the positioning of leadership of the white buddy over the buddy of color. For example, when Tonto enters the town alone, and subsequently challenges and punches down the sheriff, who is about to strike an Indian woman, Tonto stands tall as a man defending another in need of help. This incident and others demonstrate that Tonto displays no fear of white men. He perceives himself as an equal, and though his broken English and complexion might bring some resentment from white characters, Tonto never carries himself in a servile manner when dealing with others. However, in a salient manner, Tonto becomes more pliable when in the presence of "Kemo Sabe." When they share the screen together, Tonto defers to the Ranger's plans and pronouncements in a "yes man" fashion. Consequently, the Ranger's status becomes magnified in its importance relegating Tonto to a secondary tier beneath his white companion. The Ranger assumes control in situations and the response to them, accepting Tonto's input but ultimately making the final decisions. Their relationship doesn't contain any vitriolic exchanges between the men, but it does resonate with a discernible ranking. This type of hierarchy would surface again in later Hollywood films in which the rule of keeping a priority position for the white male buddy has been followed consistently.

In hindsight, some contemporary critics delivered more splenetic evaluations of the duo. With a psychoanalytic view, scholar Michael Kimmel concludes: "*The Lone Ranger* provided a new homosocial interracial couple in which the moral and innocent white Ranger, removed from society and left for dead, is then nursed back to health by the male mother and Native American spirit guide, Tonto."[13] With this assessment, the man of color functions primarily as the emotional and psychological caretaker of the inherently righteous white protagonist. With a scathing dismissal, scholars Harry M. Benshoff and Sean Griffin reflect: "*The Lone Ranger* attempted to draw the white man and the Indian together as a team that fought injustice. Yet Tonto, the Native American half of the team, was always clearly subservient to the Lone Ranger (and in fact, Tonto means 'crazy' in Spanish). Tonto is a good example of the Indian as noble savage stereotype, playing helpful sidekick to white men and white culture."[14]

Tonto, unlike Cochise in *Broken Arrow*, never insists to his white buddy that fighting "injustice" should have a priority in regard to Indians; instead, the impact of "injustice" on white men and white culture serves as the primary concern. Without a more three-dimensional rendering during the civil rights age, the Lone Ranger and Tonto were short-lived heroes on the big screen, gaining a more sustained presence in 30-minute episodes on television until 1957, before finding an audience again in reruns. Under the umbrella of simplistic storytelling, and despite strident criticism, the duo have survived as indelible icons of frontier heroism and interracial harmony.

By the beginning of the 1960s, the screen presence of Sidney Poitier — along with black actors such as Harry Belafonte and Ossie Davis—facilitated the transition of Sammy Davis, Jr., from an acknowledged song-and-dance man to an actor with comic and dramatic potential. But he never attained that renown as an "actor," as both critics and popular audiences assessed him continually as a "multitalented entertainer." His immersion into buddy films has remained his most memorable screen presence and, simultaneously, the cause of much of his pejorative criticism.

Davis's career includes two sets of buddy pictures — one with the Rat

Pack and a second with only one member of the pack. The latter set — the two films *Salt and Pepper* (1968) and its sequel, *One More Time* (1970), which was directed by Jerry Lewis— teams Davis with white actor Peter Lawford, but both movies failed to win the laudations of critics or scholars. *Salt and Pepper* follows the title characters— Davis is Charles Salt and Lawford is Christopher Pepper —who are British nightclub owners pulled into the dangerous world of spies in order to solve two murders at their club. One critic calls the film a "congenial but tepid spy spoof,"[15] while another publication declares that "the pseudo–[James] Bond action and the slapstick comedy are excruciatingly ill-timed."[16] In a scathing rejection of Davis's roles in both films, critic Donald Bogle insists the actor "returned to his comic coon figures ... as [h]e portrayed Lawford's loyal man Friday ... a regrettably embarrassing figure with little spunk or artistry."[17] In the sequel, *One More Time*, Salt and Pepper return to solve the death of Pepper's twin brother, who was involved in smuggling diamonds.[18]

By the time Davis assumed the role of Charles Salt, he seemed an anachronism amidst the changing image of black masculinity in the late 1960s. In particular, athlete-turned-actor Jim Brown fashioned a different persona that emphasized a physical toughness, sexuality, and ethnic pride absent from the black male characters of the Civil Rights era. In films such as *The Dirty Dozen* (1967), *100 Rifles* (1968), *Riot* (1969), and *Tick, Tick, Tick* (1970), Brown's angry and radical roles reflected the black male image of the inner city and black power, making the integrationist brotherhood emphasized by Davis's character irrelevant to the social and political changes at the end of the decade.

Unfortunately for Davis, his earlier set of buddy films brought no better response to his acting or characterizations but were celebrated more as commercial vehicles that gathered together the group of male entertainers called the Rat Pack — including Davis, Frank Sinatra, Dean Martin, and Peter Lawford as the central four. Known to be friends off-screen, and interactive in each other's personal and professional lives, the group completed three movies between 1960 and 1964, with two gaining box office popularity.

The first, *Ocean's 11* (1960), developed a buddyhood within the "caper genre." The titular protagonist, Danny Ocean (Sinatra), is a sergeant in the Army's 82nd Airborne Division, and he brings together his army buddies from fifteen years earlier to pull off a robbery of five Las Vegas casinos on New Year's Eve. Using their special skills learned in the service, the ex-soldiers carry out a seamless plan, which goes awry at the end when one member dies of a heart attack and is cremated in a coffin that contains the stolen money.

As with most heist movies, gathering the participants from their sundry backgrounds becomes part of the plot device. Sam (Martin) makes a living as a womanizing lounge singer; Josh (Davis) drives a garbage truck; and Jimmy (Lawford) lives an affluent life of privilege. The men complement one another through their previously formed alliance during the war, and their heist rekindles the flames of friendship that lay dormant for years. Josh, specifically, becomes the primary racialized character since Italian or Irish ethnicities are not emphasized in the plot. In fact, Josh's black identity finds its underscoring primarily through the character's own speech patterns and antics. At places in the story, Josh punctuates his ethnicity by affecting a stereotypical black vernacular, or by sarcastically stating lines such as, "I knew my color would come in handy one day." At the same time, Josh has his screen moments when he mumbles in a black vernacular that is audible to the audience, and at places a pronounced "who dat?" emerges.

In another racially charged image, when Josh first enters the film, he sings and dances in his work clothes with other men of color while taking a break on the job at the garbage company. Significantly, Sammy Davis, as Josh, is presented first as an entertainer. On the other hand, though Sam sings in a lounge during the night of the robbery, he first enters the film in a suit and tie flying into the airport to connect with Ocean. Dean Martin, as Sam, first appears as a dramatic character, and then the character's entertainment segment serves as his skill for the heist.

Yet, as expected for the times, among his white comrades, Josh remains colorless, which affirms the lack of bigotry among his fellow ex-soldiers. One particular racial issue avoided in discussion revolves around the interaction of Ocean's army buddies in World War II. Since blacks and whites were segregated in the military during that war, how was Josh a part of Ocean's unit? This racial issue, which receives far more dramatic attention in the film *Home of the Brave*, floats away without comment here.

One issue that does receive varying degrees of comment revolves around women. In this story of men, women are tangentially presented — as Ocean's alienated wife, Bee (Angie Dickinson); Jimmy's spoiled and indifferent mother; Ocean's off-and-on girlfriend, Adele (Patrice Wymore); and a lonely, intoxicated drunk (a cameo by Shirley MacLaine). Danny Ocean and his buddies inhabit a world where men rule and serve as the center in the lives of women. When Danny and Jimmy are first shown on screen, they lounge in a hotel room, being massaged by two women who are quickly dismissed when the two men need to discuss business. Later, after confirming each man's responsibility in the Vegas robbery, the men discuss their plans once they've stolen the millions. Sam remarks: "I'm the one going into politics … repeal the Fourteenth and Twentieth amendments. Take voting away from women and make slaves of them." To this futuristic, misogynistic dream, all the men chuckle in comprehension, including Josh, who doesn't appear concerned by the plans for slavery.

Tough, smart, loyal, and ambitious—these are the men of Ocean's crew. And as interracial buddies, they support, protect, and trust one another, including their black comrade, who never is made to feel different due to his race. And on his part, the black buddy blends in with their masculine banter about the old army days and the joys of pulling off the impossible robbery. These 40-something buddies find rejuvenation in the challenge of the dangerous and the hunt for riches. Their masculinity, ignited again, targets the achievement of the unthinkable, therefore defining their courage, ambition, and fearlessness.

The antics continue in the same manner in *Robin and the Seven Hoods* (1964), with a story loosely based on characters found in the Robin Hood legend. Framed as a musical-comedy, this movie exists merely as a vehicle for fun for the three stars—Sinatra, Martin, and Davis—and their fans.

The *Ocean's 11* crew rally before their big heist. From left to right: Tony Bergdorf (Richard Conte), Vince Massler (Buddy Lester), "Mushy" O'Connors (Joey Bishop), Josh Howard (Sammy Davis, Jr.), Danny Ocean (Frank Sinatra), Sam Harmon (Dean Martin), Jimmy Foster (Peter Lawford), Spyros Aceros (Akim Tamiroff), Roger Corneal (Henry Silva, in background), "Curly" Steffens (Richard Benedict, with mustache), Peter Rheimer (Norman Fell, with tie) and Louis "Cowboy" Jackson (Clem Harvey, in plaid shirt).

Set in Depression-era Chicago, the story follows the ongoing conflict involving a North Side gangster called Robbo (Sinatra) and his crew, including Little John (Martin) and Will (Davis), who are protecting their power structure against the aggression of mobster Guy Gisborne (Peter Falk) and his gang.

Once again, the racial line becomes erased between the two white lead characters, who accept Will — who seems to be the only black person in the city — as an equal in their land of gambling. Will, on his part, is comfortable and integral to the crew, even as his deference to Robbo, "the boss," looms saliently. But for the most part, Will is integrated into the gangster machine as emphasized in two song-and-dance sequences that he shares with Robbo and Little John.

In Will's solo number, two noteworthy aspects find visualization. First, after attacking and destroying their rival's night club, Will performs an up-tempo, high-energy tune with the lyrics, "I like the fun of reaching for a gun and going bang-bang!" Here, Will pulls out two handguns while tap dancing, shooting the interior randomly, and following up by spraying the walls with a machine gun. Will, who is diminutive in physical size, utilizes the guns to affirm his masculine prowess — which is important since he has no romantic moments with the opposite sex as Robbo and Little John do. However, at the same time, his gun handling and violent nature are softened by the musical number that frames the scene. He is a heterosexual black male — by virtue of the phallic weapons — but not threatening to any of his white comrades. His aggressive actions come from his affiliation with Robbo and Little John, but his behavior is kept within the realm of the benevolent sidekick. So, curiously, he's the traditional cinematic black clown, but at other places, he's just one of the white guys.

* * *

The 1950s–1960s were years that maintained the interracial buddy motif within the vicissitudes of the civil rights agenda. As such, the standards of maleness were rigid and always associated with white male images. As Robert Bly summarizes, "the '50s male ... was hardworking, responsible, fairly well disciplined ... was vulnerable to collective opinion ... [was] supposed to like football games, be aggressive, stick up for the United States, never cry, and always provide.... The '50s man had a clear vision of what a man is, but the vision involved massive inadequacies and flaws."[19] Under this umbrella of traits, the interracial buddy pattern during this time worked effectively to assure audiences of a dominant masculinity that could transcend racial differences.

3

Urban Grit, Crossover, and the Philly Southpaw: 1970s

Against a backdrop of social and political milestones, the 70s began with the tragedy of Kent State and Jackson State in 1970, evolving to a cease-fire in Vietnam in 1973. The Watergate break-in in 1972; Wounded Knee in 1973; Southerner Jimmy Carter becoming president in 1976; anti-nuclear activists in 1977; the Bakke decision in 1978; and the burgeoning women's movement were some of the markers of a decade that began with fervent political confrontations and ended with disco.[1]

In American cinema of the '70s, black urban action films, deemed "blaxploitation," saved Hollywood studios from bankruptcy, as a new phase of graphic sex and violence became integral to American feature films. Profane and scatological language flowed from the lips of movie stars in stories showing a new era of cynicism and moral ambiguity. Feature films were diverse in genre and scope, though, as film historian David A. Cook suggests, the decade saw Hollywood nurturing the "blockbuster" as the desirable form, sending production costs escalating in the hopes of the big box office payoff. Cook astutely concludes that the "seventies also marked a conscious return to the production of genre films, sequels, and series, which were more typical of classical Hollywood than the post-studio era."[2] The major studios hit their target audiences with a mélange of mainstream hits, including *Love Story* (1970), *The Godfather* (1972), *The Exorcist* (1973), *Jaws* (1975), *Star Wars* (1977), *Saturday Night Fever* (1977), *Annie Hall* (1977), *Apocalypse Now* (1979), and *Alien* (1979).

While the decade underwent a magnitude of changes, the inter-racial buddy film served as a forum for resolving cultural, class, and ethnic conflicts while affirming the conventional notions of masculinity visualized on the screen decades earlier. Fostered in two particular types of films—the comedy and the sports film—humor and athleticism functioned as the best methods for cradling male bravado and the buddy paradigm.

The decade began with a western that attempted to show, in epic proportions, the manner in which one white man travels in a picaresque fashion between cultures fraught with antagonism. *Little Big Man* (1970) chronicles the fate of Jack Crab (Dustin Hoffman) who, when 10 years old, survives an ambush by the Pawnee tribe and is taken in by a group of Cheyenne who call themselves human beings. Critic David Denby remarks that the "movie tells wonderful lies, but it often has the *spirit* of actuality in a way that ordinary lying Westerns do not…. It's a movie that is reverent about certain human qualities—particularly those embodied in the slaughtered Cheyenne."[3] Narrating his story at age 121, Crab vacillates between humorous, tragic, and mystical experiences from his past, emphasizing the enduring relationship he shares with the senior chief of the human beings, named Old Lodge Skins (Chief Dan George). Through his acculturation with the Cheyenne, Crab develops a number of relationships with other braves—growing up together, fighting the enemy, fighting one another, and trusting one another. However, it is the connection with Old Lodge Skins that frames Crab's masculine education. Through direct instruction and sagacious promptings, Crab acquires those traits—riding, hunting, weaponry, killing, and temperament—essential to his male status in the Cheyenne tribe. In fact "temperament" plays an essential part in a warrior's manhood, as shown through Little Horse (Robert Little Star), whose effeminacy requires him to stay behind with the women. Crab learns that as a Cheyenne man, he must conduct himself in a manner that makes him fit in with the expectations of other tribe members, rather than standing individually. Manhood is taught through specific physical and emotional actions, while being discernible to those who watch. For example, once married, Crab must show his manhood not only by impregnating his wife, Sunshine (Amy Eccles), but also by having sexual intercourse with Sunshine's three husbandless sisters in the same night in the same tent. And later, when unable to kill George Custer for pillaging the village and killing Sunshine, Crab observes that he was a "total failure as an Indian." Virility and killing one's enemy serve as conspicuous traits of masculinity; failing at the latter, Crab drifts back into white society and alcoholism.

From his earliest days among the tribe, Crab's lessons in being a warrior and a genuine Cheyenne man are reinforced through Old Lodge Skins's continual presence. Though Crab calls him Grandfather, Old Lodge

Skins serves as many male figures—father, brother, and buddy. It becomes clear that the senior Indian takes to Crab immediately, nurturing the young white boy who becomes the man that the elder envisioned. Later, when his eyesight is gone, Old Lodge Skins literally relies upon Crab to be his vision through the temporal world. At the same time, the elder shares his inner visions of the spirit world with his white protégé. Crab becomes a confidant, and his race ceases to exist for Old Lodge Skins, who views him as an Indian just like himself. Out of all the Indians in their village-family, Crab becomes the escort for Old Lodge Skins to his burial grounds at the end. There, Old Lodge Skins confesses to Crab his innermost sadness at the manner in which white men have destroyed the Indians and the land. Asserting that he is ready to die, the elder reasons: "There is no other way to deal with white men.... There's an endless supply of white men, but there's always been a limited number of human beings." The double meanings in Old Lodge Skins's statement carry a particular significance for Crab. Although white by birth, Crab reaches an equal cultural, racial, and gender standing with the senior Indian. As such, their bond surpasses the socially prescribed rules that dictate that the two must be enemies. On the contrary, the two discover that their personal losses—Crab's loss of his biological family and Old Lodge Skins's loss of his way of life—produce the fabric of their common destiny. Their constructed connection represents the ideal nature of a white–Indian male relationship.

The symbolic value of the white–Indian bond between Jack Crab and Old Lodge Skins speaks to the ideal that racial animosity could be assuaged and cultural assimilation could be attained. Additionally, the bond anointed the Indian culture as the more admirable of the two, intrinsic with systems of interconnected gender roles, respect for life forms, and self-dignity.

Moving forward into a twentieth-century setting, the concept of dignity finds itself on a back shelf when three sailors express their wild natures in *The Last Detail* (1973). In this dramatic comedy, the elements of masculine behavior surface through those actions popularly associated with single military men. The story presents two petty officers who receive orders to escort a young sailor from a Naval base in Virginia for an eight-year sentence in the New Hampshire Naval prison. White officer Buddusky (Jack Nicholson) and black officer Mulhall (Otis Young) seize the opportunity to travel and break the monotony of their naval careers by guarding a naïve white seaman named Meadows (Randy Quaid), but along the way, they grow fond of their prisoner, who committed a minor offense and who will miss out on years of carousing. Deciding to show the kid one last good time, Buddusky and Mulhall stretch the rules a bit, bringing the reluctant and socially retarded young man out of his shell.

Over the period of several days, the three cuss, get drunk, fight marines, argue with vendors, gamble, peruse a sex shop, attend a party, smoke grass, and visit a prostitution house. And though they fail to transform Meadows completely to their reckless level, they do liberate his moral restraints, making the duty to surrender him to the prison more difficult.

Buddusky and Mulhall serve as a complementary duo. In many ways they share a disdain for what they are doing. As "lifers," both men assert their need for the Navy, but underneath, a common resentment simmers about their status in the military's pecking order. Both men have the same rank and the same obstinate attitude about taking orders. The Navy becomes their source of purpose and simultaneously the limiting factor in their lives, and they don't or can't see a life outside of the service.

It is that aspect of sameness that ligates the two, who previously didn't know one another, but who, by the end of the detail, recognize their connection. The primary tie is the uniform and all that it symbolizes, and while wearing those colors, the men are interchangeable. Despite the contrast between Buddusky's instigative and prankish personality versus Mulhall's voice of reason, the parity that exists resonates through various scenes. Notably, at a bar when a white bartender refuses to serve Mulhall because he's black, Buddusky leaps at the "redneck," pulling a gun and scaring the "cracker" into some manners. Afterwards, they celebrate their victory over the racist by getting drunk on beer in a parking lot. Later, at a party with white Buddhist-chanting pacifists, Buddusky and Mulhall make their seductive moves on the available women. The former never challenges the latter on approaching a white woman, as race never emerges as an issue in regard to sexual prowess. Both men are soon bored with the women, who would rather talk politics than sexual positions. Then, at the house of prostitution, while waiting in the lounge for Meadows to consummate his visit, Buddusky and Mulhall discuss marriage. Buddusky confesses that his short-term marriage made demands he didn't want to accept; Mulhall states that he never married but supported his mother financially. Both men, now married to the Navy, see little room for romantic involvement and commitment, but believe that sexual pleasure always comes with a price. For example, earlier, when Meadows attempts to use a Buddhist chant to bring about a sexual liaison, Mulhall tells him: "Chant your ass off kid, but any pussy you get in this world, you're gonna have to pay for it ... one way or another." Buddusky confirms by saying, "Hallelujah."

Buddusky and Mulhall demonstrate the manner in which Hollywood cinema presents an easy alliance across racial lines. Once in the Navy, any racial history and baggage of negative experiences disappear; instead, a

On the streets of New York, the naïve Meadows (Randy Quaid, left) learns to enjoy himself with buddies Mulhall (Otis Young, center) and Buddusky (Jack Nicholson) in *The Last Detail.*

mutual respect and understanding surfaces. In their world of men, the two view the arrogance of higher-ranking officers as their primary enemy. Although frustrated with the rigidity of that Naval life, they connect as buddies for the basic purpose of showing a maligned sailor a good time. Together, they function as a united voice against self-serving authority, and a mutual heart that extends itself to the well-being of a fellow seaman.

As *The Last Detail* did its best to avoid racial politics, *The Wilby Conspiracy* (1974) rushes into the subject of one of the most controversial racist regimes—apartheid in South Africa.

With a starring role by Sidney Poitier, the film presents the popular actor in a role edgier and more sexual than previous characters during the 1950s and early '60s. With its emphasis upon the interracial protagonists, at places the film resembles one of Poitier's earlier works, *The Defiant Ones* (1959). Similar to that film, the black/white duo begins on antagonistic terms but is forced to rely upon each other to survive, reaching an understanding and friendship by the story's end. Unlike that film, however, *The*

Wilbur Conspiracy failed to earn audience or critical popularity. It gained some semblance of praise from critic Stanley Kaufmann. Writing for *The New Republic*, he concluded: "There is not a credible moment in it, but there is not one boring moment.... When the conventions of [a thriller film] are as well supported by dialogue, acting and direction as they are here, the lunacy of the action recedes to a corner of the mind's eye, and some fun can be had."[4]

With an abundant number of plot twists along the way, *The Wilby Conspiracy* follows a black activist, Shack Twala (Poitier), and white British journalist, Jim Keough (Michael Caine), who, after a fight with police officials, must escape from Capetown to Johannesburg to fly to freedom in nearby Botswana. As they elude the law during their 900-mile car journey, they grow to know one another, and despite initial differences politically, both at the end choose actions that demonstrate their mutual belief in democracy and racial equality.

This initial personality clash serves as a staple in buddy films. This inherent tension between reluctant partners suggests the improbability of any friendship, making the amelioration between the two more dramatic. In scene and after scene, the tension between the protagonists decreases, and the men commit their trust to one another. At the beginning, Keough watches dispassionately when Twala faces rough physical treatment by the police at a checkpoint, and Keough confronts the authorities only after they also strike his girlfriend, who is the lawyer representing Twala. Throughout their subsequent flight, Keough remains self-serving and concerned only about his situation, not Twala's politics or the racist system in South Africa. But through the life-and-death moments of escape and during heated conversations, the two men begin to bond.

Some of that bonding is played for humor. For example, in one scene that presages a similar situation in *The Crying Game* (1992), a handcuffed Twala comments upon his weakened bladder from the electric shock torture suffered in prison. This statement reveals both the inhumanity of the prison system on one hand and Twala's courage as a man on the other hand. Still in handcuffs, Twala needs assistance in order to urinate at the side of the road. Keough, realizing his role in unzipping Twala's pants, bristles at the thought of touching another man's pants. But he concedes as the unthinkable, unmanly action occurs off-screen.

In a more tension-filled moment, when the car overheats, police arrive and offer assistance. Both Keough and Twala immediately wear their metaphorical masks. The former speaks with the white officers, espousing the appropriate racist attitudes, while the latter assumes the silent, subservient role of "kaffir." Though both men hate their roles—Keough a closet liberal and Twala an adamant radical—they must rely upon the manipulation of the system at that moment in order to survive that system.

But the character that cements the tie between Twala and Keough is the embodiment of the evil apartheid system, Major Horn (Nichol Williamson), the chief of State Security. With his slick arrogance, Horn represents whites whose myopic vision and racial chauvinism have distorted their perceptions of humane behavior. When confronted by Horn directly and cornered into assisting him in exchange for his life, Keough despises Horn's fascist philosophies. Keough finally recognizes the blatant hatred that Twala and his comrades are fighting against. At the end, both men attack Horn, i.e., apartheid, in a direct, physical way: Twala jumps onto the rudder of a helicopter that's attempting to lift Horn away, and Keough shoots Horn in the head to prevent him from securing an escape through political asylum.

Twala and Keough, though different racially and culturally, both possess the heroic strain that feeds their courage to confront authority. Though apartheid remains the law of the land, their basic natures force them to resist. As men, they must rise above conformity to the system and challenge any effrontery to their manhood.

They both, however, share another recognizable trait of cinematic manhood as well—their easy access to women. This access substantiates their heterosexuality, which is needed to contextualize the urination scene described above. At the same time, it confirms that both exercise their masculine rights to sexual pleasure as a given rule of their gender. For Keough, his relationship with the attorney, Rina (Prunella Gee), is established early in the story, allowing for their later sharing of a Johannesburg apartment and bubble bath to fit neatly into their intimate screen moments. Rina, on her part, has placed herself in danger with the State Security by helping Keough and Twala escape, keeping secret the escape route and address of the Johannesburg apartment. When interrogated by Horn, Rina's caustic retorts to the questioning solidify her commitment to Keough, her lover, as much as to her anti-apartheid efforts.

Twala, having just served ten years in prison on Robbin Island as the film begins, becomes a bit more problematic. There is no one woman whom he mentions or seeks when escaping, so the viewer assumes there was possibly no woman in his life before his prison term. Then, while stopping at a cantina during the roadway evasion, Twala lustily eyes a number of black women dancing with partners near a bandstand. But he doesn't allow himself to approach anyone in that social setting, perhaps choosing to remain anonymous while fleeing. Yet later, in a very abrupt manner, he does allow himself to engage in a sexual tryst, while the police are searching the very building in which he hides. Twala's contact in Johannesburg, an Indian dentist named Mukherjee (Saeed Jaffrey), has a beautiful dental assistant, Persis (Persis Khambatta), who hides Twala in a secret closet behind bookshelves. In the tight proximity, while exchanging salacious stares, they begin to undress, kiss, and fondle. As the sequence intercuts between the closet and the police, Twala grapples and gropes Persis in a manner that's rather tame for a man who has been incarcerated for ten years. Although not graphic by the standards of the early '70s, the scene confirms Twala's libido and perhaps the sexy appeal that a revolutionary can possess. Later, in one of the story's twists, Persis selfishly attempts to steal diamonds belonging to the anti-apartheid forces, and she dies for her treachery. At the end, Twala again, unlike Keough with Rina, remains womanless, but an affirmed heterosexual.

Sexual liaisons take on more complexity in the action film *The Yakuza* (1975), a feature that capitalizes upon the popular interests in the Asian martial arts and the pronounced cultural differences between Japan and the United States. In a story filled with deceit and secrets, manhood becomes defined by discernible, ritualistic codes and practices.

Together, Jim Keough (Michael Caine, left) and Shack Twala (Sidney Poitier) survive the oppressive policies of apartheid in *The Wilbur Conspiracy.*

Manhood is synonymous with responsibility, obligation, and regimented actions.

The story follows Harry Kilmer (Robert Mitchum), an ex-cop who travels to Japan in order to help out an old friend, George Tanner (Brian Keith), whose daughter is kidnapped by the Yakuza when a business deal goes sour. In an otherwise lukewarm assessment of the movie, one critic praises Mitchum for "[l]ooking as menacing as a middle linebacker and doing his weary-warrior turn with a nice tension beneath his turtlenecked exterior."[5] In order to save the girl, Mitchum's Kilmer, in turn, calls on an old Japanese acquaintance, Ken (Ken Takakura), a former Yakuza member and the brother of Eiko (Keiko Kishi), the woman that Kilmer had a romantic affair with after the war. On this return after twenty years, Kilmer saves the daughter; discovers that Tanner lied and used him; and finally understands Ken's quiet hostility towards him over the years—Eiko is actually Ken's wife, not his sister.

This layered story contains a similar complexity about masculine behavior. On the one hand, there are typical kinds of concepts—such as duty, courage and honesty—yet due to cultural shapings, discrepancies in masculinity emerge. Kilmer's sense of duty to his friend Tanner springs from the notion that old war buddies are connected on and off the battlefield. In contrast, Kilmer struggles to comprehend Ken's sense of duty to him, which is based upon Kilmer assuming Ken's responsibility to take care of Eiko. In order to repay that obligation, Ken believes he owes Kilmer a favor. Even more extreme to Kilmer is Ken's obligation to repay an offense through a more pronounced Yakuza ritual. Specifically, as a way of seeking forgiveness and/or repentance for injuring someone, a Yakuza cuts off the top portion of his little finger and presents it to the injured person. Ken performs this ritual for his brother, Goro (James Shigeta), after killing Goro's son. Then, at the end, with the revelation of the Ken-Eiko spousal relationship, Kilmer performs the ritual for Ken, asking forgiveness for destroying their marriage.

But in true action fashion, the real bond between these two emerges when they agree to launch their assault of revenge upon one of the Yakuza families. Outnumbered, Kilmer, with his western weaponry of guns, and Ken, with his eastern samurai sword, attack with determined attitudes, offering up the film's most visceral sequence. Fighting beside each other, and at times protecting each other from harm, Kilmer and Ken have taken to a battlefield, tacitly pledging to die for their common cause and to sacrifice their lives for one another.

This masculine code of courage and sacrifice in the face of death squarely fits into Ken's cultural biases in regard to gender, as his attitudes and actions resonate as normalcy among his peers. At the same time, though confused by aspects of that Japanese culture, Kilmer's gender biases merge with Ken's. In their world, men protect women, possess women, and show respect to an enemy (through bowing and/or speaking formally); at the same time, they resolve the breaking of codes through physical violence. Their world holds a rigid and stern attitude, where men interact devoid of perceptible emotions.

In a striking contrast to *The Yakuza*, the comedy film *Silver Streak* (1976) offers a variation on the "man-who-knew-too-much" plot, and it showcases one of the more popular black/white comic duos during the '70s and '80s—Gene Wilder and Richard Pryor. After *Silver Streak*, this "crossover" pair teamed up twice more in *Stir Crazy* (1980) and *See No Evil, Hear No Evil* (1989).

In *Silver Streak*, George (Wilder) takes the train from Los Angeles to Chicago to attend his sister's wedding, falling in love along the way with Hilly (Jill Clayburgh), and after an intimate moment together, he sees a dead body falling from the train. When George begins to solve the mystery of what he saw, he's pulled into a dangerous web of art fraud, finding himself thrown off or jumping off the train on three occasions. Along the way, he teams up with Grover (Pryor), a thief with a heart of gold.

George, a book editor, and Grover, a professional thief, come from strikingly different worlds with race as an added qualifier. However, at the point where they meet in the film, they are both evading the law and consequently find their common link as fugitives. Their conventional masculine traits are demonstrated during their flight — handling guns, fighting, talking tough, and driving fast cars. Yet, interestingly, the two feel an affinity with one another while discussing the topic of "love" during their road trip from the law. When George explains to Grover his need to get back onto the train, he also confesses his affections for Hilly. Grover adds his sense of helplessness with emotions as well, stating: "I always lose my memory when I fall in love." Grover commits himself to helping George's efforts to save Hilly, and the two lock into their heroic mode.

Just as easily as the two admit that they're fools for love, they also relate across racial and class lines. They certainly recognize their racial differences, but never articulate those differences as being barriers to their partnership. Instead, the acknowledgment of racial issues serves more significantly in one of the film's most humorous sequences. Seeing that the authorities have established checkpoints at the train station with photos of George, Grover uses the supplies from a shoe shine stand to blacken George's complexion, a la minstrelsy, and to dress him in urban street apparel. Informing George that "Al Jolson made a million bucks looking like that," Grover then attempts to teach George rhythm and physical movements to complete his masquerade as a black man. Both are cognizant of the stereotypical image and behavior designated as "black" without ever discussing the political framework of such stereotypes. Instead, George ad-libs a "black" cadence in his voice, as he moves wildly: "Come on, man ... be cool ... I feel sharp ... get down ... outta sight!" When the shoeshiner (Nick Stewart) walks into the restroom and sees George's pathetical attempts to be "black," he confirms the desperation of a situation where a white man would pretend to be black, saying, "You must be in pretty big trouble, fellow." But other than being played for laughs, the scene — and the two main characters— avoids the much deeper historical and political implications of the moment.

By the film's action-filled ending, where the authorities and George confront the villains, Grover proves his buddy loyalty goes beyond simply saving his friend's woman. After being freed by the authorities, Grover appears again, telling George that he's returning George's wallet. Although a confirmed thief, Grover remains tied to George, joining in the life-and-death situation of getting the bad guys.

Silver Streak entertains with messages that suggest that men can transcend racial and class barriers that might exist, as long as they can connect with their inherent traits toward heroism and love. Yet, it is this very erasure of racial difference and the casting of Pryor that becomes problematic for critic Pauline Kael. She remarks that he saves a rather slow-paced film with a comic irreverence against the status quo and white society. She adds that the comedian "gives [*Silver Streak*] some potency and turns it into the comedy [the filmmakers] hoped for — and they emasculate him, turn him into a lovable black man whose craziness is only a put-on. Interracial brotherly love is probably the one thing that Richard Pryor should never be required to express. It violates his demonic, frazzled blackness."[6] Though Kael's observations have merit, one objective of the interracial buddy film is to deliberately blur racial lines in regard to the potential for interracial harmony. In a comedy such as *Silver Streak*, this erasure of racial and social issues is anticipated to be accepted unquestionably, thereby elevating this homogenization as the paragon.

Yet that performance contrasts notably with a Pryor turn in a more provocative drama, *Blue Collar* (1978). In it, Pryor embodies a character whose attributes resemble the black male's in American society. As the title suggests, *Blue Collar* focuses upon a trio of working-class friends— two black and one white. Directed by Paul Schrader, who wrote the screenplay for *The Yakuza*, this urban drama simmers with an anger rooted in male characters who perceive themselves as cogs in a dehumanizing machine of commerce. Leonard Schrader, the screenwriter and brother of the director, admitted that the structure mirrored the earlier film, asserting: "I saw how to do the story, the same as *The Yakuza*, two guys, one black, one white, from different traditions, but both stuck in blue-collar autoworker jobs."[7] But in the final script, three characters became the focus, which surfaced as a challenge for the filmmakers in raising financing, as some investors rejected the inclusion of two black main characters in a major film.[8]

The story follows three buddies working together in a Detroit factory: Zeke (Richard Pryor), Jerry (Harvey Keitel), and Smokey (Yaphet Kotto) commiserate over the circumstances of their lives and desperately seek ways to escape their economic suffocation. As married men, both Zeke and Jerry suffer domestic challenges, the former with an IRS investigation and the latter with working two jobs to pay his bills. Smokey, a black ex-con, leads a bachelor's life of parties but can't shake the irritation of being exploited by the powers that be. When the three conspire to rob their union headquarters—an ineffective union that does little for its members—they uncover evidence of union loan sharking that leads them to blackmail union leaders. Up to this point, the three have grown to be friends, finding understanding and support in their shared complaints. Despite racial differences, they recognize the class affiliation, seeing the system as their mutual foe. Their frustrations are as real as their long working hours, and they feel trapped in lives that pull them deeper into debt and anonymity. Finding a unified voice, their camaraderie serves as a source of power to strike out at the system and to strike forth in asseverating their manhood.

Yet, in that very act of undermining the system, they fall prey to a divide-and-conquer strategy that destroys their friendship and baits them into individualism. After the union terrorizes Jerry, kills Smokey, and bribes Zeke with a higher-level job, their bond disappears. This dissolution of the pact among the three emerges as one of the themes of the film: Namely, despite the common economic exploitation, male friendship cannot thrive in a capitalistic patriarchy where competition and power validate selfishness and exploitation. In this cynical perspective *Blue Collar* functions as a cinematic caveat about the destructive nature of lives defined by materialism and status. In such a world, masculinity assumes a primitive, Darwinian aspect that requires men to compete with one another and to view women as sexual objects. However, from a more pejorative view, critics Al Auster and Leonard Quart insist that the film fails by straying from an early ridicule of the capitalistic system as it "shifts gears and lays the blame on the union.... [I]t is the union that becomes the ultimate source of terror and coercion.... [B]oth the company and the government

In *Blue Collar,* Smokey (Yaphet Kotto, left), Zeke (Richard Pryor, center), and Jerry (Harvey Keitel) are three buddies who become enemies.

have been left off the hook."[9] Significantly, however, it can be argued that for the characters in the film, the union and the system (capitalism) are interchangeable monsters, and their individual and collective exploitation is no less real before either entity. *Blue Collar* still remains one of the few Hollywood features to consider the crucial eco-political factors weighing upon working-class men and to link those factors to the deleterious nature of capitalistic greed.

Perhaps the most dominant images of buddies at the end of the decade evolved from the five films that made up the *Rocky* series, beginning in 1976. Framed by the world of boxing, the ultimate professional world of one-on-one physical combat, the series follows a relationship between Rocky Balboa, the Italian stallion southpaw, and Apollo Creed, the black champion that exemplifies the positive and beneficial fulfillment of male bonding across racial lines. Receiving the Academy Award for Best Picture and Best Director, *Rocky* is viewed "as the most striking and exhilarating of the second chance films.... Rocky is a modern-day Horatio Alger who tells us the Dream is still there, if only you are kind, generous, and hard-working."[10] Indeed, one of the driving forces behind both Rocky and Apollo is the work ethic, that mythical component possessed by all good men who measure their accomplishments by the result of their individual hands-on efforts and physical prowess.

Although mentioned in dialogue in the final episode of the series, Apollo actually appears in only the first four films. Initially, in *Rocky*, Apollo surfaces as the nemesis of the title character. As artist and author Tim Miller observes: "Men are socialized to see one another as potential adversaries, strange creatures, bogeymen almost, to vanquish or die trying."[11] Certainly, the boxing arena functions as that symbolic battleground of enemies, where blood lust and battering find social sanction.

Arrogant, garrulous, affluent, black, and physically adroit in the boxing ring — Apollo contrasts strikingly with Rocky's low-key, quiet, awkward-moving pugilism. With an obvious nod toward the public flare of boxing legend Mohammad Ali, Apollo postures himself as an unbeatable fighter who has it all. Manipulating a promotional stunt of plucking a working-class boxer, Rocky, from the shadows of obscurity, Apollo shrewdly uses Independence Day and aphorisms about opportunity to frame the bout. Although surprised by Rocky's resilience in the climatic fight, Apollo retains the title, but Rocky triumphs by having gone the distance of fifteen rounds and never giving up.

The world of heavyweight boxing works on various levels in this series to demonstrate the imperative aspects of masculinity for both Rocky and Apollo. Muscular, physically taut, and determined, both boxers strike the optimal pose of the tough, aggressive male. In addition to being physically superior specimens, the two possess the mental focus and commitment to winning that conventionally define the male athlete in popular imagination. Their power and endurance extol the very nature of what a man seeks to be, their brutal match a clashing of larger-than-life warriors.

This collection of qualities that both men claim is the very element that bridges their differences. Despite race and class distinctions, their training, bodies, and respect for the sport eclipse all else. During their fifteen-round battle, as they deliver and receive punches and jabs, they connect via the physical touching of "pain." When men touch physically through competition, they assess their own sense of confidence and worth, while measuring the opponent. By round thirteen, with puffy eyes, bloody faces, and near exhaustion, both fighters warn their corners not to stop the fight. For Rocky and Apollo, they must complete their mission in order to be the man each seeks to be. The boxers see this code and commitment within the other, and their hugging at the end of the fifteenth round, as they both state they don't want a rematch, serves as the embracing of a comrade-in-arms (gloves) and a brother-in-spirit; at that moment they are a mirror image of one another — in Philadelphia, the city of brotherly love.

By *Rocky II* (1979), the palpable respect intensifies as the boxers use one another as the definitive measurement of manhood and success. Written and directed by Sylvester Stallone, the second installment gave "film audiences a glimpse of the boxing world and ... used the 'rags to riches' formula well to produce an entertaining and highly successful sequel," one critic has written.[12] As a sequel, this feature does surpass the former in regard to extending and deepening the boxers as rounded, complex characters.

While recovering in the hospital after the fight that ends the previous movie, Rocky makes his way to Apollo's room asking: "Did you give me your best?" Apollo responds: "Yes." With that knowledge, Rocky can move forward with the rest of his life, including marriage to Adrian (Talia Shire), purchasing a house, obtaining a car, and starting a family. But even with Apollo's respect for Rocky, the former struggles with a lingering doubt about his championship. Apollo tells his trainer: "I won, but I didn't beat him." Consequently, Apollo's egotistical need for dominance over his opponent leads him to the ring again. On his part, Rocky's inability to shape a life outside of boxing leads him back to do battle. When criticized by his wife for going back into the ring, Rocky confesses: "I think I'm becoming a nobody again.... I never asked you to stop being a woman ... don't ask me to stop being a man." Clearly for both Apollo and Rocky, being a man and being a boxer become synonymous.

The rematch between the two emanates as the same brutal battle as their first fight. And though not intrinsic within the script, the partisan Italian crowd at ringside suggests a particular racial aspect, as Rocky appears to be the "great white hope" who can defeat the loud-mouthed black champion. But in the end, Apollo's pride defeats him, when, leading in points, he chooses to go for the knockout, causing him to ultimately lose.

Following the validation of masculine codes in the first two films, the next two installments solidify the bonding between the two. As Rocky becomes wealthy by becoming the new heavyweight champion, the class difference with Apollo disappears. With their racial distinction and class status neutralized, Rocky and Apollo's friendship strengthens through their dislike for common enemies: Clubber Lang (Mr. T) in *Rocky III* (1982) and Drago (Dolph Lundgren) in *Rocky IV* (1985).

Lang, with his Mohawk haircut and guttural voice, represents the urban savage, the brute whose offensive and sneering demeanor only

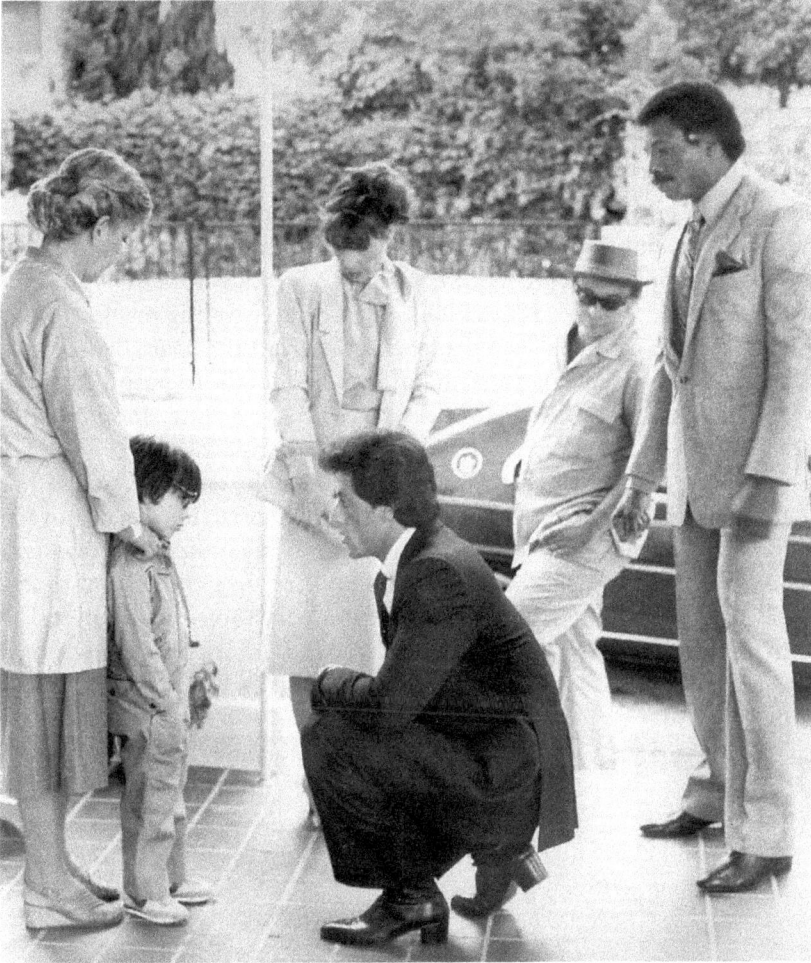

By the release of *Rocky III*, former opponents Rocky Balboa (Sylvester Stallone, center) and Apollo Creed (Carl Weathers, far right) have become buddies. Paulie (Burt Young, second from the right), and Adrian (Talia Shire) look on as Rocky bids farewell to Rocky Jr. (Ian Fried).

inspires adversaries. Devoid of the honor worshipped by Rocky and Apollo, Lang functions as the example of the despicable force threatening the stability of the masculine world defined by the buddies. In fact, throughout a number of direct public confrontations and insults, Rocky avoids responding to Lang's challenge—until Lang makes a lewd suggestion to Adrian at a dedication ceremony. Rocky, knowing that a man must protect his woman, flares into a response, accepting the challenge. At the beginning of the big fight, Apollo takes a bow in the ring as a former champion, extending his well wishes to Lang. The latter insults Apollo, and despite their common black identity, Apollo and Lang fail to connect. In essence, Apollo's true "brother" is Rocky.

As for Drago, his Russian nationality serves as the clashing force against the interracial buddies. As arrogant and single-minded as Lang, Drago's lacks the braggadocio; instead, in a machinelike fashion, he pummels fighters and displays superior physical attributes in terms of height, weight, and muscularity. Drago's challenge to Rocky, who's still the heavyweight champ, revolves around the goal of demonstrating just how weak Americans are. But Apollo, unable to retire from the sport that defines him, steps in and schedules an exhibition fight with the imposing Russian. When Apollo dies in the ring, Rocky takes up the mantle, committed to avenging his brother-buddy, which he does in heroic fashion.

In *Rocky III* and *Rocky IV*, Rocky and Apollo reach a new level of bonding, as the two men enjoy an easy, casual interaction outside of the ring. Having both been to the mountaintop of their shared profession, they understand one another in ways that others around them fail to see. Even though Rocky and Apollo enjoy a close father-son-type relationship with their trainers—Mickey (Burgess Meredith) and Duke (Tony Burton), respectively—the boxers intuitively respond to each other through the

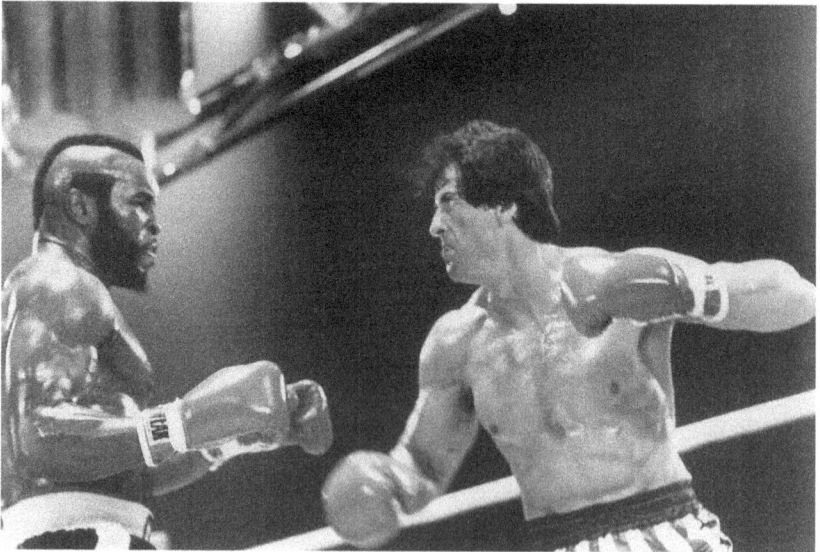

The menacing Clubber Lang (**Mr. T**, left) confronts an angry Rocky Balboa (Sylvester Stallone) in *Rocky III*.

unspoken tenets of manhood. That code goes beyond simply winning, but taking the world on one's own terms— an important element of masculinity in regard to control and self-respect. Just before the fatal fight with Drago, Apollo says, "I feel born again." This assertion acknowledges both the physical and spiritual elation that Apollo can experience only within the boxing arena, the world where he is truly a "man." Rocky comprehends that combined exhilaration and fulfillment, so that even as Apollo loses, demanding, "Don't stop this fight no matter what," Rocky obeys, never literally throwing in the towel of defeat and concession. Rocky and Apollo share a common purpose in their lives, willing to die to be what they were born to be —fighters. Rocky confirms that fact when he tells Adrian of his need to fight Drago following Apollo's death: "I'm a fighter.... That's the way I'm made.... Can't change what you are!"

At the same time, from another perspective, the institution of marriage serves to show the traditional aspects of both boxers in regard to their duty and responsibility as men. Due to Rocky's position as the protagonist, the audience perceives his romancing of and marriage to Adrian (Talia Shire) in more detail that Apollo's marriage to his wife, Mary Anne (Sylvia Meals). For Rocky, Adrian becomes the center of his life outside of the boxing profession, as often her voice warns of the dangers inherent within that professional world. Like a good husband, Rocky — and by association Apollo— provides those material items, economic security, and family rituals (joke-telling, singing, holiday celebrations) for his wife and, later, son. Significantly, in *Rocky V* (1990), the loss of the family's material riches results from Paulie's (Burt Young) mismanagement, not Rocky's inability to provide as a man should. As Adrian shifts between the voice of inspiration and the voice of doubt regarding Rocky's chances of succeeding in the ring, she always functions as that one person who serves as his support system and the key to his compassionate side. Adrian surfaces as the beauty who transforms Rocky's beastly nature into the appropriate husband-father-consumer that a successful American man should become.

The Echo Films of the 1970s

With the transforming black male images of the "blaxploitation" cycle early in the decade and the dominating visage of Richard Pryor as the crossover star of the latter half of the decade, the films discussed above were the major efforts to assign the buddy motif to interracial affiliations among men. However, two films— both comedies— appeared midway through the 1970s that did not adhere to bona fide interracial buddy film patterns but did employ some traces of the paradigm to tell their stories, making notable attempts to address manhood and race relations.

The first, *Blazing Saddles* (1974), is a satirical treatment of the western transfigured into a postmodern vehicle of conflicting styles, mixed genres, conspicuous anachronisms, and acerbic racial commentary. In its utilizations of slapstick, sight gags, verbal humor, puns, and the breaking of the fourth wall, the movie manages to attack and/or defend blacks, Indians, Latinos, Jews, gays, and incompetent politicians. Sometimes the sarcasm reveals insightful humor about society, but at other times, the styles of comedy oscillate from the silly to the extreme.

The story takes place in 1874, when a crooked state politician, Hedley Lamarr (Harvey Korman), convinces an equally crooked governor (Mel Brooks) to appoint an ex–chain gang black man named Bart (Cleavon Little) as the new sheriff of Rock Ridge, a frontier town of racist white citizens. Sheriff Bart befriends the recovering gunfighter called the Waco Kid (Gene Wilder) to help him win over the town and to fight off Lamarr's gang of cowboy thugs, who plan to seize the properties of the townspeople as their own.

The partnership between Bart and the Waco Kid is one of the relationships given screen time and symbolic significance in this irreverent story. Unlike the other whites who immediately refer to Bart as a "nigger," the Waco Kid addresses him as "black" in their first encounter. Through their exchange of personal backgrounds, their common resistance to the outlaws, and their protection of each other, the Bart–Waco Kid duo demonstrates the racial interdependence suggested in the film's more lucid moments. Bart and the Waco Kid have been ostracized by society for race and reputation, respectively, and they link in an acceptance and respect for one another. Both men are survivors who display an understanding about the foibles of their frontier society, and at the end as they ride off into the sunset together—first on horseback before transitioning into a waiting limousine—they both comprehend that they're going "nowhere special," perhaps another town just like Rock Ridge. However, the film doesn't linger on extending the depth to the Bart–Waco Kid buddyhood due to its objective of parodying historical events, racial generalizations, sexual stereotypes, and Hollywood filmmaking in general.

Blazing Saddles offers up a different style of comedy than the contemporary setting in *Car Wash* (1976), which nonetheless contains its own brand of slapstick. *Car Wash*, set in Los Angeles, follows one working day's antics of numerous male characters laboring to earn a wage and to fight away the boredom of repeatedly cleaning vehicles. Cultural critic Donald

Bogle assesses the film as "an affectionate although misconceived feature" with a talented cast that provides the "film with moments of truth and a moral authority it otherwise lacks."[13]

From a variety of racial and cultural backgrounds — black, white, Puerto Rican, Indian, and Jewish — most of the men share a good-natured feeling and camaraderie on the job. While some see the job as a stepping stone towards their dreams of future success, others appear content to merely survive the day to receive their paycheck. Slipping from one vignette to the next, the story remains a chain of visual and verbal gags with some poignant moments sprinkled in appropriately.

One of the interesting characters is (Antonio Fargas), a black gay male who openly displays his effeminate mannerisms and proclivity for women's apparel and makeup. His presence punctuates the strong heterosexuality of the other men who work beside him but who clearly draw the sexual orientation line through direct comments and/or cautionary stares. Irwin, the Jewish liberal and boss's son, attempts to hang with the workers to show his brotherly acceptance of the working class, following his reading of Chairman Mao. Then there's Scruggs (Jack Kehoe), the Caucasian cowboy who takes his woman problems to Chuco (Pepe Serna), the experienced Chicano stud. At the same time, Abdul (Bill Duke), a radical black male articulating Afrocentric viewpoints, continually reminds his black co-workers of their oppressed positions as laborers to their boss and the white-dominated system.

The car wash becomes not only the place of work but the social setting where these disparate personalities can find connections and a forum to express themselves despite the urban grit and grind. Beyond the teasing and often cruel pranks, the men comprehend that they can exhibit their true identities because they're interacting with other workers who seek that same solace in the job. Although they don't face any life-and-death moments as in action or drama films, these men bond around their working-class status and their optimism that the next day will bring opportunities.

* * *

Despite the various types of entertaining comedies during the 1970s, the dramas provided more provocative and noteworthy treatments of interracial male associations. As the *Rocky* series ended the '70s and moved into the '80s, it demonstrated the manner in which prescribed, incommodious attributes of masculinity still held popular appeal. Although *The Wilby Conspiracy*, *The Yakuza*, and *Blue Collar* explored more complex dimensions of contemporary societies that affect masculine traits, Stallone's working-class character who rose to the top reflects a male mythology that romantically called out to viewers. In that romantic, cinematic view, any man who chooses to could go the distance and fulfill his dream, and despite hard knocks along the way, any man could eventually become a champion.

4

Beverly Hills Bad Boys and the Lethal Law: 1980s

In a noteworthy contrast to the comedy genre, the action film in its various forms found a new audience during this decade. Against the conservatism of the decade, the action genre was laced with liberal doses of graphic violence, scatological language, and cynicism. In his study *American Cinema/American Culture*, author John Belton contends: "The big-budget exploitation films of the 1980s reflect[ed] the new conservatism of Reaganite America. A handful of films and filmmakers resist[ed] this reactionary tide, but ... they failed to match the success of the more conservative, mainstream films at the box office. For every *Platoon*, there were a couple of *Rambos* and three or four *Rockys*."[1] The 1980s became an era "to rewrite the recent past and put a positive face on our nation's more negative experiences."[2] With a philosophy of trickle-down economics by the political administration and growing corporate conglomeration, the popular political rhetoric extolled the messages that class and race did not matter in regard to the average American achieving dreams and fulfillment. A combination of dogged individualism and a belief in the American system was the primary weapon for accomplishing success.

For the above reasons and other marketing factors, many critics saw the 1980s as the years that fostered the interracial buddy as a principle paradigm for numerous Hollywood films. With the rise of the white buddy films—from *Easy Rider* (1969) to *Star Wars* (1977)—viewed in general as a response to the exploding feminist movement, black scholar-critic Ed Guerrero argues that in regard to race, "With the biracial buddy formula Hollywood put the black filmic presence in the protective custody, so to speak, of a white lead or co-star and therefore in conformity with white sensibilities and expectations of what blacks, essentially, should be."[3] And with a knowing perspective, Guerrero adds: "Because it wants to bring the broadest box office possible with the installation of crossover thematics and a few token black stars ... Hollywood has been reluctant to cast black stars without a white 'buddy' as ideological chaperone to ensure its box office."[4] The interracial buddy movies produced during this era include one of the most popular and profitable series, the *Lethal Weapon* films. In addition the dominance of one black actor, Eddie Murphy, indicates the type of black male image that mainstream America was willing to accept — edgy and ethnocentric, but funny.

Having already captured box office profits via *Silver Streak* (1976), the Gene Wilder–Richard Pryor duo provided a marketable pair who could perform both physical and visual humor, lacing their characters with sufficient pathos to connect to audiences. In their two films during the '80s—*Stir Crazy* (1980) and *See No Evil, Hear No Evil* (1989)—Wilder and Pryor demonstrated how opposite personalities between men could find compatibility and lasting friendship.

In the former, playwright Skip Donahue (Wilder) and his actor friend, Harry Monroe (Pryor) decide to relocate to California for their professions but run into legal trouble in Nevada when their vehicle breaks down. In a case of mistaken identity, the two friends are convicted of a crime and sentenced to prison, where they meet an eclectic group of inmates as they plan an escape.

With the majority of the story unfolding in prison, much of the humor revolves around the Donahue-Monroe duo's efforts to survive their hostile surroundings. When Donahue displays a talent for mechanical-bull riding, he ingratiates himself and Monroe with the warden, who conducts a rodeo competition with a rival prison. It becomes clear that Donahue's fortunes and mishaps in prison, as well as before, remain inextricably tied to Monroe's. The two, though distinctive in personality, surface as the same in heart and mind. They think for one another, protect each other, and plan for one another. This unusual union gains emphasis with "the now-famous 'that's right, we bad' sequence; when the two are first placed into prison, taking turns at fits of insanity; and when the two are placed in the same cell with [mass murderer] Grossberger."[5]

Importantly, with their confirmed closeness, the two never cross over into the erotic zone while serving time together in prison. Donahue flirts with and expectantly shapes an affection for his lawyer's cousin, Meredith (JoBeth Williams). Their lustful gazes quickly suggest a future relationship, reinforcing Donahue's attraction to the opposite sex and avoiding a physical attraction to his close male friend.

Wrongfully imprisoned in *Stir Crazy*, Harry Monroe (Richard Pryor, left) and Skip Donahue (Gene Wilder) endure a stressful moment.

In this comedy, all relationships remain on a surface level, and the story sidesteps the more sobering issues of the penal system and men behind bars. As a showcase of the Donahue-Monroe duo, the film achieves its goal as "it struck a note of admiration among audiences that made it the number three top-grossing film of that year."[6]

By the end of the decade, when *See No Evil, Hear No Evil* was released, the two comedians were exploiting physical disabilities as a gimmick to link their disparate characters. Even with five credited screenwriters, including Wilder, and the impressive resume of director Arthur Hiller, the story relied too heavily upon visual gags and an inconsistent verbal comedy. The plot revolves around two disabled protagonist who find themselves suspects in a murder, but who together manage to solve the mysteries of the killing, a rare gold coin, and international assassins. Wally (Pryor) is an adventurous blind black man who lives on the kindness and tested patience of his sister, Adele (Kirsten Childs). Dave (Wilder) is an adventurous deaf white man who works as a clerk in a newsstand in the lobby of a business high-rise. Wally applies for a job at the newsstand, and their initial meeting marks the structure of much of the film's efforts at humor. Wally stumbles, pretending he can see while speaking assertively, and Dave reads lips pretending he can hear while acting "normal." Perhaps, the filmmakers sought to make a positive statement about disabled people who actively participate in the mainstream without deference to their physical challenges, but any progressive statement gets lost in the exploitive humor that plays on those very disabilities.

In an interesting manner, Wally and Dave become buddies by bonding through their disabilities. Since neither was born with his respective physical losses, they connect through mutual tragedies, finding understanding in the other for the changes that life has imposed. Their racial identities, consequently, take a position of least importance. The most pronounced racial remarks comes in a sequence when Wally rides the subway with Adele as she cautions her brother to take life carefully because he's blind *and* black. He stands and screams aloud in mock surprise: "I'm black? Oh, my God!" With Pryor's humor selling the scene, it becomes obvious that racial identity exists more as a joke than a political or cultural reality in this story.

However, of interest, it is the black character who triggers most of the dialogue about sexuality. Wally initiates questions about sexual activity in street language, while Dave's character responds consistently about sex and intimacy in a romantic and joking manner. When Dave tells Wally about his wife, who deserted him when he lost his hearing, he comments poetically: "One day she turned into this amazing creature who could sit on the end of a broomstick and take off into the air." Strategically, Wally becomes the buddy who articulates most crudely about sexuality, as both men's heterosexual orientation is proclaimed. This affirmation extends also to Dave's infatuation with the female assassin named Eve (Joan Severance), who, following her killing of one victim, can only be described by Dave as having the best pair of legs he's even seen. And when it comes to this woman, a possible love interest for Dave, the word "seen" is operative here, as in one sequence when Dave secretly enters her hotel room looking for a stolen gold coin. Eve finishes her shower, stepping into the main room in just her towel. Dave, pretending his hand is holding a gun in his pants pockets, forces her to raise her hands and drop the towel. As Dave studies her naked body, he remarks: "This is the best relationship I've had with a woman in ten years." The ensuing sight gag is that when Dave removes his hand from his pocket, the audience sees that the assumed bulge of a gun was actually his erection. But, notably, since Wally is blind and black, he cannot *see* the white woman — naked or clothed — though he is allowed to accidentally fondle her breast in a later scene.

As heterosexual heroes, the scenes of emotional confessions between Wally and Dave remain in the appropriate context of friendship. Despite their physical setbacks, they are true men, particularly in their sexuality.

This trait becomes accentuated when they meet Eve's comrade in dishonesty, Kirgo (Kevin Spacey), who displays an English accent with a shade of effeminacy. Providing the male villain with this sense of being "foreign" and "soft" underscores the masculinity of Wally and Dave. And when the action sequences develop, the use of violence also has an acceptable status. Wally and Dave endure fistfights, attack dogs, and shootouts; in one chase scene, Wally even resorts to driving a car, as he and Dave evade both the villains and the police.

Wilder and Pryor maintained a rather interesting innocence in their three films together. With Pryor's presence, there was certainly the irreverent confrontation with conventions and the status quo, but Pryor's menacing attitude was always tempered by the respect he held for Wilder's characters, who in turn confirmed the suitability of the status quo. The movies were devoid of cynicism, but brimming with the possibilities of working together despite racial differences.

The notions of innocence and racial harmony took on an exaggerated twist in the two installments of *48 Hrs.* (1982) and *Another 48 Hrs.* (1990), which brought together buddies from opposite ends of the legal spectrum. However, Jack Cates (Nick Nolte) and Reggie Hammond (Eddie Murphy) possess some common traits; they're both crude, selfish, sexist, and head-

In another buddyship, Wally (Richard Pryor, left) and Dave (Gene Wilder) are blind and deaf, respectively, in *See No Evil, Hear No Evil.*

strong. When Cates loses his fellow officers and his gun during a shootout with two psychopaths, he journeys to prison to interrogate Hammond, a former member of the killers' gang. In order to locate the psychopaths on the street, Cates signs out Hammond into his custody for forty-eight hours. Cates needs to bring the killers to justice; Hammond wants to gather $500,000 that he hid during a botched holdup. With this premise Cates and Hammond set out for the streets, as they argue, cuss, and fight one another along the way. Disliking each other, and not very likeable characters themselves, these anti-heroes hurl racial insults and sexist diatribes from one scene to the next. Cates assures Hammond: "We ain't brothers, we ain't partners, we ain't friends." This statement confirms what becomes increasingly visible throughout the first half of the film; however, as events develop, the statement becomes the antithesis of the relationship that develops between the two.

Significantly, the Cates-Hammond duo remain palatable due to their identity as the "good guys" in comparison to the interracial duo of psychopaths that they chase: Ganz (James Remar) is Caucasian and Billy Bear (Sonny Landham) is Indian. Despite their disdainful and insensitive interaction with one another, Cates and Hammond are not cold-blooded killers who exploit and terrorize at random. At the same time, Cates and Hammond grow to respect one another due to the "manly" behavior each displays.

For example, in one scene, they enter a country and western bar to follow a lead on Billy Bear. Hammond, using Cates's badge, rousts a couple of the good old boys as he stops the music and revelry in the club. Hammond announces: "I don't like white people, and I hate rednecks. You people are rednecks, and I'm a nigger with a badge." Though the scene is improbable, Hammond's chutzpah in taking charge in the hostile environment of the club impresses Cates, though he doesn't admit it at the time. Then, later, when frustrated with one another, Cates and Hammond begin to physically fight on the streets. Punch for punch, Cates's wild-man fighting style matches Hammond's boxing style. When a police squad car arrives, Cates shows his badge and covers the incident, leaving the two men as equal fighters with no clear winner. These two events help to meld the two opposing personalities together, for in their primacy as hyper-masculine individuals, Cates and Hammond can respond to the physical prowess of the other.

Added to these aspects of courage and physical strength emerges the element of sexuality. Cates, already involved with his girlfriend, Elaine (Annette O'Toole), acknowledges to Hammond the difficulties of maintaining a demanding relationship. After an initial bedroom scene between

Cates and Elaine, the former keeps the latter at a distance for the remainder of the film via telephone conversations and broken promises. The bottom line remains that beyond sexual pleasure, Cates has little use for a woman in his life. Cates's stand on relationships mirrors Hammond's obsession with getting some "trim." Having been in prison for almost three years, Hammond continually pleads with Cates to allow him a few moments to "go get some pussy" because his "dick gets hard when the wind blows."

In another bar scene, in a black club where the theme song "The Boys Are Back in Town" is performed, Hammond directly propositions a black woman named Candy (Olivia M. Brown), inviting her to go across the street to a convenient hotel. Although the plan is delayed, Hammond finally gets his wish, confiding in Cates: "I was great ... should have my dick bronzed."

The blatant sexual talk and sexual activity imbues Hammond with a prurient attribute that becomes a valorization of sexual stereotypes about black men. As Hammond's character merges with Murphy's profane comedic image, the result is a blistering excess of profane language and sexuality. Despite the character's irritating, sexist attitudes, one visual cue to Hammond's acceptability becomes the suit and tie worn throughout the film. Although ostensibly for "looking good for the ladies" and contributing to his "cool" attitude, the wardrobe serves an additional function here. It softens the maniacal and vulgar expressions displayed by Hammond, giving him a proper and respectable veneer.

Yet, those same expressions endear Hammond to Cates, who never questions Hammond's sexual appetites due to his own peculiar interaction with Elaine. Elaine, Candy, and the women with the two psychopathic villains all become mere objects for the masculine need to have sexual satisfaction whenever needed. The women, devoid of depth, serve the pleasure of men as pliant and patient creatures of convenience.

By the film's final act, Cates and Hammond have forged a connection based on mutual admiration and mutual confirmation of masculine attributes of physical violence, emotional stoicism, and heterosexual proficiency. In a scene when the precinct's *black* police captain dismisses Hammond as a "nigger convict," Cates vehemently defends Hammond by responding: "I'm gonna tell you something about this man. He has more brains than you'll ever know. He's got more guts than any partner I ever had." In Cates's own limited way, he confirms Hammond into his world of masculinity where strength and trust coexist. The bond develops between the two in just forty-eight hours, and though not articulated aloud to each other, the union is worth defending and worth dying for as the two have a final showdown with Ganz and Billy Bear.

Teaming up again in *Another 48 Hrs.*, Detective Jack Cates (Nick Nolte, left) confers with his buddy Reggie Hammond (Eddie Murphy).

Eight years later, the "boys are back in town" as Cates and Hammond reunite in *Another 48 Hrs.*, though in the story line the time span has been only five years. As before, the movie opens with the two in an antagonistic position. Hammond is angry because five years were added to his sentence and particularly because Cates has not come to visit him. Cates, on his part, has been holding Hammond's money, which he uses as the bait to get Hammond to help him on another case. But Hammond refuses to assist Cates until Hammond realizes that he's targeted for a hit by an anonymous crime lord whom Cates calls the Iceman. Though the Iceman is anonymous to the cops, Hammond has seen him and therefore can finger him, and one of the three biker hit men hired is Cherry Ganz (Andrew Divoff), the brother of the psychopath killed by Cates in the first film. With these plot points in place, the film moves on to explore the relationship between Cates and Hammond. Basically, it replays what occurred in the first. Cates, older and obsessed with catching the Iceman, is no longer with Elaine after a short marriage. Hammond, older and still without a steady relationship, remains the profane, fast-talking hustler more obsessed with money than sex in this installment.

The important elements of action, violence, and masculine posturing shape the film's content and characterization. The closest the film comes to any political observation is expressed through Hammond's dialogue with Cates: "If shit was worth something, poor people would be born with no assholes." And though the notorious Iceman is revealed to be one of Cates's fellow detectives in the precinct, the story avoids an indictment of corruption of power and public trust. The exposing of the Iceman functions primarily to show that Cates is a hero whose hunches and instincts are primal and accurate. The film celebrates the resiliency of the bonding of Cates and Hammond as indicated in the end when the former confesses to the latter: "You're my friend. Besides, I had to save my partner." The sanctity of their friendship is raised to an ideal level, where all other concerns and issues disappear.

Of the interracial buddy films that prevailed in the early '80s, one popular comedy — *Trading Places* (1983) — with its notions about gender, race, and class invites detailed scrutiny. In this Eddie Murphy and Dan Aykroyd vehicle, the buddy relationship has to leap formidable differences to allow the male bonding to occur, buffered by the insertion of the stereotypical hooker with the heart of gold. Beginning with a pampered, arrogant personality, Louis Winthorpe (Aykroyd) works at an investment firm owned and managed by the equally pompous brothers Randolph Duke (Ralph Bellamy) and Mortimer Duke (Don Ameche). Hustling the streets, a fast-talking con man, Billy Ray Valentine (Murphy), gets pulled into a pleasurable if unethical bet between the Duke brothers; specifically Randolph believes that environment shapes a person's behavior, while Mortimer argues that one's natural heredity and gene pool dictates. To test their theories, the brothers manipulate events so that Valentine comes to work at their firm in the place of Winthorpe, who is thrown to the streets on drug charges. Winthorpe's one oasis in his desert of reclaiming his old life is Ophelia (Jamie Lee Curtis), a prostitute who has earned and saved a five-figure nest egg that she wants Winthorpe to help her increase through his investment skills.

In an all-too familiar persona by the early '80s, Murphy once again assumes the role of the obscene, obstreperous black male with a defiant and devious attitude. From the streets to the jail to the luxury home, Valentine becomes the ethnic outsider who wisecracks his way through unfamiliar situations. His main concern when approached by the Duke brothers to come work with them is whether "these dudes are a couple of faggots." Being all male, Valentine feels compelled to clarify his sexual orientation, and once dressed and pampered in tailor-made suits, he can extol the level of suavity and "cool" he naturally possesses. Saliently, wardrobe and fancy lifestyle have an effect, as Valentine becomes less scatological and surprisingly astute in his business observations. With no background provided, one can deduce that if given a suit, a mahogany desk, and a chauffeured limousine, anyone can become a successful investment banker.

At the same time, Winthorpe's journey through deprivation and urban blight triggers his anger and aggression toward Valentine and the Duke brothers. Winthorpe also tends to prove Randolph's theory of environmentalism as he becomes overwhelmed and suicidal by his living conditions, lack of material comforts, and loss of his high-society fiancée, Penelope (Kristin Holby). Although the men clash during the first half of the film, when Valentine and Winthorpe finally realize their common exploitation and manipulation for the sake of a bet, they join forces to get their revenge against the Dukes. By this point, the Valentine-Winthorpe duo have overcome their disparities, and indeed their racial and class distinctions disappear as they carry out their scheme to use insider information to bankrupt the Dukes. In a short space of time, they bond and solidify their mutual respect via vengeance. With the story set in Philadelphia, the city of brotherly love, the two buddies have become family, along with Ophelia and Coleman (Denholm Elliot), the proper but good-hearted butler. Specifically, securing wealth has provided the buddies, as well as Ophelia and Coleman, the opportunity to live within the structure of the affluent

In *Trading Places*, Billy Ray Valentine (Eddie Murphy, left) develops a buddy-ship with Louis Winthorpe (Dan Aykroyd, right), helped out by friendly prostitute Ophelia (Jamie Lee Curtis).

status quo without questioning the fundamental exploitation that serves as the foundation of their elite status. The film suggests that anyone can have access to wealth, and the interracial buddies who work together will accomplish the ideal goal of affluent homogeneity. Played for laughs, *Trading Places* avoids the urgent political issues that initially separate the interracial buddies, resolving them tidily for a happy ending that oversimplifies class mobility and the racial identity.

With the enormous box office success of *48 Hrs.* and *Trading Places*, Hollywood was not about to let Eddie Murphy or the interracial buddy formula slip away. By 1984, Murphy's next vehicle, *Beverly Hills Cop*, arrived profitably and eventually prompted two sequels—*Beverly Hills Cop II* (1987) and *Beverly Hills Cop III* (1994). The first two films worked effectively together developing relationships and particularly showing changes in the white buddies, but the third installment seems disconnected from the spirit and camaraderie of the previous two movies.

But in all three films, Murphy's role as Axel Foley dominates the stories, and as Ed Guerrero observes, "All of these films are driven by the disruptive effects of Murphy's irreverent and cocky interpretations of Blackness on the dominant White social order."[7] The clash plays off of the "fish-out-of-water" scenario where Foley's outrageous behavior in solving crimes takes him into the milieu of "a city whose very name is emblematic for ostentatious displays of wealth and privilege, as well as racial/social exclusivity."[8]

In the first film of the series, Foley reunites with Mikey (James Russo) a white buddy with whom he grew up. After Mikey, Foley's best friend, is killed, evidence takes Foley to Beverly Hills, where he charges a white businessman named Victor Maitland (Steve Berkoff) as the kingpin behind the murder and an international smuggling ring. Being black and dressed in casual street clothes and sneakers, Foley's appearance targets him as a troublemaker for the Beverly Hills Police Department. But in a short period of time Foley befriends three white conservative detectives in the process of solving the case.

Foley's link with the three white detectives forms the basis for the buddyship that drives the first two films. His loutish, rule-bending personality repels the white cops, but eventually Foley transforms Rosewood (Judge Reinhold), a shy, soft-spoken follower; Taggart (John Ashton), a grisly, gruff hardliner; and Bogomil (Ronny Cox), the officious, diplomatic lieutenant of the squad room. In particular, it is the Foley-Rosewood-Taggart trio that forms the noteworthy union in the film. Rosewood and Taggart perceive their jobs the Beverly Hills way — by the rules and limitations of the legal system. Foley, a blatant transgressor of rules, insists that the three have one important aspect in common — they're cops. For Foley, the identification of "cop" overrides any possible differences that might exist; indeed, Foley appears committed to his job at the omission of a personal life. So, in the process of bending and circumventing the system's rules, Foley is instructing Rosewood and Taggart on the methods of being a good "cop." The flashing of his badge affirms Foley's membership into the community of law enforcement, and if not for that badge, his behavior and attitude would guarantee extensive jail time. Underneath, Axel Foley — like his predecessors Reggie Hammond (*48 Hrs.*) and Billy Ray Valentine (*Trading Places*) — is a con artist and self-serving manipulator, but with title of "cop," his antics are elevated to investigative techniques.

But the "cop" identity functions as the device that converts Rosewood and Taggart, as they witness Foley's ability to read crime scenes, to cover for their mistakes with their boss; and to respond in a tough, aggressive manner. For example, in yet another strip club scene, while encouraging Rosewood and Taggart to loosen up and enjoy the naked white woman dancing nearby, Foley surmises the suspicious behavior of two would-be robbers, leading to a successful disarming and cuffing of the perps. In another example, in the final shootout, Foley orchestrates his two buddies into an assault upon the villain's estate, leading the courageous gunfight into an outnumbered situation. For most of the film, Rosewood and Taggart are used in comic setups as clumsy or naïve cops, but with Foley's tutoring, they move closer to graduating to another level of proficiency via shootouts, chases, fistfights, and explosions.

But the most telling examples of Foley's conversion of his white buddies become their willingness to steal and lie by the film's end. Foley, having demonstrated the benefits of deception throughout the story, influences Rosewood and Taggart to loosen up their attitudes. Even Lieutenant Bogomil becomes infected by the Foley virus as the former creates a lie to his chief of police to cover up the costly destruction of the Foley-Rosewood-Taggart trio.

By *Beverly Hills Cop II*, though Rosewood and Taggart grimace in disgust at Foley's investigative guises, by this installment they are close buddies, alluded to by references of fishing together. In fact, Bogomil, now a captain, phones Foley to cancel a fishing trip together just before Bogomil is shot as a victim of the alphabet criminal. Foley rushes from Detroit back to Beverly Hills and teams with Rosewood and Taggart to discover the source and reasons for the shooting. As Bogomil recovers, in critical condition, Foley consoles the fallen buddy's daughter, and he has access to their home to look for evidence, letting himself in and out at will.

Spending more screen time together than in the first film, the Foley-

The Beverly Hills Bad Boys — Axel Foley (Eddie Murphy, left), Billy Rosewood (Judge Reinhold, center), and John Taggart (John Ashton) hurry into action in *Beverly Hills Cop*.

Rosewood-Taggart buddyship flourishes. Rosewood has become a self-styled "Rambo," with a kick-ass attitude and with his apartment a cache for weapons of all kinds. Taggart, bemoaning a separation from his wife, breaks out of his reserved mode through his wardrobe and willingness to back Foley's stunts and challenges to authority. Foley releases the real men inside of Rosewood and Taggart, which is synonymous with being real cops. This maturation is punctuated at the film's end when both Rosewood and Taggart scream, cuss, and confront their new boss in defiance. Their spirited masculinity impresses and pleases Foley, who states to the two: "You're getting more and more like me every day. Next thing you know you'll have afros ... and big dicks." This praise of "big dicks" connects back to the strip-club scene in the first movie when Foley assures the two buddies that it's acceptable for them to have "hard dicks," implying that his own sexual organ as a black man was responding appropriately to the stripper's gyrations. As Herman Beavers emphasizes: "Because his [Murphy] comic approach is so heavily grounded in racial intervention ... we can conclude that Murphy's characters and comedy routines fail to dislodge sexual myths about black men."[9] In a blatant fashion, Foley articulates the sexually charged typing that has been suggested in quips and phallic symbols—specifically language, bananas, guns, cars, and rocket launchers—throughout both films.

A confirmed heterosexual in words and attitude — but not through a romantic relationship — Foley's hyper-sexualized nature is palatable for its comic relief but still potent in its messages about black heterosexual proficiency. In the first film, Foley's humorous interaction with two effeminate males—Serge (Bronson Pinchot), a museum receptionist and the Banana Man (Damon Wayans), a hotel vendor — is augmented by his disguise as a gay male suffering from herpes as a ruse for admittance into a members-only club where the villain dines. In these references, homosexuals are consistently rendered as jokes with no balancing images to suggest otherwise. Soft and ineffective in Foley's world, the gay man is not to be taken seriously.

With his sexual orientation never in question, Foley leads Rosewood and Taggart in the second film into the Playboy Mansion, where they enter a backyard of bikini-clad women playing volleyball. Foley touches his groin area and speaks to his penis saying: "Wake up! Isn't this what we always talked about? So look alive, you may never see it again!" In a later scene, Foley, upon hearing that Taggart's wife has returned to him, commends his buddy's sexuality:

> Foley: "The man's a stud, and we didn't even know it.... She
>   couldn't live without you, right?"
> Taggart: "No, her mother didn't have cable TV."
> Foley: "Don't think it was her mother's cable TV. It was *your*
>   cable that brought her back!"

When *Beverly Hill Cop III* appeared seven years after the second film, Foley character's played like a cliché. Taggart, who didn't appear on-screen, was a retiree living in Phoenix, and Bogomil wasn't mentioned. In this episode, Foley travels from Detroit to Beverly Hills to chase down the killer of his beloved boss, Inspector Todd (Gil Hill). Although Rosewood is still on the force as a sergeant, he and Foley spend little time together in resolving the case; instead, they team together for a brief fight scene and a shootout at the end. The camaraderie and interaction of their professional and personal lives, highlighted in the first two movies, is absent here. In an abrupt scene, Serge returns as a vendor of survival weapons, which conveniently gives Foley a source for guns for the final shootout. Conspicuously, Foley meets Janice (Theresa Randle), a black woman who helps him in his investigation of the case, but though a romantic attraction is suggested, the two never share a screen kiss.

The Echo Films of the Early 1980s

In the first half of the decade, a number of films that did not have genuine buddy patterns presented males who connected in notable ways across racial lines. Works such as *Beat Street* (1984) and *A Soldier's Story* (1984) held interest for their consideration of male reconciliations across racial and cultural divides, but the interracial buddy scenario was not the cornerstone to building the films' themes. In addition, several other popular vehicles, specifically *The Empire Strikes Back* (1980); *Nighthawks* (1981); *Sharkey's Machine* (1981); *An Officer and a Gentleman* (1982), the *Police Academy* series (beginning in 1984), and *The Killing Fields* (1984), suggested some juxtapositions of masculinity and race, but did not achieve bona fide interracial buddy status.

That erasure of racial differences pervades the science-fantasy vehicle *The Empire Strikes Back*, considered by one critic to be "the richest, eeriest and most daring episode in the series."[10] In a movie where good and evil are simplified and father-son struggles emphasized, this second installment in the series leaves no doubt about the heroic status of Lando Calrissian (Billy Dee Williams). By mere association with the white heroes from the previous film, Calrissian assumes acceptability as he rallies to the support of the "good" Rebel Alliance. Both raceless and sexless (in contrast to prior romantic leading-man images of Williams), Calrissian appears to be a pleasant marketing addition to the ensemble of heroes who commit themselves to their destiny. Although his name suggests an Armenian background, Calrissian remains a black space traveler whose racial identity receives no mentioning, and whose personal life is rendered ambiguous. A similar rootlessness and colorblind heroism continues in the sequel, *The Return of the Jedi* (1983).

Williams's role as Matthew Fox assumes a similar ambiguity in the cop drama titled *Nighthawks*. Paired with Sylvester Stallone as Deke DaSilva, the story assumes the veneer of an interracial buddy action piece, but it really serves as a Stallone vehicle. Though DaSilva and Fox work together as an undercover decoy team that ensnares mugging and drug-dealing criminals, they never really interact convincingly as working partners, let alone buddies. The story fails to demonstrate their trust and involvement with one another, whether working or off-duty. At a crucial point in the movie, when the infamous international terrorist for hire, Wulfgar (Rutger Hauer), arrives in New York, DaSilva and Fox are reassigned to an anti-terrorist task force due to their military backgrounds in the Vietnam War. In the bombings, battles, and brutality that ensue, DaSilva surfaces as the primary hero who challenges and eventually kills Wulfgar. The DaSilva-Fox duo never achieve the level of shared humor, experiences, or bonding that define other buddy films of the decade.

In a parallel manner, the urban cop fiction *Sharkey's Machine* provides a black detective who is part of the titular "machine" of detectives. As such, the black detective Arch (Bernie Casey) functions as an integral component in the heroic ensemble that distinguishes itself, the "good guys," from the drug-running "bad guys" who are intent upon destroying Atlanta. Like Calrissian, Arch's race is visible to the other characters, but emerges as no consequence for the relationships among the men. Arch, in fact, serves as an intellectual and philosophical center to his comrades, who rush to judgment and physical actions. Arch's priority is to rationalize all situations, endowing him with a noble, spiritual quality unexpected from the motley members of the crime-fighting "machine."

The award-winning and popular *An Officer and a Gentleman* explored military culture and the men who gravitated to that career choice. In the story, aspiring Naval officer candidate Zack Mayo (Richard Gere), despite a tortured childhood, matures to a point where he can express his emotions and love for a woman. Importantly, Mayo also experiences a parallel emotional journey with his black drill sergeant, Sergeant Foley (Lou Gossett, Jr.). More of a son-father dynamic, the Mayo-Foley relationship indicates the common thread of courage and honor that supposedly exists in all men who are committed to seeking those attributes. Foley's demanding persona insists that Mayo adapt to a group vision over his individuality. Critic Donald Bogle writes that "there was a kind of crazy, perverse joy in seeing Gossett as Foley upset past movie traditions; here was a black sergeant taunting the white hero (whom he calls 'boy') and other recruits as he puts them through the rigors of military life. Gossett portrayed Foley as a black man, like millions of others in America, who works in a white environment/culture, operating there successfully without losing his own personal cultural identity."[11] Despite being the most dynamic aspect about the film, the Mayo-Foley relationship serves as a subordinate story line to the love story in the movie.

On the other end of the quality spectrum was *Police Academy* (1984), "which spawned six sequels and two TV series (one animated)."[12] Against the backdrop of the culture of law enforcement, two black male recruits — Larvell Jones (Michael Winslow) and Moses Hightower (Bubba Smith) — find a world into which they fit equally with other eccentric white males and one white female. Jones functions as a "human beat box [using] his mouth to get out of all sort of sticky situations" and massive, muscled Hightower is "an overgrown florist-cum-cop."[13] In a movie that elevates silliness to a nauseating level, an interracial buddy relationship never received any particular examination. One critic simply wrote: "*Police Academy* is, without a doubt, the most painfully embarrassing, shameful and unfunny series in all the history of filmmaking."[14]

Far removed from the comic vein, a serious cultural and political dynamic drives the engaging drama *The Killing Fields*. Again, avoiding the conventional shaping of an interracial buddy film, the film nonetheless roots itself in friendship and caring between males that moves from the professional to the personal. Sydney Schonberg (Sam Waterston), a white American journalist, and Dith Pran (Haing S. Ngor), a Cambodian journalist have a common enemy during the Vietnam War. But Pran's story of survival rightfully assumes center stage in an emotionally wrenching study of inhumanity, American imperialism, and media manipulation. Pran's fight for existence eclipses Schonberg's efforts to find and locate his kidnapped friend. Though genuine in his motivation, Schonberg's American identity allows him to avoid the horrific condition imposed upon Pran.

The Interracial Buddy Pattern in the Late 1980s

By mid-decade, a more provocative, political vehicle — *White Nights* (1985) — constructed the story of interracial buddies developing a trust while surviving the machinations of both American and Soviet powers. In regard to the buddy duo, this film offered a notable variation to the traditional symbols of masculinity. Specifically, neither buddy used a gun to confront the anxious moments of danger, and dance, the artistic expression often associated with feminine sensibilities, functions as the source of passion for both male protagonists.

While on tour as a ballet dancer, Nikolai Rodchenko (Mikhail Baryshnikov), sustains critical injuries in an emergency plane landing in the Soviet Union. Recognizing Rodchenko as a Russian defector from eight years earlier, the manipulative Colonel Chaiko (Jerzy Skolimowski) lies to the American Embassy about Rodchenko's whereabouts while placing the dancer in the home of an American-born, black tap dancer named Raymond Greenwood (Gregory Hines). Greenwood, now married to his Russian wife, Darya (Isabella Rossellini), defected from the United States years before, attempting to find artistic freedom and relief from American racism. The two dancers clash politically, yet eventually meet a common understanding that artistic freedom cannot be obtained in Communist Russia, and they agree to the dangerous plot of escaping to the American Embassy for refuge.

The significant point of disagreement between the two males at the beginning of the film carries the film's most captivating dialogue, as both men argue the manner in which their love for dance was strangled by their respective native lands. Rodchenko, who attained distinction in the Kirov Theater, insists that the Soviet regime was strangling his artistic expression, forcing him to suppress his emotions and individuality. In contrast, Greenwood reminds Rodchenko that in the United States the latter could indeed find freedom because he was white. In a memorable sequence, a drunken Greenwood combines his improvisational tap dancing with his bitter recounting of the racism he experienced in America.

However, another contentious point exists between the two in regard to the styles of dance. Rodchenko's classical, choreographed ballet moves clash with Greenwood's more rhythmic, aggressive movements, which spring from the immediate emotions. The film allows each man to perform in solo sequences to highlight his own distinctive techniques. But the dance sequences remain integrated into the story, serving both as aspects of the characters' personalities and as symbols of the characters' drive to survive as artists. But later, when the two have decided to devise a common plan for escape, their shared dance number amalgamates elements of ballet, tap, modern dance, and the martial arts. As the two move in a uniformed choreography, the literal expression of their grace, athleticism, and balance fills the screen, even as the similar movements become a metaphor for their resolve to resist the Soviets and work together.

Greenwood's angst reveals itself slowly throughout the film, as his poor living conditions, his alienation from contemporary music, and his suspicions of Colonel Chaiko merge. And when Greenwood discovers that his wife is pregnant, he realizes that he doesn't want his child to be born in Russia. The audience also observes that the hypocritical Colonel Chaiko, and by association Russia, holds racist attitudes, as the colonel on several occasions refers to Greenwood as a "black stud," a "nigger," and a "black bastard." The movie, therefore, implies that despite its racism, the United

States remains the best place for Greenwood to live — though, as an African American expatriate artist, the story never explains why he chose Russia as opposed to France or Switzerland.

Once united in their plan to escape, the Rodchenko-Greenwood duo display the resourcefulness as other buddy heroes, with the major exception being their lack of violence to initiate their victory over the villainous Russians. Knowing that they are under constant surveillance, the two use their fabricated arguments and antagonistic behavior to combat the Communists.

Yet, in another deviation from the conventional buddies, both of these heroes cry. In one scene, after the sadistic Colonel Chaiko has his officers take Darya away from Greenwood, and possibly to a labor camp, Greenwood confesses to Rodchenko that she's the best thing that ever happened to him. In his emotional anger, Greenwood cries, and Rodchenko comforts him with an embrace. In another scene, in a solitary moment on the Kirov stage before his escape, Rodchenko dances a few steps and studies the impressive interior architecture. Remembering his time there in the past and all that's been lost, he begins to weep.

The most troubling aspect of the film that detracts from its accomplishments revolves around a seeming racial hierarchy that the white male has over the black counterpart. This element haunted numerous films in earlier decades, making its ghostly reappearance in this drama. Specifically, though both men experience a demoralizing set of circumstances, Rodchenko possesses a self-control and confidence that is missing in Greenwood. The former, despite his loss of native land, retains his belief in himself. The tears he cries at the Kirov are tears of loss of a childhood dream. On the other hand, Greenwood views himself as a failure, a man who has lost his sense of self-worth and value. Consequently, he gains those qualities of manhood back at the end due to his white partner, who saves him emotionally, psychologically, and physically in the film's finale. The black male possesses a confusion and weakness that isn't demonstrated in the white male hero.

However, in its engaging effort to both uphold and challenge certain gender traits, *White Nights* remains a film worth visiting. It chooses an intellectual path rather than a strictly visceral one to stimulate the audience's connection to the buddies. Its title alone carries several possible meanings, as both heroes reshape lives that have been affected by racial discrimination and racial privilege. At the same time, the title identifies that season during the Russian year that was twenty-four hours of daylight, which effects and, perhaps, distorts one's vision. This same distortion occurred for both buddies when they defected, but by the film's ending, both have regained clear perceptions about the significance of their lives.

In the same year as *White Nights*, the revisionist western *Silverado* posed a different perspective on the frontier for the audience, as various interracial connections and diverse characterizations pervade the story line. Presaging other revisionist westerns that would follow, such as *Unforgiven* (1992), *The Ballad of Little Jo* (1993), *Posse* (1993), and *Bad Girls* (1994), the film *Silverado* challenged the traditional assumptions about gender and multiracial participation that composed much of western lore.

Silverado possesses the frontier scapes, sprawling vistas, dusty streets, smoky saloons, and shootouts expected in the western genre, while driven by a musical score that's bold and sweeping in its rhythms. Beyond that, however, the filmmakers seem intent upon shaping a movie that is not just a buddy story, but a fiction that has contemporary sensibilities and ethics in its criticism of wealth and oligarchic powers that are inherently corrupt. At the center of this story with numerous characters are four heroes who are all looking for a place to belong. One of those heroes is black cowboy Mal Johnson (Danny Glover) who throws his fate in with three white riders after two of them defend him to the sheriff following a barroom brawl. Although Mal's personal story deviates from that of his three companions, the characters all come together at the film's end to battle Silverado's local tyrant and paid-off law officers.

Traveling from Chicago to the West, Mal finds his father murdered, and he tells his errant barmaid sister, Rae (Lynn Whitfield), "All we got is each other." Mal wants to reclaim his family, but the cost is to defy the powers that be. By teaming with his white partners—Paden (Kevin Kline), Emmett (Scott Glenn), and Jake (Kevin Costner)—Mal's stoicism, courage, and violence serve as his tools to accomplish his goals. He is indeed a frontier male on an even level with his white partners, whose acceptance of Mal embellishes their heroic qualities even further. Although it serves as a minor theme here, the interracial coalition of these four men signals their defiance to bigoted traditions and social rigidity. Their frontier justice would be decisively a democratic system where race would not prevent the completion of one's dreams.

Running Scared (1986) returns the interracial buddy formula shaped by films from earlier in the decade. In this action-comedy, two urban cops are inseparable buddies, completing one another's sentences, reading each other's thoughts, and walking in and out of personal lives with easy access. At the heart of their union is a careless, childlike pursuit of laughs, which creates some problems in the film's tone when situations become dramatic. At the same time, race exists as a minor issue, though Ray Hughes (Greg-

In *Silverado*, the good-guy characters, from top to bottom, Conrad (Rusty Meyers), Mal (Danny Glover), Paden (Kevin Kline), and Emmett (Scott Glenn) survey the bad guys in the canyon below.

ory Hines) is obviously black and Danny Costanzo (Billy Crystal) is identified as Italian. Whether in the city or while vacationing in Key West and dating women of various ethnic backgrounds, racial concerns never shape the lives of the protagonists.

Ray and Danny have been Chicago cops and partners for sixteen years. In their wild, unorthodox style of fighting crime, their captain allows them a bit of room for blurring lines of procedure. In their zeal to bring down Julio Gonzales (Jimmy Smits), an aspiring drug lord, they shatter various rules of conduct and ethics. The Hughes-Costanzo duo avoid taking many things seriously, until they visit and contemplate retirement in Key West, transforming them into cautious crime fighters, which almost gets them killed. The image of wisecracking, death-defying buddies has been a recurring facet in the buddy paradigm, but here, the silliness is so excessive that the film loses believability and tension. With ample chase scenes and shootouts, the movie remains true to the action genre, and the Hughes-Costanzo duo display the required profane and tough talk expected of such buddies.

The interesting area of attention is the manner in which these two males are shown in connection to female characters. The buddies are without question heterosexual, and they display the expected macho response to women. Both Hughes and Costanza are divorced, both bitter in their attitudes, but Hughes copes with it better than his buddy. In one bar scene, they meet a black woman named Maryann (Tracy Reed), who also announces that she's divorced though presently with a boyfriend. Hughes and Maryann lock eyes, and the next morning, they're in bed together in his loft apartment. Without knocking, Costanzo enters Ray's apartment with doughnuts and jokes, waking the two up as Maryann sashays into the bathroom, allowing both buddies a view of her naked posterior. In a later scene during an emergency, Costanza again enters Hughes's apartment unannounced while Hughes and Maryann are being intimate between the sheets. In both cases, Hughes doesn't become upset or irritated, and his attention immediately shifts from Maryann to Costanza — true buddies.

As for Costanza's personal life, he still harbors feelings for his ex-wife, Anna (Darlanne Fluegel), who obviously carries a flame for him as well. Costanza's mixed signals to Anna illustrate the argument that "[m]ales develop higher anxiety than females with response to divorce."[15] After announcing her impending marriage to a dentist, Danny attempts to joke away his hurt during various scenes, until finally the two admit they love one another. And at the end, when the villain Gonzales kidnaps Anna, Costanza gathers Hughes to go and rescue Anna despite the deadly circumstances.

For these buddies, the women seem to be occasional distractions. Their relationships with women appear so matter-of-factly that the attraction the women have to Hughes and Costanza is difficult to understand. The buddies' irresistible charms are a given, which is amplified during the Key West vacation segment, as a montage shows that numerous 20-ish, bikini-clad women delight in dating these two. Whether clubbing, beaching, skating, or motor-scootering, Hughes and Costanza acquire female companionship easily and always pleasurably.

Fortunately, *Running Scared* doesn't ever seem to take itself seriously, nor does it attempt to travel beyond the familiar trappings of the interracial buddy riff and action genre. With generous portions of sight and verbal antics, the film accomplishes the major entertainment objective of thrilling the audience before disappearing from thought after the images leave the screen. Perhaps, the fact that the two buddies are so similar, there's little room to connect to different contours that would make the bonding more captivating.

In contrast, this differentiation between protagonists, along with an

Buddy detectives Ray Hughes (Gregory Hines, second from left) and Danny Costanzo (Billy Crystal, far right) handle another tense conflict in *Running Scared*.

engaging story line, contributes to the appeal of the interracial buddies in the *Lethal Weapon* series. Beginning in 1987, and over the next eleven years, four films were produced that followed the development of perhaps the best-known interracial buddies of the decade — Martin Riggs (Mel Gibson) and Roger Murtaugh (Danny Glover). With a winning combination of over-the-top action and ongoing visual and verbal humor, the series kept the Riggs-Murtaugh duo at the center of the stories, as various family members, friends, and fellow cops connected to the two. With an emphasis more on the generational differences than the racial differences, the *Lethal Weapon* series displays the idealization of friendship, family, and the legal system.

In *Lethal Weapon*, Riggs and Murtaugh are introduced as two diametrically opposed characters. Riggs, an eccentric white loner, lives with his dog while getting over the loss of his young wife in a car accident. In despair, Riggs is suicidal, taking risks on an already dangerous job as an undercover cop. As reviewer Roger Ebert assesses: "In the space of less than 48 hours, they become partners, share family dinner, kill several people, survive a shootout in the desert, battle with helicopters and machine guns, toss hand grenades, jump off buildings, rescue Glover's kidnapped daughter, drive cars through walls, endure electric shock, have a few beers and repair the engine on Glover's boat — not in that order."[16]

Above all else, Riggs and Murtaugh depict the ideal of the American way of life, excluding the thorns of racism that would prick a true democratic system — though their masculinity remains enhanced via the violence and language.

Riggs is young, fearless, and alone, except for his dog, Sam. By making the white buddy the most extreme, nihilistic of the two, Riggs's violent nature becomes more acceptable to a mainstream audience. In essence, Riggs emerges as a white rebel whose enemy is never the system, but the "bad guys" who abuse and disrespect that system. Although his behavior sometimes sweeps over the top, Riggs remains a likeable individual who lives in his beachfront trailer with his pet. Riggs's martial arts skills and proficiency with various guns designate his toughness, as does his high tolerance for pain, be it in the form of torture, bullet holes, knife stabbings, car crashes, high-level falls, or a dislocated shoulder. He is the titular lethal weapon who faces down any challenge with a controlled rage.

On the other hand, making the black buddy the more conservative of the two ensures a mainstream acceptance of Murtaugh. As a reflection of Sidney Poitier's Virgil Tibbs from *In the Heat of the Night*, Murtaugh displays how the system can indeed work for blacks. Living in his two-story house in a predominately white neighborhood, Murtaugh — along with wife, Trish (Darlene Love), oldest daughter, Rianne (Traci Wolfe), son, Nick (Damon Hines), and second daughter, Carrie (Ebonie Smith) — exemplifies the hard-working crime fighter who desires quiet time at home or while fishing on his boat. Murtaugh and his family are consistently shown in all four films, emphasizing the sanctity of the family unit into which Riggs is eventually integrated. Murtaugh, whose mantra, "I'm too old for this shit," indicates his preference for avoiding violence; nonetheless, he can jump into fistfights, engage in car chases, survive explosions, and shoot it out with any set of villains. Often serving as a voice of reason to Riggs's adrenaline rush into violence, Murtaugh eventually joins in the fray to either support or save his partner. First and foremost, despite department policies, ethics, and the warnings of long-suffering Captain Murphy (Steve Kahan), the partnership of these buddies, once established in the first film, becomes impregnable.

Murtaugh, at age 50, is near retirement and therefore wants to play out his final time on the force as carefully as possible. Yet, despite their age and racial differences, Riggs and Murtaugh eventually connect, and together they dismantle numerous "bad guys" while entering the personal corners of each other's life. This personal interaction strengthens their professional skills, as they intersect in agreement on issues of justice, the family, and manhood. Commenting on the Riggs-Murtaugh union, Robyn Wiegman states: "In an interesting reversal of paternalistic ideology, it is the white male [Riggs] who, debilitated by grief, can be restored to life only through the aid of the black 'father' [Murtaugh]—the figure responsible in the film's resolution, for drawing the alienated white male back into the folds of sanity and the bourgeois family."[17] With this burden of restoration the black male exists as an essential reinforcer of the system's values both within the diegesis of the film and the world of the audience.

The two buddies merge in acceptance and understanding in the sequels, intent upon violently removing evil from the world. In *Lethal Weapon 2*, the duo take on a group of South African diplomats who manipulate their foreign credentials to cover their illegal deals in the United States. In the third installment, the buddies pursue a former cop who sells confiscated weapons to street gangs. In *Lethal Weapon 4*, while solving the smuggling of Chinese workers into Los Angeles, the heroes uncover the production of counterfeit Chinese currency. The series remains popular by introducing into the sequels new characters who reveal different aspects of the main duo, but despite all else, the interaction between Riggs and Murtaugh remains the center of each film.

In *Lethal Weapon 2*, perhaps the most racially charged story, the duo opposes the fascist attitudes of South African villains. Critic Sharon Willis notes that in a "spectacular gesture of displacement, the adversarial figures ... are all South Africans, controlled ... by the South African government, so that the perpetrators of racism are located elsewhere ... in a comforting counterbalance with our own U.S. racism, which is made to appear manageable by contrast."[18] When addressing the tight-lipped white villains, Riggs deliberately calls them "Adolph" and "Aryan," instructing them to "fold up your tents and get ... out of my country." Their insult of "kaffir lover" inflames Riggs, and he purposefully uses his badge to intimidate and violently confront them. When Riggs attaches his American pickup truck and chains to pull down the villains' private house built on stilts, he symbolically destroys the foundation of their racist, apartheid politics that have directly targeted his black partner. At the end, when the leader of the South Africans, Arjen Rudd (Joss Ackland), shoots down Riggs, Murtaugh takes aim and, despite Rudd's assertion of diplomatic immunity, the black hero kills the racist white villain. While embracing Riggs, in what scholars Vera and Gordon identify as "the pieta image of [a] black man holding his wounded white partner,"[19] Murtaugh jokes that the South Africans are dead, explaining, "they've been de-kaffir-nated."

The racial issue surfaces again in *Lethal Weapon 4*, as Murtaugh takes in a family of illegal Chinese immigrants. Murtaugh tells Riggs that the Chinese family's inhuman smuggling is similar to black slavery, as he reasons: "I'm freeing slaves ... like no one did for my ancestors." Although Riggs knows that Murtaugh is breaking the law by harboring the family, he supports his partner's stand on human rights.

Unlike other buddies, Riggs and Murtaugh do not chase women, and hence their masculinity is not connected to their virility and numerous sexual conquests. Instead, they celebrate family and monogamy. Although Riggs has a sexual encounter in the second installment with Rika van den Haas (Patsy Kensit), a secretary to the South African diplomats killed by her bosses, in the last two films, he becomes committed to Lorna Cole (Rene Russo), a fellow sergeant with whom he eventually has a child and plans to marry. When Riggs and Lorna first become intimate, their sexual foreplay is comprised of undressing by comparing various wounds and body scars attained on the job. Lorna, who rushes to use her martial arts skills rather than her feminine nurturing, surfaces as a formidable match for Riggs. She relies on more brawn than her beauty, fascinating Riggs in using her body as a lethal weapon as opposed to a sexual ornament to showcase.

At the same time, Murtaugh displays the type of family life that Riggs ultimately desires. Their sense of masculinity, partnership, and family all merge into one system. In the third film, following an argument just days before Murtaugh retires, Riggs confesses to his partner: "We're partners. What happens to you happens to me. When you retire, you're retiring us. You're the only family I got.... I got three beautiful kids and I love them and they're yours.... Trish does my laundry. I live in your ice box. I live in your life."

In many ways, Riggs and Murtaugh's relationship surpasses the standard fare in the interracial buddy motif. It lifts itself to what Hernan Vera and Andrew M. Gordon refer to as "a symbolic marriage between black and white."[20] In that vein, their bonding reaches a spiritual level when the duo display their inextricable link to one another. For example, in the aforementioned scene from *Lethal Weapon 2*, when Riggs is dying, Murtaugh clutches him, insisting, "You're not dead until I tell you ... breathe!" Murtaugh "wills" Riggs not to die, exerting his power of buddy love over death. In a similar fashion, in *Lethal Weapon 4*, following a bloody battle with villain Wah Sing Ku (Jet Li), Riggs is trapped underwater beneath cement pilings. When Murtaugh searches the topside calling his name, he prays aloud, "Will me, Riggs!" Receiving what appears to be a telepathic response, Murtaugh knows where to dive beneath the water to free Riggs from drowning.

But to maintain that spiritual realm and to disclaim any homosexual tendencies, the duo continually remind one another not to show their affection to others. When Murtaugh successfully "wills" Riggs back to life in the second story and approaching sirens blast, Riggs jokes through the pain, telling Murtaugh: "You really are a beautiful man.... Give us a kiss before they come." Earlier in the same film, when Riggs helps Murtaugh dive into the bathroom tub to escape the toilet seat rigged with a bomb, Riggs states in the aftermath of the explosion: "Get off me man. I don't want anybody to see us like this." Another example occurs in the fourth story, when the possible gay identity of a fellow cop becomes an issue. Unknown to Murtaugh, Detective Butters (Chris Rock) has secretly married his daughter, Rianne, so Butters attempts to develop a "closeness" to Murtaugh, but those efforts are mistakenly viewed by the latter as a homosexual attraction. Murtaugh repeatedly articulates his sexual orientation to avoid misjudgments by fellow officers and Butters in particular. Finally, the filmmakers successfully prevent any question about the heteronormativity of the heroes by introducing a third male character, Leo Getz (Joe Pesci), in the last three episodes. Getz's annoying personality; his inept fighting skills; his dependence on the duo to be saved; and his function as the target of their practical jokes help to reify the

Detectives Roger Murtaugh (Danny Glover, left) and Martin Riggs (Mel Gibson, right) keep control over their sidekick, Leo Getz (Joe Pesci) in *Lethal Weapon 3*.

traditional masculine traits of the heterosexual buddies. As a third wheel to their bonding, Getz assures the audience that Riggs and Murtaugh are just two regular guys who allow their emotional sides to surface on occasion, but who are, at their foundation, "straight," average, hard-working buddies.

Alongside the indelible interracial buddy images in *Lethal Weapon*, two additional films in the late '80s utilized the popular scenario. The first reinstated Gregory Hines into the third such film in the decade. Paired with Willem Dafoe in *Off Limits* (1988), Hines assumes a more cynical, loose-cannon character than in his earlier roles. Set in Saigon in the late 1960s just after the Tet Offensive, the movie follows Sergeant First Class Buck McGriff (Dafoe) and Sergeant Albaby Perkins (Hines) who are CIDs, that is Criminal Investigations Detectives, attempting to solve the murder of a Vietnamese prostitute. The evidence and witnesses in a series of six similar murders lead them to several American officers as suspects. With the support of Sergeant Dix (Fred Ward) and ongoing antagonistic confrontations with the local Vietnamese police official, named Lime Green (Kay Tong Lim), the buddies find themselves pulled into the seedier side of the city, the war zone, and an orphanage run by nuns, included a young French woman, Sister Nicole (Amanda Pays).

The story is gritty and graphic, as the McGriff-Perkins duo cruise the dangerous streets with their own dogged commitment to solve the crime. And as Cynthia J. Fuchs remarks, "The front seat of their car situates McGriff and Babe's [Perkins] bond, delineating their incorruptible morality as proximity and loyalty to one another."[21] McGriff, more cerebral and sensitive, and Perkins, more unpredictable and edgy, are rendered as the tough crime fighters who rely upon one another instinctively. Their camaraderie is grounded in their military service, but their plainclothes cop techniques seem to be based upon their experience of dealing with the particular nature of Saigon's wartime environment. In fact, the film's more engaging segments stem from the political currents running through the story; in an anti–American environment, the volatile streets erupt with violent cultural clashes. At places, the film raises some provocative questions about the relationship between the United States and Vietnam, as the exploitation of the Vietnamese women by an American officer works as a metaphor for the history between the two countries. However, though questions are raised, their possible answers take a secondary role to the action, in the form of explosions, foot chases, shootouts, a car-and-motorcycle chase, zooming helicopters, and war-zone battles.

But, awkwardly, an unevenness surfaces in the connection between the protagonists. At times, their friendship flows like a synchronized machine, but in other places through the dialogue, or lack thereof, McGriff and Perkins do not appear to know one another beyond the surface. They work the case as partners, but often they do not seem close, displaying attitudes that swing between belligerent and affectionate. When they share a good-natured moment, it comes off as being forced and awkward. The two often demonstrate an affiliation that would not be there if they were not partners professionally. And, even at the movie's end, as the two plan to fly back to California together, one wonders whether they will even stay in touch over the phone.

Certainly, the McGriff-Perkins duo possess the expected heterosexual proclivities, as the former develops an infatuation for the young Sister Nicole and the latter expresses a possible relationship with a bar girl with "big tits and huge nipples." In addition, the solving of the serial murders allow the two a peculiar voyeuristic gaze of the nude, female Vietnamese victims. Their gaze, along with the camera's, speaks to a privilege of objectifying the women, and in the scene where McGriff watches an American officer and a Vietnamese woman playing out a sexual fantasy, his lengthy staring suggests a curious enjoyment with the proceedings. McGriff's frustration with lusting after an unattainable nun and viewing nude women mirror the situation of the war; America suffers from being active in a country that's both unattainable and alluring at the same time. Nevertheless, the McGriff-Perkins buddyship proceeds with a duty to close the case despite its dangers.

One movie that deserves attention from the end of the 1980's is the action-drama *Black Rain* (1989), with Michael Douglas taking the major role and adding his name above the title as a producer. The first half of the story presents Nick (Douglas), a New York detective under scrutiny by the Internal Affairs Division for confiscating drug money, and his partnership with Charlie (Andy Garcia), a likable, upbeat detective. When the two witness a Japanese Yakuza named Sato (Yasaku Matsuda) kill two men in a restaurant, their chase and capture of Sato leads to their escorting the man back to Japan to face charges. In Japan, Nick and Charlie mistakenly hand Sato over to the wrong men, and from there the chase is on to find Sato, who later viciously murders Charlie. The second half of the film follows the uneasy partnering between Nick and Japanese detective Masahiro, or Mas (Ken Takakura), who have suffered an ongoing cultural and personality clash.

Nick and Mas's tense alliance eventually becomes one of trust as they survive a final shootout to capture Sato and take him into Japanese headquarters. Importantly, on his part, Mas faces suspension by his superior

Sergeant Albaby Perkins (Gregory Hines, left) erupts violently as Sergeant First Class Buck McGriff (Willem Dafoe) looks on in *Off Limits.*

officers for deliberately backing Nick, who has become a persona non grata, in an assault of a Yakuza meeting.

Although actor Andy Garcia is Latino, his character isn't identified as such in the story. So, the intent here is not to show a white-Latino buddy film, but, as in the earlier film *The Yakuza*, to underscore the Western-Eastern dynamics of the American and Japanese pairing. A significant statement made by Mas to Nick summarizes the contrasts between the two: "Think less of yourself and more of your group." Comprehending Nick's Western individualism, Mas challenges the New York cop to examine his thinking and behavior. Nick's struggle with his own weaknesses, as he eventually admits to Mas that he indeed stole money, parallels Nick's defiant efforts to capture Sato. The Nick-Mas bonding is tenuous but nurturing in the personal changes that Nick undergoes. In that process Nick uses the action hero's profane language, defiant attitude, and physical violence to gain his revenge and validation. The gun, in traditional fashion, serves as a symbol of the hero's masculinity and power, as Nick pursues his manly obligation to avenge Charlie's death. Yet, Nick has indeed learned compassion and control from his brief partnering with Mas, as the former chooses not to kill Sato but to turn him in alive with Mas at his side. Nick embraces the Eastern perspective to help reinstate Mas into his job and to avoid further personal disgrace in Japanese culture.

Black Rain vacillates in its adherence to the buddy film pattern, unable to concede its efforts to be a character study of Nick. However, in order to examine Nick, the film has to integrate Mas as the catalyst for the former's maturation and reflection on masculinity. The film's graphic violence is distracting at places, and its upbeat ending with Nick and Mas exchanging gifts, smiles, and respect for one another, attempts to erase the brutality visualized earlier.

The Echo Films of the Late 1980s

By the latter half of the '80s, a number of films, such as *Gardens of Stone* (1987), *Shoot to Kill* (1988), and *Glory* (1989) included masculine messages and race-related themes, though the buddy factor was merely echoed due to the demands of genre. Two additional films worthy of attention were military-related dramas, and one a hit action vehicle, but they sought to highlight men searching to define manhood amid deadly circumstances.

Hamburger Hill (1987), set in the Vietnam War, "develops the characters and at the same time gives ... food for thought about the immorality of war, juxtaposing tranquility with horror."[22] One critic praised the "adept leading man" performance of white actor Dylan McDermott, as

In *Black Rain*, American detective Nick Conlin (Michael Douglas, left) discusses his Western cop philosophy with Japanese detective Masahiro Matsumoto (Ken Takakura).

Sergeant Franz, and black actor Courtney B. Vance as Doc Johnson in a film that's "more about the soldier than the war."[23]

At the same time, the film *Bat 21* (1988), which also places its characters in the Vietnam War, is about the actual incidents of a U.S. Air Force colonel, code name "Bat 21," who is "shot down during a reconnaissance mission over North Vietnam."[24] Colonel Hambleton (Gene Hackman) develops a crucial relationship and communications via the radio with a black pilot named Bird Dog (Danny Glover) as the military strategizes a rescue. The two "form a 'Diehard-esque' comradeship, a couple of right guys spiritually connected by wireless."[25]

The major echo film was the immensely popular contemporary action story *Die Hard* (1988). In this box office prize, multiculturalism seems a key ingredient as heroes and villains appear across cultural lines—Irish American, African American, Japanese, German, and Russian. But the link between the white hero, John McClane (Bruce Willis), and the likable black police officer, Al Powell (Reginald VelJohnson) functions as the clearest statement of American racial harmony. Although communicating via radios, McClane and Al navigate the life-and-death situation within the high-rise tower that traps the former and the office workers, including John's wife, Holly (Bonnie Bedelia). McClane and Al finally meet face to face in the final moments of the movie, connecting their kindred professional souls with a physical embrace. The essential element to their relationship stems from their interrelated identities as working-class cops. Scholar Robert Kolker recognizes this dynamic in his observations about the two characters: "*Die Hard* is a great riff on the buddy film. Al and John are given a multifaceted relationship. They are father and son, mother and child; they embrace almost like lovers.... Al, once afraid to shoot his gun, redeems his manhood by shooting the last of the bad guys" in order to save John.[26] Without the ability to "see" one another, John and Al must "feel" one another, providing them with the emotional exchanges that temper violent impulses while sharing their desires to be good family men. But always at the center of the story, McClane's character assumes the spotlight and endures the rigorous tribulations that must be confronted by an action hero.

* * *

With the interracial buddy paradigm reaching a heightened level of popularity during the 1980s, the pattern framed numerous genres, verifying its legitimacy as a storytelling tool and an effective marketing strategy to reach mainstream audiences. Viewed as an enticing commercial package, particularly for teenage males, interracial buddyship garnered audiences that attended the first weekend screening and perhaps made for repeat ticket sales. Collectively, the increased quantity of interracial buddy films in the 1980s became the harbinger of a pattern that flourished further in the 1990s and was stimulated by the multicultural movement that erupted in academia and popular culture.

5

Mayhem, Multiculturalism, and the Male Gaze: 1990s

By the 1990s, the interracial buddy film had found an ongoing depiction in America's commercial cinema. Carrying on the images from the previous decade, many of these male-oriented films were nurtured in genres where action, adventure, and tough individualism framed the dimensions of manhood. During a decade optimistic with the Clinton administration's progressive approach to racial and social issues and a marked improvement in economic recovery, American cinema maintained the familiar dimensions of masculinity, even as the public discourse hinted at ways of transforming the familiar.

In both popular literature and academia, the established dimensions of manhood were being debated and assessed for their value to both genders. Masculinity Studies, viewed by some scholars as the complementary progression from Women's Studies, collectively explored the complexities of maleness across racial, class, and political lines as issues of sexual orientation and queerness entered many discussions and debates as well. In the '90s, numerous books invited readers to revisit and rethink the repercussions of conventional notions of masculinity: *Iron John* (1990); *To Be a Man: In Search of the Deep Masculine* (1991); *Cool Pose: The Dilemmas of Black Manhood in America* (1992); *Making Things Perfectly Queer: Interpreting Mass Culture* (1993); *The Assassination of the Black Male Image* (1994); *The Masculine Mystique: The Politics of Masculinity* (1995); *Manhood in America: A Cultural History* (1996); *Rethinking Masculinity: Philosophical Explorations in Light of Feminism* (1996); *Stiffed: The Betrayal of the American Man* (1999), just to mention some of the many titles of the decade. In a significant manner, the decade became a forum for multilayered debates about manhood, and American cinema entered those discussions through the notable films released.

Often cited as the decade of political correctness, the '90s also brought on variations on the concept of multiculturalism. For some, multiculturalism offered a practical way of making society more inclusive of its various ethnic and cultural voices. Historian Ron Takaki supported multiculturalism in concluding that "the people of America's diverse groups are able to see themselves and each other in our common past ... affirming the struggle for equality as a central theme in our country's history.... America does not belong to one race or one group."[1] Dismissing the trivialization of assessing various ethnic voices as simply being "politically correct," cultural critic Douglas Kellner asseverates that "[m]ulticulturalism affirms the worth of different types of culture and cultural groups, claiming, for instance, that Black, Latino, Asian, Native American, gay and lesbian and other oppressed and marginal voices have their own validity and importance."[2] In Hollywood films, the visibility of people of color on movie screens increased substantially, even as some critics dismissed the trendy revisionist approaches to traditional stories, such as the Peter Pan fantasy in *Hook* (1991) and established genres, such as the western *Posse* (1993).

Another mixed response of criticism was targeted directly at a cycle of films that placed more black and Latino male images on the screen — the "hood" films. Appearing in the first half of the '90s, these films, such as *Boyz N the Hood* (1991), *Juice* (1992), and *Menace II Society* (1993), connected directly to hip-hop urban culture and the generalized homicidal behavior of young men of color. Often viewed as extended promotional films for hip-hop soundtracks, the masculinity depicted in these films was based upon nihilism, materialism, and misogyny.

However, the mistreatment and objectification of women was not just the province of the "hood" cycle. Hollywood movies posed some contradictory representations of women during the decade. On the one hand, the female form — most often naked or barely clothed in bedroom, party, and strip-club settings— remained a staple in numerous films, including those utilizing the interracial buddy pattern. Serving as an affirmation of critic Laura Mulvey's assertion that the "determining male gaze projects its fantasy onto the female figure ... women are simultaneously looked at and displayed,"[3] the female body functioned as the primary object of the lingering look by male characters within the film and simultaneously by the spectator watching that film. On the other hand, the revisionist approach with various '90s films constructed female characterizations with feminist contours. Across genre lines, movies such as—*Robin Hood: Prince of Thieves* (1991), *The Ballad of Little Jo* (1993), *Bad Girls* (1994), *Fargo* (1996), *G.I. Jane* (1997), and *The Matrix* (1999) positioned female protagonists and supporting characters with authoritative attitudes, independent behavior, and self-sufficiency.

The interracial buddy paradigm in the '90s thrived as it pervaded a decade of films that incorporated mayhem, multiculturalism, and the male gaze. Maintaining elements of earlier films, the '90s interracial buddy formula framed big-budget and more modestly developed projects; at the same time, a number of movies merely echoed the pattern, taking only some of the conventions of the formula to serve thematics or marketing.

The Interracial Buddy Films of the Early 1990s

One of the first interracial buddy films of the decade was also one of the most award-winning westerns in American cinema — *Dances with Wolves* (1990). Committed to the same respectful presentation of particular Indian cultures as the earlier westerns *Broken Arrow* (1950) and *Little Big Man* (1970), *Dances with Wolves* eschews the humor and satire of the latter movie to develop a dramatic story that underscored the Indians' survival of their frontier environment. However, similar to the aforementioned films, once again the protagonist of focus is a white male who becomes transformed by living with Indians.

In the film, following the Civil War, Lieutenant John Dunbar (Kevin Costner) travels to a frontier military post to find himself in the solitude and raw challenge of the plains. When he crosses paths with a nearby Sioux tribe, Dunbar and the Sioux begin a long but mutually beneficial relationship of understanding and peace. Although Dunbar eventually becomes accepted and feted by the entire tribe, the key male relationships here evolve between Dunbar, a holy man named Kicking Bird (Graham Greene), and a fierce warrior called Wind in His Hair (Rodney A. Grant).

Told through Dunbar's voiceover and from his perspective, the divergent personalities of Kicking Bird and Wind in His Hair mark the realization on Dunbar's part that not all Indians are the same. Kicking Bird, a man of thought and calculation, sees Dunbar as a solitary soldier who can perhaps give information about the arrival schedule and numbers of other whites. More a man of decisive action, Wind in His Hair merely views Dunbar as the white enemy who should be eradicated. To his credit, Dunbar, who wears his military uniform at first, refrains from putting on his racial arrogance and tries through gestures and body language to communicate his goodwill. Kicking Bird patiently tolerates Dunbar's awkward movements and pantomime, while Wind in His Hair dismisses the white man as being insane.

The filmmakers' choice to show the Indians speaking in their own language with English subtitles enhances the importance of cultural differences that are eventually overcome. Helping in this area is the important, if a bit too convenient, character named Stands with a Fist (Mary McDonnell), a white woman raised from childhood by the Sioux. Stands with a Fist is forced by Kicking Bird to recall her native English to help him communicate with Dunbar. But the communicating works both ways, and soon Dunbar is learning the language of the Sioux.

Consequently, the interracial enemies become interracial buddies, particularly following three events. First, Dunbar alerts the tribe that the buffalo have migrated into the area, and he joins the Indian males on horseback to hunt the animals, in the process saving the life of an adolescent Indian named Smiles a Lot (Nathan Lee). Second, while Kicking Bird and Wind in His Hair have led a party of braves to track down an enemy tribe, the Pawnee, Dunbar has been given the responsibility to protect those left behind. When the Pawnee move in on the Sioux village, Dunbar gathers rifles from his fort and joins the Sioux in defending their family and village. These two courageous acts amend the hostility that Wind in His Hair feels toward Dunbar, which is punctuated when they make a "fair trade" and exchange clothing. Third, Dunbar marries Stands with a Fist, and afterwards begins wearing Sioux clothing and ornaments while speaking in their language. Through these three acts, Dunbar earns his position of acceptance into the tribe. Having demonstrated the courage, physical skills, and spirit of a male warrior, his taking of a wife in the Sioux ceremonial fashion confirms his acculturation process and seals the bond.

The test of this bond occurs when the Army arrives at the remote fort, and seeing Dunbar in Indian apparel, they shoot his horse and beat him severely. After ascertaining his identity, they send him back to "civilization" in chains to stand trial for being out of uniform and refusing to disclose the location of the Sioux. But in transit, several Sioux rescue Dunbar from the cavalry as Dunbar fights alongside his Indian comrades to kill the arrogant white soldiers. Dunbar's willingness to choose his Sioux identity over his white identity testifies to his life-and-death commitment to his Sioux brothers.

Dunbar, who becomes anointed with the name Dances with Wolves, is a man who journeys outside of his birth identity to find his true identity in an adopted culture. He has literally danced with the wolf that visits his fort, but is a more symbolic way, he interacts with whites whose imperialism and greed make them wolves preying on the indigenous people of the frontier. From one perspective, film historians Joseph M. Boggs and Dennis W. Petrie surmise that Dunbar "has softened the edges of the traditional hero, making him more sensitive to Woman."[4] Yet, it must be argued that Dunbar crosses racial lines without losing his masculine attributes demanded by the challenging environment of the frontier. His maleness is not threatened by the Sioux traditions or vice versa, suggesting that the frontier survival requires fundamental codes of masculinity — riding, hunting, shooting (bows or guns), fathering, protecting, and weathering the natural elements — regardless of racial background.

Turning to a movie that's set in a contemporary urban enclave: *Hangin' with the Homeboys* (1991) proves to be an effective mixture of entertaining and thought-provoking elements. One critic expressed that the movie "ought

Lieutenant John Dunbar (Kevin Costner) and Sioux warrior Kicking Bird (Graham Greene, top) find common understanding on the frontier setting in *Dances with Wolves.*

to do for the South Bronx what [the film] 'Diner' [1982] did for Baltimore ... both [are] bittersweet and boisterous recollections of working class camaraderie."[5] In the South Bronx, two African American friends—Willie (Doug E. Doug) and Tom (Mario Joyner)—spend a Friday night with their two Puerto Rican buddies—Johnny (John Leguizamo) and Fernando, who wants to be called Vinny (Nestor Serrano). With four divergent personalities all in their early twenties, the four men, despite their complaining, look forward to the nights out together. As Willie says at one point: "I wait all week to hang out with you guys ... bored all week ... I die for these Fridays. I want to hang out with my homeboys."

For Willie, the time together gives him a much-needed social life. Unemployed and quick to use his black identity as the reason for not getting a job, Willie is the freeloader friend who understands and defends the sensitivity possessed by Johnny. Johnny, working at a neighborhood market, wrestles with his fear of going off to college as he romanticizes about his life and Daria (Christine Claravall), a neighborhood girl on whom he has a crush. Vinny, however, gets annoyed at Johnny's pensive moods and his prideful claiming of his Puerto Rican identity. Vinny, the ladies' man of the group, hides his ethnicity by using an Italian sounding name, seeking to avoid any restriction to one cultural group or one woman. As a struggling actor, Tom works as a telemarketer, hoping for his break, as he leads the group in improvised scenes of "ghetto theater" on the subway as a way to rattle the unsuspecting public.

The four find a much-needed source of support with one another, even as they often argue when verbal taunts become too truthful. Their shared friendship is both what's good and bad about their environment. On the one hand, as minority members living in the same neighborhood, they relish the sense of power in knowing places, people, and expectations. At the same time, due to their knowledge of the milieu, they know that they can be stuck in future lives that will go nowhere other than in the same circles. The result is a conflicting ambition to leave, but a fear to move away from the familiar—including hanging together on Friday nights.

The sexual orientation of the four never comes into question, though Johnny's possible virginity is a target for Vinny's jokes. Johnny's anger ignites when the four stop off at a peep show and see a porn clip where his romanticized Daria is in flagrante delicto for the spectator's gaze, and his rage explodes later when he sees her at a Manhattan dance club. Tom's luck with women runs just as tragic, as his girlfriend, Vanessa (Kimberly Russell), claims to be sick but is seen on the streets with another man. Yet, despite the heartbreaking events, the homeboys support each other even if it means articulating the truth about notions of love.

One of the more thought-provoking aspects of the film revolves around the handling of race and ethnicity. The film never paints the group's union as a color-blind friendship. Instead, the assertion of racial differences peppers the dialogue, and it becomes offensive at places. Yet, they make one another accountable for any racial stereotyping or prejudicial statements, revealing Willie's flawed Afrocentrism and Vinny's ethnic shame. The discussions about race remain authentic and believable regarding these men whose environments are consistently steeped in both intraracial and interracial confrontations.

In looking at one picaresque night, *Hangin' with the Homeboys* offers a much different look at urban men of color than other "hood" films appearing in the early '90s. These characters know the streets, but are not defeated by those streets. These four friends are not homicidal gangsters, nor are they gun-toting thugs plotting the exploitation of their neighbors. As critic Roger Ebert confirms: "One of the undercurrents in this movie is that these four young men are all essentially good. That needs to be said in films like this, and such films need to be seen."[6] With its open ending, the film is presenting a brief glimpse into the lives of four buddies who care about one another, even as they're attempting to find answers in their own personal lives, which are works in progress.

In a much more accentuated manner, the action film *The Last Boy Scout* (1991) reached an irritating level of cynicism, brutality, and abuse. In appropriate assessment, critic Sharon Willis states that the movie "exaggerates the action film's commitment to the surface — where any pretext for wildly implausible and prolonged violence suffices and where dialogue consistently reduces to ironic patter, a steady rhythm of aggressive jokes bouncing back and forth."[7] In this Bruce Willis vehicle, the action star appears to be reprising his John McClane character and suffers from a constant hangover and cigarette addiction. As Joe Hollenbeck, a sardonic and Laodicean private investigator, Willis is a stoic and wounded spirit who has lost his purpose in life. Though existentialistic in his attitude and behavior, Hollenbeck's actual value lies in the people that surround him — his wife, Sarah (Chelsea Field), and his daughter, Darian (Danielle Harris). However, his mistreatment in his past job as a bodyguard for a pompous senator renders him defeated, and consequently alienates him from his family. His wife has an affair with a man he called a friend and his pre-adolescent daughter swears and screams incessantly.

While taking a job to make quick money, Hollenbeck crosses paths with Jimmy Dix (Damon Wayans), a former pro football quarterback who leans heavily upon alcohol and cocaine after being ejected from the league for gambling problems. Similar to Hollenbeck, Dix has recoiled from others, as the death of his own athletic career and pregnant wife left him bitter and caustic. Without focus, he roams aimlessly between parties and various women. Dix perceives his situation as futile, leaving him to view life dispassionately.

Although antagonistic at first, Hollenbeck and Dix come to understand one another's pain and loss, as they are forced to fight "the bad guys" together along the way. In this case, the bad guy is a pompous, overweight owner of a pro team who wants to legalize sports gambling but manipulates events in order to kill the aforementioned pompous, slender senator who heads a commission on sports gambling. The major problem here, however, is that the story's heroes—Hollenbeck and Dix—are as repulsive as the villains. The interracial buddies are self-absorbed, self-pitying whiners, and as such, they are an irksome pair. In typical fashion, they begin in opposition, preferring different music, cars, and lifestyles, but the revealed personality traits that they have in common make them an unlikable duo.

The issue of race follows the usual structure, as the white hero possesses no animosity in that area. Instead, Hollenbeck saw Dix as a hero before they met, having followed the latter's career and statistics. More than race, Hollenbeck disdains the athletic gifts and privileges that Dix has tossed away, emphasized by the occasion when the white hero punches Dix for snorting cocaine. Ironically, Hollenbeck can clearly view Dix's weaknesses, but has difficulty assessing his own until life-and-death pressures wake him from his self-absorbed quagmire. Finally, at the film's ending, Hollenbeck—clean-shaven and wearing fresh clothes—has reconciled with his wife and daughter, extending an invitation to Dix to be his partner in a private investigation business.

As a significant aspect of this film, and other buddy films in general during the decade, women enhance the main characters' masculinity but at the price of reducing those same women to inferior levels. First of all, Sarah cheats on Hollenbeck with his best friend, and her infidelity is presented as yet another injustice imposed upon the hero. Despite her dialogue, which suggests Hollenbeck's part in the estrangement that fed the affair, Hollenbeck stoically accepts the adultery as an assault to his effort to be a good man. Throughout the film, Hollenbeck confesses his love for Sarah to Dix, but he doesn't express the feelings directly to her. In the closing sequence, Sarah begs for Hollenbeck's forgiveness, and he replies, "Fuck you, Sarah," and then smiles. The combination of his profanity and his smile must be interpreted as his anger and forgiveness for his affair, as they embrace. Second, Dix's girlfriend, Cory (Halle Berry), is first shown working in a strip club as a waitress and exotic dancer. Dix visits her in the club after spending the night with another woman at a wild ballplayers' party. Although Cory is a spectacle to all the men in the club — which doesn't seem to bother Dix — he becomes annoyed with the attention she's receiving from Hollenbeck during this initial meeting between the two. Later, while leaving the club, Cory is gunned down on the streets with automatic weapons, but apparently there's no funeral service. Cory thereafter functions as the motivation for Dix to work with Hollenbeck to discern the killers. At the mentioned party, where Dix emerges from a bed with a strange woman, he saunters to the pool area where a Neanderthal lineman tries to drown a woman for refusing to perform fellatio. Dix casually intercedes by throwing a football into the lineman's face, freeing the woman to escape the Jacuzzi. The point here is that Dix has an accurate toss of the ball but not excessive concern for the woman, who luckily escapes death. Finally, the matter of Hollenbeck's daughter becomes exploited to enhance the emotional turmoil of the white hero. The young girl's litany of profanity, her outbursts, and disobedience are targeted at the resentful Hollenbeck, who early on appears incapable of winning the daughter's respect. But by the end of the film, after saving the girl from the bad guys through excessive violence, she contritely responds to Hollenbeck's parental instructions. These female characters and designated scenes contribute to the film's abusive treatment of women through depictions that maintain their objectification and their value only in connection to male characters.

The Last Boy Scout pairs the tough duo of private investigator Joe Hollenbeck (Bruce Willis, left) and ex-pro football star Jimmy Dix (Damon Wayans).

A more impressive movie, the revisionist western *Unforgiven* (1992), comments upon external dynamics that affect an individual's display of conventional masculine traits in a genre that historically valorized those traits. The movie "has not come to praise the western, but to deconstruct and deglamorize its myths."[8] Set in Wyoming, the story follows the partnering of three unlikely gunmen who travel to earn money by avenging a prostitute who was physically abused. Will Munny (Clint Eastwood) is an over-the-hill white gunslinger turned pig farmer and father. Ned Logan (Morgan Freeman), a black farmer, is Will's partner from the old wild days. And the Schofield Kid (Jaimz Woolvett), is a young white braggart who aspires to be an infamous outlaw. The crucial relationship among the three is the union between Munny and Logan, as it has been established before the screen depiction begins. Closer in age and experience to one another than to the Schofield Kid, Munny and Logan have gone together where the Kid desires to be. Their common past has shaped a friendship based upon knowledge of the "wild" and violent past when the two rode together in a gang of outlaws.

Although Logan is black, his racial identity remains seen but not articulated. Additionally, Logan's interracial relationship with a woman, Sally Two Trees (Cherrilene Cardinal), is visible and discussed, not in terms of race but rather about her silent disgust of Munny's notorious past. Logan refers to Sally's stoic "injun" demeanor, but neither man weighs Logan's black identity as a significant dynamic. Even though Sally lacks the label of "wife," her companionship finds value as Logan admits to Munny that he misses her as the two men adjust to an uncomfortable outdoor sleep by the campfire.

This lack of racial acknowledgment surfaces later in two notable sequences. First, the prostitutes of Big Sky have pooled their resources to pay the hired guns, and they advance Logan and the Schofield Kid "free" sexual trysts against the money to be paid for killing the guilty cowboys. The white women — as well as the Schofield Kid — appear unconcerned that Logan is a black man who crosses racial lines for sexual pleasure, as he's viewed as just another man. Later, when Logan is captured by a posse and brought to town to the sadistic sheriff, Little Bill Daggett (Gene Hackman), none of the white men in the posse or in town cast any racial spite to a black man caught for killing a white cowboy. Yet, despite the absence of verbalized racial epithets, the power of the image prevails. Specifically, when Little Bill whips the bare back of Logan in the jail, the depiction of a white man lashing a black man's back to a bloody pulp connects to the similar images of slavery in films, literature, and historical texts. Messages about race in society resonate despite the filmmakers' preference to present a colorblind frontier society.

The audience is asked to accept the ethnicity as the least important factor while meditating on the manner in which alcoholism and a committed relationship with a woman can design the expression of masculinity. Both Munny and Logan discuss the effects of the former's dead wife upon rehabilitating behavior. Munny confesses to Logan: "Claudia [the wife], she straightened me out ... cleared me of drinking whiskey and all. Just 'cause we're going on this killing, that don't mean I'm going to go back to the way I was."

Munny's transformation under his wife's power redefined his life by setting borders of behavior that were missing before. His assertion of love for Claudia and his children serve as his mantra for reformed manhood, where kindness, hard work, temperance, and patience emerge as the traits of an ideal husband/father. Munny's journey to kill the two cowboys, therefore, is merely a business deal, and needing money for his kids and the ranch, Munny rationalizes his gun-for-hire as a one-time contractual arrangement.

However, Munny backslides into his past ways based upon two interrelated elements: first, the killing of his buddy, Logan, and the ensuing lapse into drunkenness. When Munny hears that Logan has been caught, whipped, and killed, he immediately drowns out his pain by swigging down a bottle of whiskey. As he numbs his emotions, he disconnects from the reformed man and assumes his former male self — violent, sadistic, vengeful, and unforgiving. Riding into the town and seeing Logan's dead body displayed in front of the saloon sanction his drunken state and thirst for a bloody shootout.

The Munny-Logan relationship emanates as a union of two men over numerous years, and that connection runs deep, as Logan nurses a beaten and sick Munny back to health and as Munny insists that Logan receive an equal share of the bounty. The two speak to one another about inner feelings and questions without shame or hesitation, assured that the other will not judge. It is a buddyship of enduring life-and-death trust and defense of the other's defined manhood.

A movie in a contemporary setting, *White Men Can't Jump* (1992) cashes in on the popularity of basketball and the appeal of film tough Wesley Snipes and television favorite Woody Harrelson. Set in Los Angeles, Snipes plays Sidney Deane, a self-employed craftsman who uses his court skills to hustle up money between jobs as an independent contractor. Harrelson, as Billy Hoyle, is also a court hustler whose shady college career has left him in debt to the Stucci brothers, two gangsters who lost money when Hoyle chose not to throw a game. When Hoyle outhustles Deane on the Venice Beach courts, the latter strategizes a way to make considerable

In *Unforgiven*, the experienced, aging gunslingers Ned (Morgan Freeman, left) and Will Munny (Clint Eastwood) ponder the value of being hired guns.

money. Using the expected attitudes about Hoyle, who'll be perceived as a "slow, white, geeky chump," Deane and Hoyle travel inner-city courts to lay bets and win big as they play two-on-two games.

Unlike other contemporary movies, the objective of the interracial buddies is not to get the "bad guys," but to make money and survive. And in that process, Deane and Hoyle grow closer despite their obvious differences in background and personal life. Deane is married with a child, and his wife, Rhonda (Tyra Ferrell), understands and supports his efforts to be his own man. In exercising that manliness, Deane prefers to hustle jobs so his wife can stay at home with their child. On the other hand, Hoyle lives with his girlfriend, Gloria (Rosie Perez), who commits her life to preparing for being a contestant on the television game show *Jeopardy*. Although Rosie tries to support Hoyle, his past gambling weakness and hiding out from the Stucci brothers wear on her patience. But both Deane and Hoyle excel at their sport, and their abilities to "talk trash" undermine their opponents.

With this last aspect, the film carries an interesting twist in that the culture of the black buddy becomes more pervasive. On the basketball courts, the ongoing "playing the dozens" rules as much as physical skills. Scholars Richard Majors and Janet Mancini Billson note that the "dozens is a verbal contest of young blacks" reflecting the "expressive nature of black talk with its special rhythms, inflections, slangs, and grammar ... as two protagonists [hurl] insults against each other and their families," particularly mothers.[9] Hoyle realizes that by venturing onto the street courts, he faces a constant challenge, verbally and physically, due to his race. In street ball, Hoyle's whiteness becomes a detriment rather than qualifier for privilege, forcing him to prove himself each time. But once he accomplishes that feat, then the game neutralizes race as one's skills in ball handling, shooting, passing, fast-talking, and "playing the dozens" emerge as the criteria for remaining on the court.

Yet in an honest fashion, race never entirely disappears from the discourse off-court. Hoyle, with his Puerto Rican girlfriend, opens himself up to various comments about their relationship. When listening to music, Hoyle and Deane argue about the ability of a white listener to understand the feelings of black musicians. Additionally, at one point in the story, the issue of whether a white player can jump high enough to dunk the basketball ignites a bet that leads to Hoyle's loss of his earnings. Hoyle masks his inability to jam the ball with his homespun philosophical statement: "White men want to win first and look good second. A black man wants to look good first, and win second." Eventually, however, when Hoyle does indeed dunk to win an important match for him and Deane, the action functions as a metaphor for the former's maturing attitude and potential ability to achieve in his personal life. Comprehending this personal victory in Hoyle, Deane offers Hoyle a job to freelance as a contractor with him.

Rather than being superheroes, the Deane-Hoyle duo come across as average guys who have their understandable passions and weaknesses. Although using excessive profanity as a masculine marker in the same manner as *The Last Boy Scout*, the Deane-Hoyle masculinity displays a more respectable approach to the women characters. These interracial buddies— Deane in his marriage and Hoyle in his monogamous union — acknowledge their women as integral people in their plans. Deane, who appears to have a solid romance with his spouse, consistently tutors Hoyle about the value of maintaining an emotionally healthy relationship with Gloria, though to no avail at the end. Neither buddy equates his manhood with a sexist notion of dominating or exploiting women.

The popular response to the on-screen pairing of Snipes and Harrelson prompted a reteaming three years later in the urban action drama *The Money Train*. In this vehicle, the two are foster brothers who have entered the same profession as cops working a decoy squad on the New York subway system. As undercover officers, John (Snipes) and Charlie (Harrelson) protect and serve citizens from nefarious individuals, such as the Torch

(Chris Cooper), a sadistic pyro-terrorist who drenches female subway booth clerks with fuel before lighting a match. However, the main source of friction between the brothers develops when they both fall in lust-love with Grace Santiago (Jennifer Lopez), a fellow officer who transfers into their unit. At the same time, driving the plot is a series of confrontations, either with Chief Patterson (Robert Blake), the misanthropic subway boss, or Mr. Brown (Scott Sowers), a small-time gangster to whom Charlie has an outstanding gambling debt.

Having been raised together, John and Charlie have an established relation-

Two basketball hustlers — Sidney Deane (Wesley Snipes, left) and Billy Hoyle (Woody Harrelson, right) — find their buddyhood in *White Men Can't Jump.*

ship before the movie begins. Their brotherhood, questioned by other characters because of their racial difference, remains immune to outside doubters and attackers. They have a bond and trust fashioned since their childhood, and the only people capable of breaking it are the two themselves. When Charlie needs $15,000 to pay off Mr. Brown, John empties out his bank account to give him money. When John and Grace are discovered in bed together, Charlie steps back and pretends not to be interested in her. When Mr. Brown sends his goons to beat Charlie up, John goes alone to the gangster's headquarters and applies his martial arts techniques to punish the hoodlums. And when Charlie decides to rob Chief Patterson's beloved money train that carries the millions collected from the city's subway booths, John intercedes in an attempt to prevent Charlie's risky crime.

Although *The Money Train* avoids the in-your-face, trash-talking dialogues of athletic prowess highlighted in *White Men Can't Jump*, the former still includes the improvised scream-fests between the streetwise characters portrayed by the Snipes-Harrelson duo. Their profanity-laced harangues accentuate the characters' masculinity in the form of verbal competition to claim victory over an opponent. Yet John and Charlie follow their masculine codes of trust, rivalry, and loyalty even when they lead to a temporary friction and discord between the two.

Snipes shows up yet again in another action film as a buddy in the Los Angeles-based thriller *Rising Sun* (1993). Snipes portrays Lieutenant Web Smith, a detective working a new position as a liaison officer. During a celebratory party in a downtown high-rise for a merger between a United States computer-chip company and a Japanese company, a white woman is found strangled on a boardroom table. Sent to investigate the crime, Smith receives orders to take along Captain John Connor (Sean Connery), a retired officer who at one time lived in Japan. From their initial meeting, the two clash as Connor gives lessons on Japanese protocol to Smith, who believes he doesn't need a teacher. When Connor suggests that they assume the role of *simpei* (senior man who knows) and *kohei* (the younger man who does the speaking), Smith interprets the term simpei as racist, asking: "That wouldn't happen to be anything like master, would it?" From there, the relationship between the two remains edgy, as Connor informs Smith on protocol and philosophy through a Socratic method. But eventually the question-and-answer technique moves the two men closer to understanding the case, as well as more trusting attitudes toward one another. However, the prevailing aspect of their developing bond positions Connor as the authority. In the world of the Japanese businessmen that they encounter, Connor knows the culture, and he has a personal connection to Mr. Sakamura (Mako), the senior owner of the Japanese corporation and his son Eddie (Cary-Hiroyuki Tagawa), the party-loving playboy.

Eddie functions as a key figure in the film's complicated plot, as his girlfriend, Cheryl (Tatjana Patitz), is the woman killed in the boardroom. Connor, while working with Smith to solve the case, shows a protective nature to and a trust of Eddie. With Eddie providing a security disc that recorded the murder and with the help of Connor's Japanese girlfriend, Jingo (Tia Carrere), who is a savvy media technician, Connor and Smith deduce the events and guilty people involved in the case.

Of interest, Connor and Smith's journey into the convolutions of the case becomes an immersion into a masculine world that the film suggests is culturally shaped. For example, Mr. Sakamura's business world and Eddie's party world are a milieu in which men dominate. There are no women in the Japanese boardroom, while there are numerous women populating Eddie's world of pleasure. Additionally, Cheryl, the victim, lives in a "love residence" protected by the Japanese Yakuza. When Connor and

Smith go to her address, they, as well as the audience, peek into various rooms where white women pleasure their guests. This visual lingering on women's bodies occurs often in the film, offering Connor, Smith, and the film's voyeuristic camera to objectify women as toys and pieces of pleasurable furniture. This latter aspect surfaces when Smith and his old detective partner, Graham (Harvey Keitel), lead a raid on Eddie's house to arrest him. Smith and Graham watch through a window as Eddie eats sushi from the torso of a naked white woman lying on her back on the carpet. Sitting next to Eddie is a nude white, red-haired woman, and Eddie lifts his sake bowl to dip her breasts before sipping the wine. When Smith, Graham, and the SWAT team finally break through the house, the naked redhead jumps onto Smith's back, scratching and screaming from the interior and out into the driveway to protect Eddie. Although played for humor, the full nudity of the nameless woman serves to titillate and expose the female form. Then, in a much more pronounced manner, the boardroom scene depicting the physical intimacy and then strangulation of Cheryl is shown in detail, with the woman's body still sprawled on the table as the male detectives and Japanese businessmen discuss the crime. And if once wasn't sufficient for that scene, the recorded disc is watched by characters, and the audience, an additional four times.

Connor and Smith fit into this world of men, as each one handles his personal relationships with women in distinctive ways. Connor never speaks openly about his connection to Jingo, a union that's not understood by Smith until the last sequence in the film, when he must decide whether to romantically pursue Jingo—who confesses in the film to being Japanese and black. And on his part, Smith handles his ex-wife with disdain, as his daughter and mother live with him. Earlier in the movie, with his ex-wife being a lawyer, Smith's outrage toward her gets placed within the framework of lawyer-bashing jokes.

Rising Sun offers the Connor-Smith duo against the backdrop of another male-dominated culture. As both buddies exemplify their independent natures, impatience with authority, and physical prowess—Connor and Smith display their martial arts skills in a sequence where they fight Japanese henchmen — they move closer to respecting one another and bridging the gap that initially caused friction. And with both men having an interest in Jingo, the film ends with a suggestion that the duo will be connected in still more complicated ways after the film ends.

Unlike the fast-paced action of *Rising Sun*, *The Shawshank Redemption* (1995) takes a more calculated character study of two men who find faith in one another, and their hope for living, at an institution whose purpose is to break the human spirit. Similar to his steadfast nurturing

In *Rising Sun*, detectives John Conner (Sean Connery, left) and Web Smith (Wesley Snipes) discover a common respect while solving a murder.

that his character did in *Unforgiven*, once again Morgan Freeman's character, this time named Red, becomes a teacher and emotional caretaker to the white protagonist, Andy Dufresne (Tim Robbins). However, an important difference in *The Shawshank Redemption* is that the white protagonist reciprocates the support. In fact, these two interracial buddies appear to be a case study for what scholars Robert A. Strikwerda and Larry May label as "comradeship." They suggests that "[s]ome traditional male experiences have led to a form of friendship that may pass for intimacy — what we call comradeship. The sharing of certain kind of experiences ... provides occasion for mutual disclosure among males. In these situations, one is in a period of some stress ... physical danger.... Such occasions can bring men to talk about deeply personal matters in their lives and hence form bonds with one another...."[10] The environment of Shawshank prison force Red and Andy to weave their comradeship as a survival tool against institutionalized demasculinization.

In the movie's voiceover, Red informs the audience about his essential status in the prison as a man "known to locate certain things from time to time." Essentially a businessman who runs a smuggling ring of sundry requested items, Red, a confessed murderer, has chiseled out a world of survival with a network of acquaintances. But when Andy arrives, convicted of murder and claiming his innocence, Red surmises him to be the typical personality that falls into the hole of the Maine penal system. But eventually the two men discern that there's more beneath the surface appearances that each must wear. The film's enduring quality becomes the growth of their buddyship that evolves over decades despite the exploitation within the prison walls.

As a period piece, covering the 1930s through the 1960s, the issue of race is, as in the period piece *Unforgiven*, given the least priority. Besides Red, only three other black characters are given brief screen time in the prison environment, but being such as pronounced minority in a world of white inmates, the probability that Red's black identity would find vocalization seems certain. Early on in the film, when Andy first approaches Red to request a rock hammer, the former questions the latter about his nickname; Red responds, "maybe it's because I'm Irish." Other than this sarcasm, which plays directly off of Red's visible black identity, the racial issue disappears. In dialogue and in the close-ups of Red's parole hearing files, the explanation for the nickname is connected to the character's surname, which is Redding.

Two issues that receive focus in the story are the connections between power and sex, as well as power and money. In Shawshank's world of incarcerated males, the bullqueers, led by the brutish inmate Bogs (Mark Rolston), are heterosexual men who rape other men, and in this victimization they acquire power and group identity in an environment that takes the same from them. Targeting Andy, their ongoing attacks upon him have little to do with sexual pleasure but more with physical control that equates to their sense of manhood. At the same time, through the dominating presence of Warden Norton (Bob Gunton) and prison guard Captain Hadley (Clancy Brown), their systemic power allows them to exploit individuals and situations for their own financial gain. Exploiting Andy's banking background, the warden scams himself toward a wealthy retirement of illegal money, and the captain discovers a method for evading the IRS. The connection between masculinity and power become inextricable for these men, and based upon their pecking order in the system, they suppress other males without conscience or remorse.

However, the Red-Andy buddyship expresses masculinity in a manner that goes beyond the conventional notions. In the restricted prison life enforced upon them, Red and Andy turn to a comradeship that thrives on affection, emotional intimacy, and trust that doesn't cross over the line into a homosexual union. Deprived of expressing the traditional abstractions of male power — independence, individualism, and freedom — the two embrace the stereotypically feminized concepts of caring, nurturing, talking, and feeling as the traits that cement their comradeship. For Red and Andy, the last line of defense against the eradication of their manhood remains their friendship that promotes "hope," because with hope the possibilities of freedom live within the individual. This type of thinking disturbs Red at first, who after thirty years accepts his institutionalized condition where other men have power over every detail of his existence. Red insists that "hope is a dangerous thing. Hope can drive a man insane." But Andy gives Red the gift of hope through their confraternal conversations, through a surprise gift of a harmonica, and through his prison escape, which inspires Red to beat the system. Andy comprehends the import of the statement "get busy living or get busy dying," and he tells Red that "hope is a good thing ... and no good thing ever dies."

The Shawshank Redemption is a splendid film that peruses the rigid constructs of manhood by showing masculinity in various forms. And the focus of that presentation are two men who propel themselves over the walls of race, traditional gender notions, and a flawed penal system to find hope and a future freedom living on "the Pacific ... in a warm place that has no memory."

Jumping forward to a film that has little innocence, *Se7en* (1995)

Red (Morgan Freeman, left) and Andy (Tim Robbins) exchange thoughts in the prison yard in *The Shawshank Redemption.*

emerges as a gritty contemporary thriller that offers little hope in an urban world driven by mayhem. Infected by the havoc of their common profession, detectives William Somerset (Morgan Freeman) and David Mills (Brad Pitt) find that their personal lives succumb to the urban malaise, resulting in an irrevocable transformation.

In fact, the film could work effectively as a character study of these two oppositional personalities: Somerset — an intellectual, methodical, literate cop — and Mills — an emotional, impulsive, impatient cop. Simply, Somerset's masculinity is forged in mental acuity, as he uses his reading of the works of Chaucer and Dante to understand clues in the case. On the other hand, Mills's sense of manhood emerges from physically responding to people and situations, as he's quick to draw his gun, kick down doors, and chase a suspect down fire escapes and across traffic-jammed streets. However, the movie creates a serial killer (Kevin Spacey) whose clever, sadistic, and interconnected crimes steal the focus from the conflicting natures of the detective buddies.

As expected, as in most buddy films, Somerset and Mills find one another irritating when meeting in the first scene. Six days away from retirement, Somerset questions Mills's motivation for transferring into a department that covers the seedier side of human behavior. Mills, on his part, enjoys the rush and excitement of the urban jungle over his former upstate, rural beat. Moving in opposite directions professionally and personally, the two are brought together through the efforts of Mills's wife, Tracy (Gwyneth Paltrow), a young woman who loves her husband but hates the city. At dinner with Mills and Tracy, Somerset finally laughs and loosens beneath Tracy's personal questions, confessing: "Anyone who spends a considerable amount of time with me finds me disagreeable." Thereafter, Somerset and Mills interact more cordially, though each holds onto his distinctive personality as they work together to solve the serial murders based on the Biblically identified seven deadly sins — gluttony, greed, sloth, lust, pride, envy, and wrath.

In a bar over drinks, the partners articulate their philosophies about the nature of society. Having revealed his retirement plans to locate away from the city, Somerset states: "I just don't think I can continue to live in a place that embraces and nurtures apathy as if it were a virtue." For him, after thirty-four years of solving a succession of crimes, he's convinced that people "don't care" and choose to "take the easy way" in life. Mills strongly disagrees, believing that his job as a cop makes a difference and that he can personally make changes. In the evolving disclosure of each man, their viewpoints emerge from the differences in age and maturity, and though Somerset's perspectives about the gray areas in people might be considered cynical, they're laced with realism, while Mills's simplistic black-and-white world rests heavily upon the premise of male heroes, such as himself, fighting valiantly for the good.

One aspect that doesn't enter their discussion is the dynamic of race. Similar to his other films during the decade, Morgan Freeman's Somerset functions as a minority male of some status in a majority white world. When Somerset visits the library after hours, the uniformed guards appear to be black and Latino, and at various crime scenes, there are uniformed police officers of color. However, for all of their deep and probing dialogues, Somerset and Mills fail to comment upon racial factors that would certainly play into their profession in an urban environment. And as Somerset mentions his extensive literary exposure, the names of black authors and thinkers, such as Franz Fanon, W.E.B. DuBois, and Ralph Ellison are not referenced.

In the film's final act, as the killer surrenders himself before the last two sins are played out in murder, both Somerset and Mills suspect his intentions. When the killer promises to show the two the last two bodies outside the city, the three share a final police-car ride filled with efforts at manipulation and power. The killer, however, maintains control of the situation as he leads Somerset and Mills to the conclusion of his meticulous plan. After stalking the detectives earlier in the film, the killer has "envy" for Mills's life, including Tracy and an unborn child on the way; the killer murders Tracy off-screen prior to surrendering at the police station, arranging commercial delivery of a box that contains her head. In his "wrath," Mills executes the killer, shooting him repeatedly despite Somerset's pleading and efforts. In the end, the killer has won his ultimate goal of creating a perfect set of killings, and Somerset, though proven correct in his assessment about people, pledges his support for the emotionally devastated and jail-bound Mills.

By the middle of the decade, the third installment starring action hero John McClane (Bruce Willis) was hitting the big screen, using the interracial buddy riff as its anchor. In *Die Hard* (1988) and *Die Hard 2: Die Harder* (1990), the cowboy individualism of McClane elevated the character to the extreme image of the white hero marshalling his superior physical skills, clever strategies, and wry humor to battle and defeat international thieves and international terrorists. In those first two movies, McClane was a working-class kind of guy who was trying to keep his marriage together while trying to simply do his job as a cop. Viewing the first two installments as echo films, traces of buddyhood emerged with McClane's trusting interaction with Al (Reginald VelJohnson), the black cop who serves as his literal and figurative lifeline to the outside world.

However, in *Die Hard: With a Vengeance* (1995), McClane develops

Merging their opposing viewpoints, detectives William Somerset (Morgan Freeman, left) and David Mills (Brad Pitt) assemble clues to the serial killings in *Se7en*.

a closer association with a black buddy who, in one day of mayhem, becomes his comrade in heroism. Set in New York, the movie pulls McClane from the comfort of his hangover by his superior officer in order to respond to the telephone demands of Simon Gruber (Jeremy Irons), a madman placing bombs around the city. In McClane's initiation to Simon's telephone games of riddles, the former must walk around a Harlem street wearing a sign stating, "I hate niggers." Rescuing McClane from a certain death by a group of young black toughs, Zeus Carver (Samuel L. Jackson), a black store owner, propels himself into a partnership with McClane in the ongoing game of riddles and bombs.

McClane's philosophy toward Simon remains simple: Simon is the "bad guy," while McClane and the police are the "good guys." Early in a telephone exchange, McClane articulates his basic male instinct, inviting Simon to "come on down to police plaza so we can settle this like a couple of men." Regardless of Simon's deadly games and the analysis of the police psychiatrist working with the case, McClane's ethos exists on primal masculinity of strength, stubbornness, and confrontation where the best man wins out — the best always being the "good guys."

By helping save McClane, however, Carver has complicated the game,

and Simon seeks to manipulate the duo. At first, Carver rejects any affiliation with the police's efforts to capture Simon, dismissing him as a "white
man with white problems." Carver's tone makes his cultural politics clear,
and in his Afrocentric viewpoints, demonstrated by his lessons of self-
determinism and black pride given to his grade-school nephews, he commits himself to his priority of protecting the Harlem community. Carver,
whose first name associates him with the god of mythology, is an articulate, intelligent, and savvy black male who contrasts saliently with
McClane's insipid, jaded demeanor. In fact, Carver emerges as such a strong
male presence during the first act of the film that he eclipses McClane's
low-key energy. Carver refuses to take orders from white authority figures,
including McClane, the police, and Simon, and his statements about race
and politics are blunt and direct.

Interestingly, midway through the film, Carver's Afrocentric perspectives are mutated into racial diatribes, emphasized when McClane impa-
tiently asks: "Have you got some problem with me because I'm white....
Have I oppressed your people somehow?" McClane, the white hero, articulates his feelings of personal injury as he delivers the questions that represent the feelings of all good-hearted whites of the 1990s. Since McClane
is not personally at fault for slavery, economic oppression, racial segregation, or hate crimes, he resents any responsibility by association and by
historical privilege to the situation of race relations in society. Carver,
consequently, has become a selfish, racist attacker of the white hero who
has only shown him respect and kindness, and therefore earned an exemp-
tion from any political criticism or collective responsibility. As film scholar
Krin Gabbard argues in his reflection upon the film: "The American cinema has perpetuated the notion that the white ruling class is not itself a
class but a legitimate element of the status quo. Like the members of that
class, the American cinema often categorizes those who talk of race and
class as, at best, misguided malcontents."[11] McClane has been transformed
into the oppressed male, a position of empathy augmented when Simon,
in his distinctive German accent, later refers to McClane as a "dumb Irish
flatfoot."

Despite the argumentative nature of the McClane-Carver duo, eventually their joint concern for protecting the public inspires them to work
together. As they do, their union increases in a caring for one another even
as racial quips, from Carver, surface on occasion. Toward the end, when
handcuffed together atop a container with a liquid bomb, McClane opens
up about his personal life, talking about his wife and their separation. Zeus
counsels McClane, criticizing his stubbornness and encouraging him to
phone his wife in California. Once his handcuffs are off, McClane makes

Connected through danger in *Die Hard: With a Vengeance*, buddies Zeus (Samuel L. Jackson, left) and John McClane (Bruce Willis) face another life-threatening situation.

the ultimate buddy gesture; he refuses to leave Carver to die as the bomb arms itself, struggling until the final seconds to free his comrade.

Amid the chases, car wrecks, gunfire, fistfights, explosions, and helicopter battles that surfeit the action genre expectations, *Die Hard: With a Vengeance* extols the virtues of buddyship. And as racial and cultural politics are transfigured to embellish the white hero's status, the film sustains the codes of male heroism made synonymous with that hero.

Echo Patterns of Interracial Buddyship in the Early 1990s

The nature of the cinematic cross-cultural liaisons in the early '90s often seemed to be a matter of reassuring audiences that the social consciousness and political astuteness of society was moving in a progressive manner. Although some movies avoided such interracial connections as the major theme, numerous works still allowed such relationships to occupy a significant place within the story, often allowing the white protagonist to be viewed in a more humanistic manner. Films such as *Heart Condition* (1990), *Regarding Henry* (1991), *Sneakers* (1992), *Last of the Mohicans* (1992), and *Geronimo: An American Legend* (1993) all contained some notable attachment and interaction between males across racial lines that led to a deeper recognition of common humanity and/or manhood. However, the three films below followed some crucial element of the authentic interracial buddy paradigm but chose to position the pattern as a secondary concern, with varying degrees of effectiveness.

First of all, the box office popularity of *New Jack City* (1991) was a measurement of the film's successful interlacing of urban cops, gangsters, and hip-hop. The film "interlaces genre conventions, music video techniques, hip-hop music and language, and slick visuals to attract a young multiethnic audience."[12] As one of the first films of the decade to journey into the urban masculinity on both side of the law, it also highlighted a set of multicultural characters who have an effective, though sometimes tense, working relationship: undercover Detective Scotty Appleton (Ice-T), a black cop dealing with the memory of his mother's murder; undercover Detective Peretti (Judd Nelson), a cynical white cop with a short fuse; Detective Park (Russell Wong), a quiet, professional Korean cop; and Detective Stone (Mario Van Peebles), who is the lead black cop that brings the team together. This team commits itself to taking out the growing power of a criminal consortium led by the sadistic Nino Brown (Wesley Snipes). Brown's world is one of intimidation and death to secure wealth and power, as women are merely objects of pleasure and recreation.

Although they're expected to leave their personal biases at home, Appleton and Peretti have an ongoing disdain for one another. The former mistrusts the latter for trying to be a white man who acts "black"; in a similar fashion, Peretti constantly questions whether the light-complexioned Appleton can be authentically black. Their face-to-face verbal sparring and near physical confrontation underscore the shared machismo that serves as their individual foundations. In essence, they are mirror images of one another in their tough, aggressive, street-shaped manhood. But with Stone refereeing, the two find a common ground of tolerance where they can work together.

But with most of the screen time given to Appleton's undercover infiltration and befriending of Nino Brown and his gang, the personal connections among the members of this multiracial detective team never receive extensive development. To its credit, however, the film attempts to reflect the times and to show that the New York urban scene included males from various cultural groups.

In a stark contrast to *New Jack City*, the film *Pure Luck* (1991) has little chance to succeed, as it's based on the silly premise that its protagonist, Eugene Proctor (Martin Short), the unluckiest white man in the world, can be used by company investigator Ray Campanella (Danny

Glover) to find a corporation's heiress, who is the unluckiest white woman in the world. Using the conventional buddy-film element of two dissimilar men who initially dislike each other, *Pure Luck* shows that the disdain that Campanella has for Proctor is justified and clearly understood. Proctor and Campanella are not only men from opposite racial backgrounds; these two hail from opposite planets. What remains unclear is why actor Danny Glover took the role of Campanella's straight man to comedian Martin Short's physical shtick; perhaps Glover was preparing himself for his equally ludicrous role as Gus Green in *Gone Fishin'* (1997).

Although Campanella's racial identity never serves as a critical point in the story, it surfaces as a target for a joke in one scene. When a distracted Proctor enters a café, he sees the back of a black man who is sitting at a table. He promptly sits down, conducting a conversation with a complete stranger, as he merely saw the man's blackness and assumed it was Campanella. In many ways, though not articulated by the characters, the film's images and story line suggest the old convention of the black male character who nurtures and protects the white protagonist. By the film's final moments, Campanella, having survived numerous misadventures with Proctor, has reached some enlightened affection for the clumsy man, calling him a "close friend"—which appears to be because it's in the script rather than due to any action shown on the screen.

In *Robin Hood: Prince of Thieves* (1991), in a Jerusalem prison in the year 1196, the English Christian Robin of Locksley (Kevin Costner) saves the Moslem Moor named Azeem (Morgan Freeman) from a sure death. In turn, Azeem helps Robin escape from the underground cells promising: "You have saved my life, Christian. I will stay with you until I save yours. That is my vow." Keeping his word, Azeem forms a union with Robin that will endure through a violent war between the local farmers-turned-warriors and the wicked Sheriff of Nottingham (Alan Rickman).

Reworking the Robin Hood legend, the film presents the unlikely teaming up between Robin and Azeem, using the shared prison time as the foundation for their ongoing connection. Their link by vow soon becomes a trusting friendship, and seemingly without any family or home of his own, Azeem abandons his world for the cause of liberty and land ownership for Robin and his band of British Christians. These same Christians mistake Azeem as Robin's servant when they first confront them at the river's edge, and later as Robin assumes leadership of the group, he chastises one man who not only refuses to share his wine flask with Azeem but also calls Azeem a "savage." Robin defends Azeem by saying, "Yes he is, but no more than you or I." This statement serves well for the moment, but in another sequence, as the wife of Little John (Nick Brimble) suffers painfully during a child delivery, Friar Tuck rants excessively about allowing the savage Azeem to touch the white woman. But Azeem successfully performs a caesarean and once again wins the accolades of his white cohorts. But throughout the movie, the filmmakers temper the issue of race by merging it with the religious identity of the characters; basically, the whites (Christians) assert their criticisms of Azeem due to his Moslem identity rather than because of his racial background.

Robin Hood: Prince of Thieves offers the potential of interracial buddyship, but the story remains focused upon Robin, emphasizing his romantic love with the independent Maid Marian (Mary Elizabeth Mastrantonio). Viewed within the context of the '90s, the appearance of Azeem as a major character and Marian's strikingly feminist attitudes were a crossover effort to appeal to a multiracial audience and both genders.

The Interracial Buddy Paradigm in the Late 1990s

Perhaps in an effort to duplicate the closeness exhibited by the characters John and Charlie in *The Money Train*, the film *Bulletproof* (1996) wanted the audience to accept its story of interracial brotherhood. Unfortunately, with a poorly written script, elliptical passages, awkward editing, and unconvincing protagonists, the movie fell flat and forgettable when compared with other buddy vehicles. Borrowing generously from previous and better films such as *The Defiant Ones* (1959), *48 Hrs.* (1983), *Midnight Run* (1988), and *Deep Cover* (1992), the movie failed to generate interest in or concern for the buddyship at its center.

Working as an undercover cop, Jack Keats (Damon Wayans) develops a closeness to a well-connected criminal, Archie Moses (Adam Sandler). Bringing Keats into the schemes of a drug kingpin, Frank Colton (James Caan), Moses is shocked when Keats's real identity surfaces. Accidentally shooting Keats while escaping a bust, Moses eventually turns federal witness against Colton, who is extradited to Los Angeles by Keats. Keats remains angry over the gunshot injury and months of physical therapy.

The barrier preventing an absorption in the film's story is the fact that Wayans and Sandler — both comedians — are not believable in the dramatic contours necessary for their characters. Wayans appears self-conscious in his efforts to embody a by-the-rules detective, and Sandler resorts to grimacing and whining when not delivering wisecracks. Consequently, their bonding doesn't seem genuine and fully developed, as it allegedly occurs before the film begins.

The elements of the interracial buddy formula are present in the form of conflicting backgrounds, shared moments or personal revelation, hetero-uniformity, and sarcasm, but these aspects are injected into wooden and paint-by-number sequences. For example, when Keats travels to Arizona to take custody of Moses from federal officers at an airport hangar, an ambush erupts killing the six officers but amazingly not Keats and Moses as they jump onto the waiting private plane, which once airborne begins to dive because the pilot has been shot upon takeoff. Conveniently, Moses knows how to pilot the plane, which crashes due to a loss of engine fuel, but miraculously the vehicle explodes just after the duo jumps out. As a result, they are forced to travel by foot through the desert with Moses in chains. Along the way, they argue about the deceit and betrayal of their alleged friendship. The degree of Moses' bonding to Keats surfaces in a mantralike statement he makes several times in the film: "I would've taken a bullet for you, Keats." Yet the lack of depth in developing the characters renders these plot events and lines of dialogue jaded and clichéd.

As the two make their sojourn back toward Los Angeles, they stumble across a remote inn that has an available cabin and a porn video selection. The only available residence is the "honeymoon suite," which is ornamented in pink and salacious decorations; this set-up allows for sight gags and one-liners about homosexuality, body functions, and toilet seats. Interestingly, the consistent manner in which Moses whines about Keats's betrayal and lying often suggests a latent romantic desire, resembling the stereotypical complaining of a girlfriend jilted by a boyfriend. Moses' tirades seem to mask a belief that he's been cheated on by Keats, who has given his passion to another lover (the law) rather than to his buddy.

The filmmakers balance the homoerotic suggestions by giving Keats a girlfriend, namely Traci Flynn (Kristen Wilson), the physical therapist who guided Keats back to his normal mobility. Mistakenly, the film never provides any on-screen physical intimacy between the two, leaving the passion of their "relationship" dangling on a long-distance phone-sex call in one scene. And, in a later scene, Keats receives a phone call from Colton, who has kidnapped Traci to exchange for Moses, but in an awkward response to the threat to his girlfriend's life, Keats, along with Moses, stops at a strip club to have a beer — while sitting in front of a near-nude pole dancer — and discuss their plan to rescue Traci. The gratuitous scene merely supplies both male characters and the audience-spectator the opportunity to look upon the gyrating female form, reconfirming that in Hollywood films women characters are "unable to be active in the way that male characters are"; therefore "a woman's ability to draw the male gaze gives her the ability to bring the narrative to a halt."[13]

The mixed tones and shallow characterizations in *Bulletproof* negate the possible value of the film. Even by the formulaic aspects of the urban action genre and the buddy paradigm, the movie never achieves even mediocrity. Instead, mediocrity was left to the film that co-starred another of the Wayans brothers. *The Glimmer Man* (1996) brought Keenen Ivory Wayans into partnership with martial arts notable Steven Seagal in a convoluted and muddled plot that misused the potent appeal of interracial buddyship.

Los Angeles detective Jim Campbell (Wayans) is forced to take on a new partner from New York named Jack Cole (Seagal), who wears Tibetan prayer beads and investigates crime scenes with philosophical and spiritual observations.

With a mysterious background, Cole's fingerprints are found at a gruesome crime scene in which his ex-wife was one of the victims, creating suspicion in the mind of Campbell and his fellow detectives. After enduring shootouts, explosions, fight scenes, the Russian mafia, a sadistic, rich business man, and a greedy CIA operative, the Campbell-Cole duo realize that they are indeed working toward the same justified end, and together they launch a violent assault against the bad guys.

But similarly to the previous film, Campbell and Cole's linkage seems forced and contrived. Again, the combination of the script and the selected actors results in protagonists who default as captivating figures. Campbell refuses to share his personal life with his partner, and consequently with the audience, and Cole's personal life — especially with his new wife and visiting children — comes off as frosty as his last name, devoid of displayed or discernible affection. In essence, both men do not really have a meaningful personal life, and at the same time, they fail to establish an open connection professionally with one another. Though they arrive to crime scenes together and work in the same office area, they continue to interact distrustfully as strangers. Repeatedly, the plot points attempt to punctuate a buddyship without the characters and dialogue assisting in the effort. Notably, in the climatic showdown with the villains, Cole — the accomplished white cop — does manage to save Campbell's life by scaling down a building on a rope, but this stunt appears to be proof that Cole indeed scaled Mount Everest as he declared during an earlier piece of dialogue. The various dramatic, visual, and verbal elements of the film never merge convincingly.

In another scene that pushes the heterosexuality of the duo, a typical weakness in the script emerges. While in the coroner's office following up on what appears to be a copycat killing, Cole and Campbell survey the body of a dead woman lying coldly on the table. As the camera shifts the audience's perspective to the nude torso of the young victim, Campbell comments that the victim has "nice tits." Cole, a bit more intuitive, concludes that the woman is Russian due to her hair and bone structure before deciding that her breasts are a bit "too nice." He then proceeds to snap on gloves, to take a scalpel, and to remove a silicon implant from the woman's breast. Cole proves his skill at recognizing breast augmentation, while the female form is exposed to the male privilege of looking, touching, and cutting it into pieces.

The Campbell-Cole buddyship attempts to merge opposites in regard to race and creed, but achieves instead the opposite effect desired. Campbell and Cole seem so awkward together physically and their dialogue so wooden that a believable chord never resonates. The performances are not strong enough to eclipse the script and dialogue, leaving the audience with a hollow reflection of the interracial buddy pattern.

A much more effective relationship centers the social commentary in the film *Gridlock'd* (1996). With a Detroit setting, two musicians— Spoon (Tupac Shakur) and Stretch (Tim Roth)— decide to break through their drug addiction when their friend-vocalist-roommate, Cookie (Thandie Newton), overdoses on New Year's Eve. With effective casting, one critic

Unorthodox Detective Jack Cole (Steven Seagal, left) joins up to serve justice with street-wise Detective Jim Campbell (Keenen Ivory Wayans) in *The Glimmer Man*.

in particular observes that Tupac Shakur possessed a streetwise, "earthy consciousness" that "threaded Tupac's art, no matter the forms it took or how much it appeared to be sacrificed on the altar of his commercial ambitions."[14] The movie chronicles Spoon and Stretch's struggle to survive all the policies and red tape of social services, as well as vengeful drug dealers and forceful cops, in order to be admitted into a detox program.

With their relationship as co-composers and roommates established before the film begins, Spoon and Stretch display an effortless camaraderie. In some ways they are mirror images of one another — talented, profane, selfish, addicted, and fearful of responsibility. Yet their interdependence on one another is telling in regards to the trust and protectiveness exhibited. During the day, they hustle as con men, selling boxes of hot appliances that actually are filled with bricks. When one buyer — Reper Man (Vondie Curtis-Hall), a drug dealer — catches on to the con, Spoon knocks out the dealer as he aims his gun at Stretch. In the same manner that they share their music, living environment, and lifestyle, they bind their lives by their actions and decisions.

For the two, race exists, but race between the two of them doesn't matter in their daily negotiating of the volatile, oppressive environment. In one sequence at the apartment of a black drug dealer, Mike (Bodeem Woodbine), and his Asian girlfriend, CeeCee (Lucy Liu), Stretch casually addresses both the former and Spoon with the word "nigger," resulting in a tense moment of a drawn gun. Spoon later admonishes Stretch: "You can't just be calling me nigger in front of other black people. They gonna be, 'Why you letting a honkie call you nigger, my brother?' You can't say that. You're not black." But Stretch doesn't comprehend the fuss, because in his world he is "black," not by complexion but by his political condition and artistic expression. Both Stretch and Spoon perceive that their class and drug habit, with all of the concomitant experiences, place them in the same condition regardless of complexion. Consequently, their shared struggle against bureaucratic forces strengthens the bond they possess as brother artists.

Additionally, their willingness to seek the other's approval occurs in a number of scenes. In one significant segment, while discussing who can easily gain access into the health care system, Stretch confesses to Spoon that he's HIV-positive from a shared needle, acknowledging that he has never told anyone else. In another example of their common trust, Stretch is shot and wounded as the two flee the imposing Reper Man and his henchmen. Spoon realizes that the only method for admittance to the hospital is via the emergency room. So, he lifts his shirt and confidently gives Stretch a target for a small pen-knife stab. After numerous unsuccessful jabs, the blood finally flows, and the two stagger into the hospital with their wounds.

Spoon and Stretch don't carry badges or guns; instead, they reside on the other side of the legal line as drug users and street cons. Yet their buddyship endures due to an intersection of artistic and class ties that override all other considerations. Their avante-garde approach to music and life filters out other political, cultural, and materialistic distractions that can weigh in on other buddy relationships. In a film that sought to ridicule the health care system in society, *Gridlock'd* went much further in presenting a duo who indeed live as integral parts of each other's lives.

A similar effort at male bonding inspires the film *Tin Cup* (1996), but the on-screen relationship that's shown transforms into a racial hierarchy viewed in films from earlier decades. In this story, the protagonist, Roy McAvoy (Kevin Costner), is a white golfer who never quite made the big-time pro circuit, and his sidekick-caddy, Romeo (Cheech Marin), is the Latino friend who assumes several roles in helping McAvoy break onto the pro tour and into the heart of Roy's love interest, Molly Griswald (Rene Russo). In another supporting manner, four of McAvoy's male friends serve as a multicultural Greek chorus to his personal and professional efforts, with one friend, Clint (Lou Myers), being black and the other three white. In this group of comrades, racial differences do not exist, nor are

In *Gridlock'd*, buddy musicians Spoon (Tupac Shakur, left) and Stretch (Tim Roth) fight the bureaucratic system to survive.

they mentioned, as the four, without any seeming interests or families of their own, hang around like ornaments to McAvoy's life.

At one point in the film, Romeo identifies himself as Mexican, and his frequent lapses into Spanish mumblings reveal his "ethnic" flair. In a rural Texas town at a golf driving range, Romeo lives in a Winnebago trailer with McAvoy, and the former serves to be a confidant, defender, business consultant, cheer leader, and golf "swing" doctor to the latter. As the "swing doctor," Romeo's function is to keep McAvoy's golf techniques sharp and consistent, and on the fairways, Romeo carries the golf bag while dispensing game wisdom to McAvoy's self-destructive tendencies. Romeo's knowledge of the game is as extensive as McAvoy's, and though McAvoy excelled as a college player, the details of Romeo's golf background remain hidden. Additionally, the reasons why Romeo chooses to live in a trailer in McAvoy's shadow also remain concealed, particularly when at one point Romeo quits during one of McAvoy's stubborn antics on the course. Disappearing for days, Romeo returns, and like a hurt lover, he coaxes from McAvoy a confession about being irreplaceable. In a manipulative voice, Romeo asks, "Am I special?" Roy responds with contrition and overt masculinity: "If you can remove the sexual overtones ... then Romeo, I'm your Juliet."

The avoidance of gayness becomes a minor concern in the film since the attraction that McAvoy has to Molly, his psychiatrist, drives the plot's romantic line. In fact, McAvoy's motivation to qualify for golf's U.S. Open springs from a conspicuous effort to impress Molly and win her attention. In a down-home, shy, boyish manner, McAvoy confesses his love for her during one of their sessions, stressing his desire to get into "her heart, not into [her] panties." McAvoy is an old-fashioned kind of guy, who loves to watch sunsets and lay around on the couch cuddling. Yet, in an odd turn of events, he finds himself indebted to his old girlfriend, Doreen (Linda Hart), who is a stripper at and the owner of a local night club. In exchange for thousands owed to her, Doreen takes the deed and ownership of the driving range, placing McAvoy on salary. Like the aforementioned multicultural chorus, Doreen also takes time away from her life to follow McAvoy's golf efforts, and at the film's end, she and Romeo dance a tango together, suggesting their romantic future. This suggestion confirms Romeo's heteronormativity, and though he winds up with McAvoy's old girlfriend, he at least finds a woman.

Unfortunately, the racial hierarchy between the white and Latino buddies pervades the film. Though they share a trailer, McAvoy's status as the center and focus of both their lives negates an equal footing between the two. The image of Romeo's caddy position operates as a metaphor for that differentiation, and his ongoing nurturing of his white friend relegate Romeo to a level of secondary importance. Then, at places, Romeo seems merely an employee, referring to McAvoy as "boss" when completing a duty, but unlike the '40s Jack Benny-Rochester relationship where salary was used as a weapon of control, McAvoy is financially broke and obviously unable to pay Romeo. Consequently, if friendship keeps Romeo available, that same type of friendship is not returned by McAvoy.

Just as the common connection of golf fails to cement an equality of buddyhood between McAvoy and Romeo, and in another film released in that same year, *Fled*, physical chains fall short of being the metaphorical link of equality between the two protagonist in the story. Black convict Charles Piper (Laurence Fishburne) and white convict Luke Dodge (Stephen Baldwin) escape a Georgia prison road crew chained together, heading desperately toward freedom. As with *The Defiant Ones* (1959), the two men detest one another as they flee the law, fighting and arguing across landscapes, rivers, and tunnels. Dodge, imprisoned for computer hacking, offers Piper half of a $5 million jackpot stolen from a criminal corporation in exchange for Piper's help to reach Atlanta. With that offer before him, Piper cooperates with Dodge, but what the latter and the audience eventually discover is that Piper, a cop, is working undercover to locate computer information stolen by Dodge.

The impetus for Piper's closeness to Dodge results is cracking a case, and consequently, the degree of concern about Dodge's safety often has

Rebounding golfer Roy McAvoy (Kevin Costner, left) and his buddy-caddy Romeo (Cheech Marin) enjoy a laid-back moment off the fairway in *Tin Cup*.

more to do with police work than personal attachment. The two possess conflicting personalities that never quite achieve compatibility. Piper carries a serious, no-nonsense demeanor, while Dodge surfaces more as a wisecracking loudmouth with a habit of alluding to popular movies when dealing with stressful situations.

The Piper-Dodge duo intersect when it comes to their masculinity and their relationship with women. This aspect is more pronounced for Dodge, as he journeys solo into an Atlanta strip club to connect with his girlfriend, Faith (Brittney Powell), who dances at the club to pay her college tuition. While sitting in the audience watching Faith's pole dance, Dodge hustles money from a black male customer by betting on successfully kissing her. As a prelude to the bet, Dodge berates the customer for not being man enough to deal with an independent woman like a stripper. By inference, Dodge *is* that kind of secure male who can accept his woman's choice to dance for money in a strip club. Later in Faith's apartment, presumably following sexual intimacy between Dodge and Faith, she — while wearing her sexy lingerie — is shot in the face by the villains when she looks through the peephole of the front door. Immediately, Dodge suffers several moments of torture before Piper arrives to rescue him, but after her death Dodge remembers Faith only as a motive for revenge.

Piper fares better with his woman, Cora (Salma Hayek), an innocent driver who's muscled and kidnapped by Piper and Dodge when they first reach the streets of Atlanta. Conveniently divorced from her husband, Cora, a Chicana, seemingly has no friends or family as she is forced to take the pair to her apartment. After providing food and clothes, Cora and Piper share an instant attraction that culminates later in a passionate kiss before Piper exits to find Dodge. Cora invites Piper to return to her after he completes his affairs, and their dialogue suggests a future cross-cultural relationship of intimacy.

The convenience of both Faith and Cora provides the necessary female presence to affirm the buddies' hetero-masculinity, and in a typical fashion, the women are killed off or dropped from the story once that duty is fulfilled. Consequently, the duo possess conventional male traits that accentuate their commonality despite being on opposite sides of the law. At the same time, Dodge's white-collar crime, as well as his Robin Hood-ish donation of part of the stolen mob money to a children's center, cushions his illegal behavior as an acceptable error in judgment. By the film's end, the Piper-Dodge duo have formulated a respectful closeness that has been attained despite racial and professional disparity.

In contrast to the action efforts in *Fled*, the fantasy contours of *Men in Black* (1997) and *Men in Black II* (2000) follow a pair of heroes serving and protecting the earth from destructive aliens while monitoring the arrival and stay of friendly intergalactic refugees. With a reversal upon the traditional meaning of black, i.e., evil, and white, i.e., good, the heroes here dress in black and deal with keeping human society conscious about the surface appearance of those around them. As critics Hernan Vera and Andrew M. Gordon observe of the tone and effects: "Like the supernatural comedy *Ghostbusters* (1984), *Men in Black* plays on somatic disgust to create horror and comedy. There is a lot of emphasis on *slime*; the evil aliens are exceptionally disgusting and repulsive."[15] When white agent Kay (Tommy Lee Jones) recruits a black New York City police detective, James Edwards, later agent Jay (Will Smith), to become one of the select, racial issues fail to be a qualifying factor for a job handling extraterrestrials. As in other films, the racial references are articulated by the black character, not the white. Early in the movie during a chase sequence, Edwards/Jay jumps onto a moving tour bus from a bridge, proclaiming: "It just be raining black people in New York." And subsequently in his young, hip-hop demeanor and language, Jay sets up his racial distinction from the other characters. In a similar fashion, in the sequel, as Jay struggles to warn subway passengers about a giant alien worm attack, the riders remain indifferent until the subway car is bitten in two by the alien, causing Jay to chide: "Oh, now y'all running…. Save us Mr. Black Man!"

But beyond the brief comedic references to ethnicity, Kay and Jay are a working team, unselfishly confronting alien bad guys in volatile forms. Although required to lead a monk-like life, Kay chooses to return to his wife at the end of the first film and in the sequel, Jay finds a love interest in Laura Vasquez (Rosario Dawson), the bi-universal Princess, who must return to her planet and assume leadership. But both men's willingness to concede their personal lives for their jobs connects to the admirable sacrifice of men courageously giving their personal happiness to maintain their homeland.

In *Blue Streak* (1999), the buddy connection between black Detective Miles Malone (Martin Lawrence) and rookie white Detective Carlson (Luke Wilson) never actualizes itself, due to the fact that the former is a jewel thief masquerading as a robbery-homicide cop. Carlson and the rest of the LAPD force appear to be unable to permeate the façade projected by Malone, whose intent is to recover a multi-million dollar jewel hidden in the department's new building. As with other '90s films, the black protagonist accentuates his ethnicity in a way that is derisive to those whites around him, making the character of color the more color-conscious member of the duo. For Carlson, despite race, he merely longs to be a good cop and to establish effective ties with an experienced professional like Malone. Carlson states: "We're gonna be partners.... We ought to communicate.... This thing's like a marriage." Malone responds, "No, it's more like a one-night stand." As Malone bungles and double-talks his way through investigations and meetings with his police peers, there's a reciprocity of admiration that emerges. By the end of the film, as Malone makes it across the Mexican border, Carlson admits that he figured out his partner's real identity, a final commentary that mutual respect between the two men surpassed the established legal codes.

In a much more delirious comedy, *Gone Fishin'* (1997) stands as a film that prompts disbelief. Specifically, with such a talented cast, how could a movie be such as frivolous waste? In this vehicle, not only is race and ethnicity absent in importance, but so too are humor and good taste. The interracial buddies—who are both "slow" mentally—consist of the characters Gus Green (Danny Glover) and Joe Waters (Joe Pesci), two childhood friends for thirty-six years from New Jersey who share the unfortunate ability to always cause havoc. Living side-by-side with their wives and children in a duplex, the two finally get a long-anticipated fishing trip to Florida, but along the way, a series of mishaps occur in an overwhelming fashion that appears to be their ruin.

Rendered as two stooges with good hearts, Gus and Joe are at the core of the expected humor that stems from slapstick, sight gags, and verbal confusion, but it all results in faulty and uninspired escapades of foolishness. In one way, the film achieves racial equality between the two men because both are similarly stupid and accident-prone, yet their racial identities are never germane to the story. Just as vague is their masculinity, which does announce itself on occasion. For example, during their journey they meet two women friends—conveniently Rita (Rosanna Arquette) is white and Angie (Lynn Whitfield) is black — who travel together searching for the con man Massey (Nick Brimble) who stole money from Rita's mother. When first seeing the two single women, Gus and Joe assume their flirtatious personas attempting to impress the opposite sex, but being good married men, they go no further than innocent dalliance. In another example, after suffering from Massey's con, which causes them to lose their car, boat, and fishing gear, Joe tells Gus: "He [Massey] made me cry. I don't feel much like a man." For Gus and Joe, both the posturing of their maleness (flirting) and the displaying of their manhood (stoic courage) must be maintained for their gender identity. In this movie, even males with simple minds comprehend the essential elements that shaped their sacred hetero-uniformity.

In another movie coming out in the same year, the male characterizations gained little improvement. *Money Talks* attempted to showcase black comedian Chris Tucker as the '90s version of the '80s characterizations by Eddie Murphy. One journalist comments that "Tucker's spontaneity makes the movie move along quickly, making the audience wonder what he will try next.... Tucker shines in this formula buddy movie."[16] Tucker portrays Franklin Hatchet, a fast-talking, streetwise, inner-city hustler who finds himself mistakenly targeted by the authorities as a murderer. On the run, he teams up with white television reporter James Russell (Charlie Sheen), who gains an exclusive story in exchange for hiding Hatchet over the weekend — the same weekend of his marriage to a Beverly Hills socialite, Grace Cipriani (Heather Locklear).

The reluctant partnering between Hatchet and Russell flows from an exploitive remote report where Russell exposed the former's sundry deal making, which led to jail time. However, as the two find themselves chased and shot at by jewel thieves, they recognize their mutual dependence for survival. Hatchet is quick-witted and opportunistic, and Russell is methodical and privileged. Indeed, the aspects of privilege and race become the ongoing targets for Hatchet's verbal barrage to keep Russell at a distance. Referring to Russell as a "punk-ass white boy," Hatchet utilizes street slang to undermine both masculinity and race.

Russell, the essence of the white liberal, must hold back on the racial remarks to be politically correct, asserting less offensive lines to Hatchet, such as "I know how your type operates." However, there is considerable truth in the term "type," as the Chris Tucker-Eddie Murphy analogy becomes inescapable. Similar to the black male protagonists in *Trading Places*, *48 Hrs.* and *Beverly Hills Cop*, Tucker's Hatchet is the black hustler who becomes the racial fish out of water, as he winds up in the social preparations for Russell's wedding with Grace. Identifying himself as the biracial son of Diahann Carroll and Vic Damone, a real-life celebrity interracial couple at the time of the movie, Hatchet ingratiates himself with Grace's father, Mr. Cipriani (Paul Sorvino), as the two become instant "Italian brothers." But the Beverly Hills milieu exists as a polarity to the "ghettofabulous" life that Hatchet seeks, and his behavior and statements confirm his ethnic difference, which he consistently emphasizes. For example, when first meeting Grace at her father's estate, Russell warns Hatchet that she's self-conscious about her weight before the wedding. Yet upon seeing Grace dressed in an elegant evening gown, Hatchet remarks that she's looking "phat," causing momentary distress for the woman.

Again, the women function here to place the interracial buddies into focus. Grace's affluence, decorum, and reserved nature underscore Russell suit-and-tie professionalism. On the other hand, Hatchet's pregnant girlfriend, Paula (Elise Neal), is loud, aggressive, and profane — similar to her man's ghetto nature. Both men have obviously conquered female territories upon which they can raise flags to their particular personalities, while making clear their orientation to the opposite sex.

The need for clarity surfaces on several occasions with Hatchet due to his mannerism of releasing a high-pitched, girlish scream when in danger. Similar to the futuristic, androgynous character of DJ Ruby Rhod that he played in *The Fifth Element* (1997), Tucker uses his effeminate scream here, which brings laughter but also suspicions about sexual orientation. In this manner, the Tucker character strongly differed from the Eddie Murphy urban characters that were testosterone driven and edgy in a dangerous way.

Still, the film itself contains a scene that serves the male gaze. Without a strip-club environment, the story takes us to a party being held by Aaron (Michael Wright), a black childhood friend of Hatchet's who sells weapons of all types. In a gratuitous segment, the camera opens on a close-up of a black woman's posterior as she joins what appears to be a sex party where Aaron and his male friends are surrounded by the bare bodies of numerous black women. This scene further attests to Hatchet's "normal" orientation, offering evidence that he and his friends enjoy the same recreational intimacy with the opposite sex.

With a much darker tone than *Money Talks*, the misleadingly titled *Gang Related* (1997) begins by presenting the undeniable bond between two undercover cops— Detective Frank Divinci (James Belushi), a white cop trying to patch up his marriage and Detective Rodriguez (Tupac Shakur), a black cop with a gambling debt. Following the opening credits and sequence that highlight women dancers in a strip club, the scene shifts to show Divinci and Rodriguez discussing their ideal retirement, but their ensuing drug sale and subsequent killing of the buyer reveal their double life. With the assistance of Divinci's stripper girlfriend, Cynthia (Lela Rochon), the buddies have been setting up, taking money from, and then killing the seedier elements of the streets.

The two interracial buddies work their scam by using drugs and guns lifted from the police department's evidence room. On their part, they believe they're merely killing those who deserve to be eliminated, though Rodriguez remains more troubled than Divinci about the life-taking results. For Divinci, other than the money, the most important thing is his relationship with Rodriguez. On one occasion, he tells Cynthia: "I'm loyal to my partner. We're closer than blood, and I trust him with my life."

But for various reasons in this plot-driven movie, the duo's lives quickly spiral out of their control. To survive the impending disclosure of their crimes, the two plot to frame an innocent man and to kill Cynthia. Then, in a final breaking point, Rodriguez wears a wire to trap Divinci, and the latter cocks a gun to kill his partner. But even in the desperation of their situation, the two choose not to hurt one another, eventually dying at the hands of criminals who earlier crossed their paths.

The male protagonists in this film offer the potential for a provocative study of morality and corruption, but the script loses its way in numerous plot twists. And though Jim Belushi's one-tone acting never breathes contours into Divinci's character, the buddy connection remains the most engaging dynamic of the movie. Unfortunately, only showing the duo in a work scenario never convincingly explains the deep connection that's alluded to earlier in the film. In short, Divinci and Rodriguez seem to be just two guys working together to exploit their power and positions as cops, going in separate directions until the next scam. When placed in different locales, the film doesn't include what scholar Sharon Willis refers to as "parallel spaces linked," which would "produc[e] ... a kind of reciprocal 'passion.'"[17]

When compared with the inadequacies of *Gang Related*, *Three Kings* (1999) is an exceptional film that tackles contemporary politics, greed, and the collision of cultures. Using the Gulf War as its backdrop, the story begins in 1991 as the war between the United States and Iraq has just ended. Two reservists serving their duty — Troy Barlow (Mark Wahlberg), a white working-class dad of one and Chief Elgin (Ice Cube), a black working-class, single man — and one white career soldier, Major Archie Gates (George Clooney), accidentally team up to make a simple recovery of hidden gold based upon a map found on an Iraqi prisoner. But in a war, where few issues are easy, logical, or sane, their secret and self-serving mission spirals into conflict with the enemy and within themselves. In a captivating integration of visual techniques and emotional tones, *Three Kings* often triggers ambiguous responses to the mayhem on screen. Critic Marsha Kinder assesses that "the fusion of laughter and violence can be found in many films of the 1990s ..." as filmmakers attempt to remind the audience of "our desensitized culture ... when the lines between all genres, tones, and feelings dissolve."[18]

Similar to other war films, the military culture shared by Barlow, Elgin, and Gates provides a structured relationship among the men. With American uniforms and weapons sealing their power, their masculinity fits inextricably with their identity as soldiers. They are the three kings, i.e., the reigning males, whose feelings of entitlement motivate their quest. Their deference to Gates's rank and Special Forces experience assign him a leadership in their adventure, but as unexpected events unfold, the symmetry of their decision making reflects the connection the three have quickly made. Eventually, their military perspectives dissolve as they understand the humanity needed to respond to the refugees they acquire during their raid for gold.

The racial markers emerge through the slow-witted Southern soldier, Conrad (Spike Jonze), who accompanies the three and who fixates on Barlow as a brother. Expressing the views of the environment that shaped him, Conrad speaks before thinking, often igniting Elgin's wrath. For instance, the two argue about black quarterbacks in the NFL, as Conrad insists that black men are incapable of successfully playing that leadership role on a team. Yet to each of Conrad's prejudiced points, Elgin identifies a specific black player who excelled at the position. Yet Conrad's litany of negativity is not rooted in logic but in the mere stubbornness of his inflexibility. The two confront one another continually, with Elgin cautioning Conrad to keep his "white cracker" remarks to himself. Yet Barlow rushes between them physically and verbally urging Elgin to maintain a mature status in disregarding Conrad's childlike mentality and stereotyped views.

Among the three kings, the only significant color is gold, and when they discover the treasure that fills two dozen or more bags, they believe they have secured lives of prosperity for their return home. However, in the small desert village where they find the bunker with the gold, Saddam Hussein's soldiers are systematically targeting civilians whom they suspect are rebels against the Hussein regime. With the war officially over, the three kings can walk away with their gold, but when civilian Amir Abdullah (Cliff Curtis), captured and gagged, must helplessly watch his wife's murder by the soldiers and watch his little girl's emotional breakdown, the three kings reluctantly intercede. Though Barlow argues against involvement, Elgin insists: "We can help these people first and then be on our way." But once the three step into the circle of caring, they can't step out as they get deeper into preventing the certain death of innocent people. A simple mission to liberate gold becomes a commitment to get fifty refugees to the Iranian border, which brings more violent confrontations with Iraqi soldiers and a status of AWOL from the American base.

Three Kings reveals the layers of chaos surrounding the Gulf War and its barren environment, but it really explores the degree to which three men extend themselves, not as American soldiers, but as human beings helping others in harm's way. Masculinity for the three becomes synonymous with a commitment to protecting and defending those who are weaker. At the end, when cornered at the border by both Iraqi sentries and American officers intent on arresting them, the three kings look at one another, tacitly agreeing to barter the gold to save the lives of the refugees.

In doing so, they also save themselves by finding redemption from a greed that almost destroyed them as much as the war had destroyed the land.

The deadly sin of greed also functions as a motivating element behind the police corruption in the action drama *The Negotiator*. Set in contemporary Chicago, the movie opens with black police detective Danny Roman (Samuel L. Jackson) displaying his skill at arbitrating hostage situations and enjoying a professional fellowship with his white peers. Following the death of his partner, Roman becomes the prime suspect for the killing and for the theft of money for a department fund. Realizing he's being framed, Roman kidnaps police officials and innocent civilians as leverage for demanding the arrival of another hostage negotiator named Chris Sabian (Kevin Spacey).

Besides the whodunit aspect of the movie, the intriguing component of the film is the connection made and developed between Roman and Sabian. Just as both men have successful marriages, both men move seamlessly between their personal and professional lives. Skilled in controlling people and situations, the duo's initial verbiage over the phone and then face to face shows similar mental agility and intuitiveness. Both men are at the top of their professional skills, and each maneuvers around the other's techniques of control. When it becomes apparent that the embezzlement conspiracy confessed to by the captured Internal Affairs Inspector leads to his death by a SWAT team assault, Sabian comprehends Roman's situation.

In a film that centers on the relationship among men whose professional lives flow from violence, risk, and precarious situations, Roman and Sabian match the masculine toughness of their peers. In one scene, Roman stands within the frame of a broken-out high-rise window, his arms stretched wide in a crucifixion gesture, yelling a challenge to his trigger-happy peers on the force to take him out: "You want my blood? Take my blood! ... I'm getting too close to the truth!" In his defiance, he soars as the matinee hero who, literally in this scene, stands above other men who seek to destroy him. On his part, Sabian launches his anger into the command chief regarding the surprise assault. Sabian states he must be in control, announcing emphatically: "We're gonna do it my way, or I walk!"

Unlike other buddy films, Roman and Sabian spend much of the film in different settings, their connecting phone line serving as the metaphor for their teamwork to expose the crooked cops. In a final sequence when they do manipulate a self-incriminating response by a corrupt senior officer, their resolve to trap him requires Roman's trust to be shot and wounded by Sabian. Accordingly, they gamble and win their bluff.

Racial identity within the Roman-Sabian duo remains an unspoken issue in the film. In fact, Roman's presence as a black officer within his majority squad of whites stands out early in the film when he's feted in one celebration scene. For all purposes race vanishes here, leaving the police culture as the only significant entity that matters. The film suggests that being a "good cop" is the only identity that has value, which will provide a man's ethos and connection to others.

On the opposite end from the cop buddies in *The Negotiator,* in terms of tone, were the *Rush Hour* films. Merging international action star Jackie Chan with popular comedian Chris Tucker, the films placed the buddy relationship within a multicultural and multinational framework. In *Rush Hour* (1999), a Hong Kong policeman named Christopher Lee (Chan) journeys to Los Angeles to find the kidnapped daughter of a Chinese government official. Attempting to keep Lee out of their investigation, the FBI manipulates a Los Angeles police detective named James Carter (Tucker) to be a baby-sitter to Lee. In *Rush Hour 2* (2002), Carter has traveled to Hong Kong for a vacation, but workaholic Lee pulls him into a case that has personal meaning for him. Together, the duo eventually fly back to Los Angeles to solve a case of a Chinese mobster who is organizing an international money-counterfeiting scheme.

Following the conventional buddy pattern, Lee and Carter collide

In a tense setting, Detective Danny Roman (Samuel L. Jackson, left) confronts fellow hostage arbitrator Chris Sabian (Kevin Spacey) in *The Negotiator.*

when they first meet. In this case, beyond the usual personality differences, the two must deal with cultural elements that cause irritation and miscommunication. Carter is further annoyed when he discovers that the FBI has used him to remove Lee from the investigation. Consequently, the first half of the movie presents the clashing of the buddies, mostly around Carter's racist assumptions.

As the character Carter, Tucker summons up his signature persona of the fast-talking, frenetic, sarcastic urban black male with an inflated sense of self-importance. He reduces Lee to a walking cliché of the stereotypical Asian male — quiet, simple, and impotent. Played for humor, Carter's biased comments about Lee, and the Chinese in general, remain safe under the blanket of Carter's own black identity. In the rules of cinematic race relations, if a black person articulates racial generalizations, particularly about another person of color, the harangue becomes acceptable within the comedy genre. If a Chinese person mistakenly uses racial language that would be normally offensive, the intent of the language is not malicious and is deemed acceptable. American cinema allows this special dispensation because both men belong to the racial "other" and therefore are already on an equal footing from the dominant group's perspective. Likewise, in a form of vindication of the dominant group, if people of color espouse racial epithets about one another, the attitudes that frame those statements do not belong solely to the dominant group, thereby turning racial slurs into merely another form of entertainment.

As Carter and Lee wage their ongoing verbal assaults upon each other, they find that they are both reprimanded by the FBI for intruding into the kidnapping case, realizing their common position as outsiders. Then, while staking out a Chinese restaurant, they reveal their shared connections to their fathers, both of whom were also policemen. As the scene continues, the song "War" comes over the radio, connecting directly to their friction-filled relationship as the lyrics reflect upon the pointlessness of war. As a method of attaining understanding, they discuss the song's lyrics and share certain cultural elements with each other: Carter teaches Lee to dance to the song, while Lee demonstrates an intricate martial arts movement. The sharing of father figures, music, cultural expressions, and a masculine code of individualism leads directly to a sharing of food, as Carter eats a Chinese take-out entrée. This sequence ends, as the duo transition into a fight scene where the two literally fight back to back against a common enemy. Carter and Lee have bonded and transcended their racial and cultural differences. Their committed and common objective, as with all good heterosexual males, is to save the life of the innocent kidnapped girl.

This goal functions not only as a bonding element for the duo, but it also affirms Lee's possession of that conventional masculine trait of protector. Without a romantic interest in the film, Lee's manhood extends from his exceptional martial arts skills and his compassion to save the preadolescent daughter. Like a courageous soldier, he risks his life and his career to resolve her abduction. On the other hand, Carter expresses his libido through his lascivious comments to colleague Detective Johnson (Elizabeth Pena), a Latina who can maintain a professional camaraderie amid a squad room of fellow male officers. Johnson's participation in the dramatic showdown with the villains underscores the multicultural aspect of the movie, as the three — Lee, Carter, and Johnson — represent traditionally underrepresented racial groups as the central "hero" of the film.

In a parallel manner in *Rush Hour 2*, an undercover Secret Service agent, Isabella (Roselyn Sanchez), is also Latina, and by the film's end, she shares a screen kiss with Lee. After unknowingly serving as the desired object of spectatorship as Lee, Carter, and the audience watch her undress through an open-curtained window, Isabella displays an attraction to Lee. Once again the multicultural crime-fighting team accentuates the perspectives of the times, even as it suggests another question. Specifically, with the two films, do both male protagonists of color have love interests who are Latina to avoid a romance with white women? Is the decision in both films a method of celebrating multiculturalism or avoiding the still prevalent taboo of interracial romance between a male of color and a white woman?

What remains clear in the sequel is that the buddyship established in the first movie deepens between Lee and Carter. In the Hong Kong setting and the later Los Angeles locale, they fight and protect one another, even as they still identify and acknowledge racial distinctions. For example, in one scene, they discuss their respective cultural groups:

> Carter: "Let me tell you something about black people. When stuff
>   goes down, we keep our cool."
> Lee: "Maybe, but not like Asians. We never panic."
> Carter: "Yeah, right, but when Godzilla comes, y'all be tripping."

In this installment, the racial comments remain, but with less vilification. And in addition to more fight scenes together, there are two symbolic scenes that include the duo physically hanging and holding on together on a high-rise scaffold in Hong Kong and dangling from high-rise wires in Vegas; the life-and-death scenarios solidify their comradeship.

The cross-cultural format of the *Rush Hour* films works effectively for entertainment vehicles that merge the tones of action and comedy. By cleverly keeping racial elements inside the lines of acceptability, the films avoided a veneer of disrespect and tastelessness. The same kind of care

Los Angeles Detective James Carter (Chris Tucker, left) and Hong Kong Detective Christopher Lee (Jackie Chan) enjoy an enthusiastic moment in the action-comedy *Rush Hour*.

regarding tastefulness seemed to be absent from another 1999 film, *Play It to the Bone*.

Considering that the film was written and directed by Ron Shelton, an audience could certainly expect the well-edited, dynamic, and up-close visuals regarding athletic performance as seen in his films *Bull Durham* (1988), *White Men Can't Jump*, and *Tin Cup*. Those movies contained insights on the emotional and psychological results for men whose sports passions function also as their livelihoods— men who find excitement in the challenge and addiction to athletic competition. As scholar Andrew Kimbrell surmises: "As competition becomes the male's main avenue of self-validation, fear of losing in competition remains the single greatest anxiety for many men…. [L]oss in competition can equal psychic anni-hilation."[19] However, in a similar fashion as *Tin Cup*, the interracial component of *Play It to the Bone* functions on less steady ground and slips into disparagement between the male protagonists.

Play It to the Bone contains some engaging dramatic moments, but misfires when it moves into comedic scenes. The story centers on the close friendship of white pro boxer Vince Boudreau (Woody Harrelson) and Spanish prizefighter Cesar Dominguez (Antonio Banderas), whose bond is already established when the film begins via boxing and their affection for Grace (Lolita Davidovich), a former girlfriend to both.

While working out in a Los Angeles gym, the two buddies receive a call from a Las Vegas promoter desperate to find an undercard match before a Mike Tyson main event. Desperate for money and over-the-hill in their careers, the two take the offer, and convincing Grace to join them, they take her car to drive to Nevada for the fight. As a provision of their contract, the men demand that whoever wins their fight would get a future fight for the middleweight crown. Boudreau, a born-again Christian who often sees Jesus in the flesh, laments a fight where his future fame was destroyed by judges bought off by a promoter. Boudreau, with a bruiser boxing style, gambles and lives an impulsive life, while Dominguez, displaying a smoother boxing style, takes life seriously, and openly expresses his insecurities. Dominguez, an immigrant from Madrid, bemoans a fight where his future fame was halted when in a brief second, he was caught by an opponent's lucky punch.

Both men possess a degree of self-pity that hampers their ability to move forward with their lives, and though they argue about a number of issues on their road trip to Vegas, they also display an unexplainable compatibility — often speaking at the same time, understanding the other's moods, trusting one another, and loving the same woman.

Their pronounced racial and cultural differences become a point of argument at places, but not a factor for dissolving their friendship. For example, when Dominguez stresses emotionally, hearing that Grace doesn't plan to return to him, he cries openly, and at a roadside stop, he wanders into the desert spouting his anger in a long, unceasing Spanish monologue. Boudreau and Grace watch patiently until Dominguez wanders and talks himself out. And though written for humor, the scene plays self-consciously and contrived. It is not only a cliché, but it also trivializes the language and emotions of the character. Similar to the characters in earlier Shelton films— specifically, Gloria (Puerto Rican) in *White Men Can't Jump* and Romeo (Chicano) in *Tin Cup*— Dominguez's lapse into a Spanish litany functions as fodder for humor, particularly for the white characters who look on and observe. It keeps the "ethnic" aspect of the character as a comic factor for the film. Additionally, another function of these three Latino characters in each film is to make "ethnic" synonymous with "erotic." Gloria is the hot Latina lover to her white boyfriend; Romeo gives his white buddy ongoing advice about romancing women; and Dominguez serves as the emotional Latino lover to his white girlfriend.

In yet another scene in *Play It to the Bone*, race and ethnicity are vilified again for comic relief when the two buddies get into an awkward argument as Grace drives. In a moment of confession, Boudreau states: "I love you, man. I love all Mexicans." Dominguez quickly responds: "I love Mexicans, too, but I'm Hispanic." In an age of multiculturalism, the comments display a conspicuous ignorance of the term "Latino," as well as confusion about the connection between Mexicans and other Spanish-speaking cultures. Whether the confusion is on the part of the characters or the filmmakers, the point is never clear, but the intent of belittling Mexicans appears primary. Their conversation continues:

> Dominguez: "We [Spanish] discovered this land."
> Boudreau: "Italians discovered it."
> Dominguez: "But who paid for the trip?"

Once more, the cultural groups that were indigenous to the areas of California, Arizona, and Texas get lost within the set-up for a joke. And as the two buddies escalate into a heated dialogue at this point, Grace intercedes and brings them back to civility. In doing so, Grace mediates as more than just the peacekeeper; she assumes her ongoing role as the desired woman who confirms the heterosexual drives of the buddies.

The hetero preference of the two characters connects to another awkward issue raised in the dialogue — namely, that Dominguez, after losing the championship fight to a boxer identified as a "fag," experimented with homosexuality for one year. In Dominguez's illogic, he believed that if he was beaten by a homosexual, he himself must have possessed such tendencies; consequently, he was no longer a "man" but a "fag." In addition to this announcement leading to various jokes, it sets off Boudreau's anger, as he can't accept his best friend's being a "fag." Such behavior cancels out Dominguez's masculinity from Boudreau's perspective, even as he avoids the contradiction that a boxer could be both gay and the champ. Even more repulsive to Boudreau is his quintessential image of homosexuality — one man performing fellatio on another man. Using much more graphic language to describe the act, Boudreau abhors the entire conversation, let alone the possibility of Dominguez's abnormal sexuality. Dominguez, however, gains forgiveness because he declares that he never performed fellatio, and after all, he was Grace's lover as well.

The clumsy dialogue about homosexuality is soon followed by a more incredulous plot twist that both proves Boudreau's normal sexual drives and fulfills a male sexual fantasy. Joining the two buddies and Grace, a character named Lia (Lucy Liu), negotiates a ride with them after leaving her older male companion with a broken-down race car. When Lia finds that no one has any drugs, she promptly announces that she wants to have sex to fight off her boredom. Boudreau takes advantage of the situation, and at the next stop for gas, he and Lia have a hasty sexual romp behind a building. In another effort at humor, Boudreau refuses to reach an orgasm before his upcoming fight, but the free-spirited Asian woman coaxes him to be a "man" and go all the way. In the following sequence, after fighting with Grace, Lia hitches a ride with a truck driver and leaves the three.

The final act of the film gets the audience to the section that works most effectively — the actual boxing match between the two friends. The two know they must put all that they're worth into the ring — that is, play it to the bone — and the film's visuals capture the brutality, courage, and skills of both who rise to their best as boxers for one more chance at glory. When the judges pronounce a draw to their match, the faces of both men show their disappointment, as well as their exhausted bodies that have matched their fighting spirits.

Play It to the Bone could have been a memorable achievement in telling a story of interracial friendship and individual courage, but it floundered into racial stereotypes, gender clichés, and sexual fantasies for its comic aspects. And the story's efforts at delivering some profound messages about human spirit failed, particularly when compared with other Hollywood boxing films such as *Body and Soul* (1947), *Rocky* (1976), and *Raging Bull* (1980).

In 1999, an interracial buddy pairing framed an expressionistic rendering of the western genre. *The Wild Wild West*, inspired by the television show of the same title and lead characters, converged several tones and visual styles in a vehicle that often seemed confused in its objective. Set in 1869, the movie features James West (Will Smith), a black stud gunslinger, and Artemus Gordon (Kevin Kline), a white inventor, intellectual, and master of disguise, as U.S. Marshals sanctioned by President Grant to carry out clandestine activities to keep America safe.

In a noticeable departure from the television series, the character of James West is portrayed as black, which means that with a historical setting only four years after the Civil War, the issue of race and slavery would have to be acknowledged. As cultural critic bell hooks notes, "Although the gendered politics of slavery denied black men the freedom to act as 'men' within the definition set by white norms, this notion of manhood did become a standard used to measure black male progress."[20] To make a black secret agent in that time would take a reconciliation between conventional masculine traits and the existing racism. One specific technique used by the filmmakers was to assign pejorative comments about West's black identity to villains who are Southern loyalists enraged at having lost the war. Dr. Loveless (Kenneth Branagh) rules as the clever villain plotting to gain control of the country via weapons developed by kidnapped scientists. Throughout the movie, there are references to the "dark stranger," "Negro," "coon," and "slave" as markers of the historical times, augmented by dialogue peppered carefully with racial allusions. For example, early in the movie when West walks into the White House to keep his appointment with President Grant, a white security agent blocks the door, stating: "Winning the war, we [the Northern whites] got you forty acres and a mule, but you can't just traipse into the president's office."

Most of the comments and puns targeted at the black James West are framed by humor and sarcasm. However, one sequence fails to work effectively to achieve either. At a costume party, West fondles the breast of a

Vince Boudreau (Woody Harrelson, left) and his buddy Cesar Dominguez (Antonio Banderas) have one final chance at the championship in *Play It to the Bone*.

white woman who he mistakenly believes is Gordon reprising an earlier disguise, but when the woman responds angrily and a rope is thrown onto the floor, the white party-goers become a lynch mob. Taking West to the nearest tree, the hero employs a psychological strategy, saying lines to the white mob, such as "the slavery thing ... who wouldn't want folks running around doing chores?" The intended wittiness fails, and the overly long sequence trivializes the horror of lynching, as well as the destructiveness of slavery. The scene ends as Gordon races up in a wagon at the appropriate moment to rescue West from the noose.

West and Gordon exchange the expected dislikes for each other in the movie's early segments. Each man adheres to his own particular way of completing his mission. Yet, by the time both are left to a torturous death by Dr. Loveless, their common efforts become the only way to survive and defeat the villain. The West-Gordon buddyship grows from a professional relationship to one of interdependence and personal trust.

The closeness is challenged only by the presence of Rita (Salma Hayek), the Latina who seeks to free her kidnapped father, who actually turns out to be her husband. But before that announcement, West and Gordon are male rivals attempting to win Rita's favor, further validating the duo's "normal" sexuality. The contrived interaction among the three also leads to a scene that allows the duo, and the audience, to catch a quick peek at Rita's exposed buttocks when donning baggy long johns for sleepwear. But this establishment of Gordon's orientation becomes particularly important, as he was disguised earlier as a woman, singing and flirting in a saloon. The transvestite image sparks a certain kind of humor — the transvestite as an object of ridicule — but the necessary confirmation of Gordon's sexuality is required for him to function as a true hero in the buddy pattern. As for West, his manliness was confirmed in an opening scene as he and Belle (Garcelle Beauvais), a black woman with straightened hair, frolic in the nude in a water tower. Additionally, the tryst serves as a convenient plot element as white bandits accidentally knock the tower over with their wagon, leading into sight gag of West standing in the nude and holding a hat over his groin area.

Additionally, the inclusion of Rita connects back to the *Rush Hour* films where a Latina love interest vied for the attentions of both buddies. Whether the films collectively emphasize the stereotype of the hot Latina lover or whether they deliberately avoid a white woman as love interest is ambiguous. Perhaps, a combination of both functions serves suitably in all three films, maintaining the preferred distance between heroes of color and white women. Regardless, the West-Gordon duo manifest the essential masculinity for the western-action film and the expected comradeship of the interracial buddy pattern. Despite the fantastical and exaggerated dimensions of *The Wild Wild West*, the film perpetuates the viable and reaffirming aspects of male bonds across racial lines.

In a grittier, realistic venture, *The Corruptor* (1999) demonstrates an enduring buddyship within the tricky and blurring lines of police work. Set in contemporary New York, the story follows Nick Chen (Chow Yun-Fat), a Chinese cop highly decorated for his work on the Asian Gang Unit (AGU) and Danny Wallace (Mark Wahlberg), an ambitious white cop joining the same unit. Through the convolutions of payoffs from and concessions to a local criminal boss, Henry Lee (Ric Young), both Chen and Wallace stumble along a slippery path to professional and personal ruin. At the end, when Wallace is exposed for his real identity as an undercover internal affairs officer sent to gather evidence on Chen, the latter must decide whether to kill or forgive his buddy.

The prominent weakness in the story springs from Chen's protective nature toward Wallace. When first introduced, Nick Chen displays an aggressive, defiant personality that dominates the screen. In several scenes, Chen's idiosyncratic mannerism — a wide-eyed, maniacal grin to a situation of violence or authority — is a visual statement of his "cool," above-reproach attitude. His nihilistic mannerism punctuates his masculinity, both controlling and impulsive all at once, without regard for established rules. Consequently, why would Nick feel compelled to safeguard a white man assigned to his unit? Chen's motivation to steer Wallace from corruption functions most conveniently as an element for irony within the story; the very man Chen maneuvers to protect is the same man who maneuvers to gather evidence to end Chen's career. Chen remains torn between two loyalties, suffering from the confused Chinese identity assessed by scholar Peter X Feng: "Being Chinese American is not a matter of resolving a duality, for proposing to draw from two cultures inevitably results in not belonging to either."[21] The flaw in Chen's characterization is this lack of clear motivation for his allegiance to a white male living outside of Chen's world.

However, once Chen's protectiveness is established, the buddyship demonstrated in the movie fulfills the expected provisions of the pattern. For example, during a stakeout, Chen and Wallace discuss their fathers— both of whom were cops. And as they analyze their connections to those figures, Chen theorizes that perhaps both he and Wallace followed in the same professional paths to prove something. Here, the implied father-son dynamic of mutual pride enters the dialogue in the same fashion as the buddy duo from *Rush Hour*. In another example of buddyhood, as an extended, violent chase scene ends, Wallace stays and protects a trapped Chen from the onslaught of the villains; later, in a climactic shootout, Chen returns the favor and pushes Wallace aside to take a fatal bullet. In a final gesture of comradeship, Wallace refuses to write a negative report about Chen to the Internal Affairs Division, insisting to his boss that Chen was a "good cop." The loyalty and trust shared by the two encapsulates them to the Unit as just an example of "yellow fever": that is, a white person's obsession with Asian culture.

Despite Chen's hard-edged exterior, his rougher qualities are smoothed out through his affection for May (Marie Matiko), a prostitute for one of Henry Lee's businesses. Indeed, Chen is as protective of her as he is of Wallace, but having been May's lover, as well, Chen's nursing and caring takes on a specific gender meaning. In one scene, Chen screens her from being arrested, and in another scene, he patiently feeds her soup as she recovers from a drug binge. Chen's furtive behavior illustrates his conflict, and as Lillian Rubin notes, "Requests for such intimacy are difficult for a man, but they become especially complex and troublesome in relations with women."[22] Chen's macho street reputation would definitely be punctured if his affection for May, a prostitute, were discovered, so his sensitivity must be shielded in privacy. May functions both as Chen's lover and his moral duty, his attempts to save her being a significant "good" deed in an "evil" environment. On his part, though Wallace doesn't have one significant woman, his heterosexuality receives confirmation through his acceptance of Henry Lee's offer for a bathhouse massage by a nude Asian woman with whom Wallace has sex.

This latter element of miscegenation connects to the discussed cultural stereotypes surfacing in earlier dialogue. As film critic Gina Marchetti notes, "Orientalia has always had a sexual dimension, associated with luxury, sensuousness, eroticism, perversity, and decadence,"[23] and Jack (Jon Kit Lee), the other Asian male member of the AGU, punctuates that fascination. Jack rebuffs Wallace's professional interest in joining with Asian culture and people, labeling the interest as "yellow fever." Reducing Wallace's noble intentions as masking his desire to have an "almond-eyed girl" who'll "lick his wick," Jack dismisses the white cop's announced commitment to mere sexual fantasies. Later, in a bar scene, a drunken Jack crudely explains his theory on sexual stereotypes: "White people believe all Asians have little dicks, so you think that when an Asian chick sees your pecker, she's going to think that it's Mount St. Helens ... and then you look at the hands of most Asian chicks, and you think your weenie's going to look like a sewer pipe in a fist.... The joke's on you. The Chinaman's hung!" Amassing several cultural generalizations together, Jack punctuates his resentment of Wallace's presence while defending his own penis size, as well as that of other Chinese men, before the white male. Jack's measurement of masculinity via the size of genitalia seeks to debunk one stereotype by insisting upon another about all Chinese men. Jack's logic is faulty, but his male praise of the power of the penis rings true according to prevailing conventional notions.

The Corruptor uses a gritty and violent lens to view the interracial buddies who find redemption from personal demons in their common pact of trust. The story flirts with issues of illegal immigration, Asian youth gangs, and cross-cultural misconceptions as a backdrop to assert the value of male bonding. The film's final image of Wallace's solemn expression at Chen's funeral procession is the coda that authenticates the depth of loss. No greater gift can be given by a buddy than to lay down his life as Chen did for Wallace.

In the gritty action vehicle *The Corruptor* detectives Danny Wallace (Mark Wahlberg, left) and Nick Chen (Chow Yun-Fat) create an uncommon buddyship.

Echo Patterns of Interracial Buddyship in the Late 1990s

By the latter half of the decade, a number of films showcased the interaction among males from different ethnicities, but often in an oblique manner that supported some major theme or character revelation about the protagonist — usually a white male. The films *Ransom* (1996), *The Jackal* (1997), *Nothing to Lose* (1997), *Blade (1998)*, *U.S. Marshals* (1998), *Primary Colors* (1999), *The Chill Factor* (1999), and *The Green Mile* (1999) depicted men in crisis who turned to one another, usually learning something about the value of working together, respecting difference, and/or redemption. But the following films that echo the interracial buddy paradigm deserve a bit more attention in regard to the substantive meaning that the male unions had for the characters and the movies' plotlines.

As entertainment fare on its own, *Metro* (1996) "provid[es] sequences that offer mixtures of humor and tension, humor and action, and humor and romance."[24] However, being an Eddie Murphy movie, it faces the inevitable comparison to earlier Murphy vehicles such as *48 Hrs.* and the *Beverly Hills Cop* series. But here in this film Murphy's character of Scott Roper — a San Francisco Police Department hostage negotiator — possesses a more contained nature, with an affection for his journalist girlfriend, Ronnie (Carmen Egojo), and a professional respect for his new white partner, Kevin McCall (Michael Rapaport).

Although Roper expresses reluctance to train McCall at first, a former SWAT sharpshooter whom Roper refers to as "Huck Finn" upon first meeting, Roper sees potential in the way that McCall handles himself during a jewelry store hostage crisis and the ensuing chase to catch the nihilistic villain Korda (Michael Wincott). Roper and McCall develop a healthy professional relationship, but never quite buddies, they don't share their private lives. The exception comes at the end when Ronnie — who has served in one scene as the object of a voyeuristic killer and camera that watches her undress through a window — must be rescued from Korda's clutches. With McCall backing him up as a sharpshooter, Roper faces down Korda, who literally has Ronnie tied down to a deadly lathe machine poised to slice her head.

Race consciousness and bias are handled in the film primarily through the villain, who, capable of exchanging high-decibel profanity with Roper, calls him a "nigger cop." Keeping the racial slurs and prejudice ensnarled within Korda's personality justifies any contempt for him and makes his death acceptable.

At the most, Roper and McCall are professional sidekicks who function effectively on the job. Their relationship doesn't serve as the focus of the film's plot and thematic elements, similar to the connection between two recurring agents in the *Mission: Impossible* films.

Although *Mission: Impossible* (1996) began with the framework of an ensemble effort, as with the basis of the television show that suggested the film, by the end of the first act, the focus upon agent Ethan Hunt (Tom Cruise) becomes apparent. Tagged as a possible double agent by his superiors, Hunt must locate a list of undercover agents and orchestrate a sale of the information in order to expose a "mole" in the agency. To complete that task, he rallies a set of operatives to help him, including Luther (Ving Rhames), the black techno-whiz. Luther's appearance comes about in the second act of the story, and having been placed on a "disavowed list" of agents like Hunt, the two men connect solely on a professional level. Yet, out of the small team that Hunt assembles, Luther becomes the one person whom Hunt admits he can trust. After the heist of a disc from the FBI mainframe, Hunt gives the disc to Luther for safekeeping. When Luther asks, "What makes you trust me?" Hunt confides: "Because if you knew what you were getting into, you never would have done it." The "it" refers to the aforementioned job, which Luther did just for the challenge and satisfaction of doing the impossible. This faith in Luther's integrity and loyalty proves correct and advantageous for Hunt, as the other members of the team have their own agendas. At the end of the film, Hunt and Luther, having survived their common ordeal, dialogue about Hunt's family and the possibilities of working with the Impossible Missions Force in the future.

In *Mission: Impossible 2* (2000), Hunt and Luther team up once more to trace down a lethal virus being sold by a rogue ex-agent, Sean Ambrose (Dougray Scott). Hunt's investment in the mission intensifies as he asks his romantic interest, Nyah (Thandie Newton), to go undercover to infiltrate Ambrose's organization, as the latter two were former lovers. In order to maintain surveillance of Nyah, Hunt recruits Luther again to help him with the mission, and the two agents click professionally as they did in the earlier mission.

Hunt and Luther's union revolves around their jobs, which include life-and-death situations for both. And though their relationship never functions as a central focus of either film, the interesting angle of their camaraderie involves both men's shrewd and calculating abilities. Their masculinity springs from the same physical agilities and cool-under-fire dispositions of other action heroes as they negotiate explosions, gun battles, helicopters, and high-speed vehicles. Yet, at the same time, their shared trait is brains more than brawn.

In *Jerry Maguire* (1996), Tom Cruise pairs with another black male co-star in a character study of a sports agent who finds integrity and love by the movie's end. The titular protagonist, played by Cruise, finds his world of slick promises and high-salaried clients crumbling, with one potential client, Rod Tidwell (Cuba Gooding, Jr.), the only hope for redemption. But Tidwell, a showboating NFL receiver, brings his own demanding and irritating personality to the table forcing Maguire to re-think his approach and commitment to his job.

On one level, both Maguire and Tidwell suffer from similar weakness: neither can commit fully to those things that each values. For Maguire, his affection for Dorothy Boyd (Renée Zellweger) leads to a marriage that he won't allow himself to surrender to emotionally, and for Tidwell, his desire to become a top-tier, overpaid player requires that he give more than just attitude on the field. But in the professional exchange, the two men help each other to recognize their flaws and the manner in which they prevent their own success. In particular, having a successful marriage and children, Tidwell mentors Maguire about the requisite honesty and expressions of love necessary for a marriage, which Maguire eventually understands.

In this romantic comedy, though Tidwell has some screen moments where his fast-talking black male conjures up thoughts of Chris Tucker or Eddie Murphy, the ethnic-showboat image finds a balance in Tidwell's scenes of sincere dialogue with Maguire and with the family moments. Both men negotiate in typical male arenas— Maguire in the high-pressure business world and Tidwell in the high-pressure world of professional athletics—but both need personal relationships with women and children more than their jobs. Their lives run parallel and then intersect around the emotional dynamics that connect the two beyond their agent-client contract to a much deeper friendship. This friendship remains a subplot, but it remains vital to the characterizations of both males. Basically, their friendship empowers each man to open up beyond a hardened veneer that he uses to navigate his life. As psychologist James Hillman notes: "Friendships are so hard to maintain because they continually demand accessibility, that you let yourself take in the other person, let your imagination be stirred by thoughts, approaches, feelings that shake you out of your set ways."[25] This ability to be "accessible" confuses some males, whose conventional notions of masculinity demand individualism and the stoic strength to face life alone.

The depth of closeness within the interracial friendship in *Phenomenon* (1996) remains as elusive as the extraordinary mental and physical powers assigned to the film's protagonist, George Malley (John Travolta). In the small Northern California town of Harmon, Malley is "an ordinary man ... who becomes a genius after being struck by lightning or, perhaps, hit by an alien force" on the night of his 37th birthday,[26] and the person he spends the most time with is his black male friend, Nate Pope (Forest Whitaker). Both men endure routine, predictable lives at first, but Malley's transformation into a creative intellectual with telekinetic powers disturbs Pope, who prefers the comfort of the slower, monotonous lifestyle.

The two men greet each other as "buddy" on occasion, and they linger on each other's porches consistently. Early in the film, their lengthy dialogue and numerous scenes together suggest that the film will focus on their connection. However, each time that the film moves toward exploring their friendship, the plot becomes busy with twists: a curious Berkeley professor, FBI agents, earthquakes, lost boys, and women. For Malley, his singular wooing of what seems to be the town's only eligible white woman, Lace (Kyra Sedgewick), transitions into the focal relationship in the film. For Pope, he eventually discovers love through Malley's arranging of a single mother Ella (Elisabeth Nunziato), a Portuguese immigrant and day laborer, to become Pope's housekeeper.

More important than the interracial buddyship in this vehicle, the multicultural characters give the small rural town an ethnic diversity that would be expected in a city. Along with Pope and Ella, another major character in the ensemble is Tito (Tony Genaro), the Latino auto mechanic with whom Malley practices his Spanish language skills. The racial toleration in the town is remarkable, particularly acknowledging the agricultural-based economy that appears to be dependent upon the Spanish and Portuguese laborers viewed in one sequence.

In a completely different tone and style, the film *Enemy of the State* (1998), highlights two male characters who join together to survive formidable political and legal threats. Robert Dean (Will Smith), a black labor and union lawyer, becomes the target of a villainous inner circle within the National Security Agency when he receives information that reveals the murder of a senator by that same inner circle. On the run from his upper-class home and life, Dean connects with Brill (Gene Hackman), a legendary, underground ex-agent. The oil-and-water mix between the two is stirred by Brill's resentment for Dean's naiveté, which leads to Brill's forced emergence from his underground life and the death of Brill's contact/confidante, Rachel Banks (Lisa Bonet). Dean, isolated from his wife and family, has only Brill to trust.

With Dean's legal mind and Brill's mastermind in technology and communications, the two work together to bring down the leader of the inner circle, Thomas Reynolds (Jon Voight), and his sycophants. Dean and Brill never reach a buddyship, perhaps due to their age, race, or class. One point that becomes clear, however, during a coffee-shop conversation is their realization of being in a critical situation with no one to save them but one another. As Brill confesses that his underground life has meant that he has no family, Dean states that he refuses to give up his life and family. He says: "I grew up without a father. I know what that is, and I will not allow my family to go through that." Dean's objective to survive goes beyond his individual preservation to his masculine mandate to maintain and protect his family.

With *The Matrix* (1999), the filmmakers guided the first half in the direction of a possible buddyship between Neo (Keanu Reeves) and his mentor, Morpheus (Laurence Fishburne). When Neo is first contacted by Morpheus via his crew, led by Trinity (Carrie-Anne Moss), Neo's motivation is to finally meet the legendary Morpheus, who has risen to mythical status for numerous computer hackers. Neo's trust and respect for Morpheus helps the former to choose the red pill that leads to the life-changing awareness of Neo's true condition. Morpheus informs Neo: "The matrix is everywhere ... all around us ... the world that has been pulled over your eyes to blind you to the truth ... that you are a slave born into bondage."

To have a male character who is visibly black allude to "slavery" in defining Neo's situation clearly underscores the severity of that status. Yet here the filmmakers move toward much larger thematic concerns than race; for the sake of their survival, characters' racial identities vanish amidst the more weighty significance of their human identities. Consequently, the series develops as a multicultural tapestry of black, white, Asian, and Latino characters whose interdependence becomes their only means of defeating the artificial intelligence of machines that seek to imprison human bodies as an energy source. In *The Matrix Reloaded*, when Zion, the last human city, is revealed and defended, the characters of color, as well as multinational characters with accents, abound in both the human world and in the matrix system. And in the last installment, *The Matrix Revolutions* (2003), as the dialogue grows heavy with reflective, philosophical suppositions, Neo seems secondary to the affirmation of a racially diverse human society.

However, in the first film, Morpheus serves as a father figure, tutor, rebel leader, and eventual friend to Neo. In fact, Morpheus's committed belief to Neo being the "One"— the reincarnated human leader returning to free the people from the machines— actually functions to elevate Neo's status to savior. Eventually, Morpheus reveres Neo in a more spiritual capacity than Neo ever revered Morpheus. So as the two men learn to understand their intertwined destinies, the movie, and the two sequels, moves beyond their buddyship and into issues of the quality of human life; the dangers of a machine-dependent society; existentialism; and romantic love (particularly between Neo and Trinity).

* * *

It would be difficult to name some of the most memorable films *and* some of the worst of the 1990s without connecting with the interracial buddy paradigm. The motif had reached such an ongoing utilization in Hollywood that it became standard fare in dealing with issues of race and manhood. With some movies more penetrating than others in examining messages of masculinity and racial progressivism, the concept of buddyship, at the very least, served a function in stimulating discussion during a decade when the dimensions of masculinity were being re-examined.

6

Capers, Chaos, and
Contemporary Cool: 2000–2003

The male presence in the cinema of the 21st century has remained firmly rooted in gender conventions while displaying some shadings of change. Within the first three years of the new millennium, at least twenty films have already been released that have incorporated the interracial buddy pattern or some aspects of the cycle. Caper films have been strong, as ensemble casting provides the genre with the desired star power to stir the marketplace. At the same time, the tragedy of 9/11, a falling economy, the outsourcing of jobs, the first term of the Bush administration, the genocide in Sudan, and the war in Iraq made a number of war films relevant metaphors for the chaos occurring both domestically and on foreign soil. Consequently, the familiar cinematic images of masculinity have connected to a term such as "the alpha male" as topics about male leadership resonate in public discourse. Similarly, the suggestion of the evolving, progressive male who carries himself with strength, sensitivity, and a cool confidence has become a popular type as terms such as "metrosexual" come into vogue.

By 2003, there were already numerous films incorporating the interracial buddy pattern to depict key male relationships. Once again, buddyhood crossed genre formats, maintaining some of the issues from previous years. The interracial buddy formula continued to be a winning tactic for appealing to wide, varied audiences.

The Interracial Buddy Films
of the Early Millennium

The dramatic tensions of men at war, both literally and ethically, designed the content for the film *Rules of Engagement* (2000), as the military careers of a buddy duo are jeopardized. Despite a contemporary setting, the film opens with a 1968 battle in Vietnam, where Terry Childers (Samuel L. Jackson) and Hayes Hodges (Tommy Lee Jones) share a command that leads to a bloody battle. To end the grisly conflict, Childers saves Hodges's life by executing a Vietnamese soldier in order to force compliance by his commanding officer, Colonel Cao (Baon Coleman). Twenty-eight years later, that act plays as crucial evidence in a court case against Colonel Childers, following his command for his troops to return fire at civilians storming an American Embassy in Yemen.

Childers and Hodges claim the soldier's code of honor that links their attitudes and behavior. As author Peter Lehman acknowledges: "War, where men go to prove and affirm their masculinity, is perhaps not surprisingly also a ... cinematic site of a great deal of anxiety precisely about losing that masculinity."[1] Although Hodges's war wounds led to a desk job and a law degree, Childers's war experiences led to his later involvement in Beirut, Panama, and the Persian Gulf. Yet, despite their different responsibilities, the two have remained close and have remained committed to the core values of being Marines. When faced with charges of murder for the 83 dead civilians, Childers doesn't hesitate to ask Hodges to represent him. Hodges, not only a friend, possesses the knowledge of what it means to be in the chaos of combat. And though Hodges hesitates, insisting that "I'm a good enough lawyer to know you need a better lawyer than me," he is indebted to Childers for saving his life in Vietnam.

Beyond the sharing of battle wounds, the bond between the two men resounds loudly in two particularly scenes. First, as the trial works against them, Hodges enters Childers's apartment to find him sitting in the dark with bourbon and a handgun. Having suffered through "an ugly divorce" and a "drinking problem," Hodges avoids preaching but responds with an understanding statement: "It's okay ... I know." With tears flowing, Childers opens up and confesses his fear: "They take my uniform away.... They may as well shoot me." Childers, still single and without a family, has dedicated his life to the service of his country, and to be stripped of his purpose would reduce him to the nadir of existence, a place that Hodges knows too well.

Second, after returning without any helpful evidence from a personal investigation of the American Embassy in Yemen, Hodges erupts angrily at Childers, and the two exchange punches. Exhausted by their brawl, the two friends laugh, allowing Hodges to confess the actual source of his anger: Hodges hates himself for being alive after losing his men in the Vietnam battle. They argue and fight, but never abandon one another. The two scenes provide the manner in which the trust between the buddies enables their candid asseveration of fears and self-doubt. The repressed insecurities find a supportive and compassionate shoulder, not a condemnatory voice.

Childers and Hodges consider themselves warriors who did the job asked of them: men who offered their youth and their very lives for the good of their country. Granted, they don't question the politics of the country until a scheming National Security Advisor named Sorkal (Bruce Greenwood), seeks to make Childers a scapegoat for military intelligence errors, but the duo view their manhood as interwoven into their military identities.

Interestingly, Childers's racial identity avoids consideration by all those involved with crowning him with thorns of guilt. This tolerance and racial blindness fits into the shaping of the buddyship between Childers and Hodges, but it seems unlikely that, even in the late 1990s, even a highly decorated black colonel would remain unscathed by racial biases about his ability to command. Likewise, Childers's absence of a family or love interest conspicuously shapes his characterization, in contrast to Hodges, whose ex-wife and adult son are signifiers of his heterosexual and romantic history. Perhaps, as scholar Cornel West asserts, "Black sexuality is a taboo subject in America principally because it is a form of black power over which whites have little control."[2] Omitting both racial and sexual dimensions to Childers's character presents him as an alienated man, floating in a disconnected manner to other characters and the audience. On that racial note, however, in the post-trial moments of being acquitted of the murder charges, Childers steps outside, sees Colonel Cao across a parking lot, and returns a salute. This gesture between the two officers of color might simply express a military respect as soldiers, but it could also be read as two men of color comprehending their mutual expendability due to racial politics of obliteration.

Appearing one year later, the film *Men of Honor* (2001) also incorporates military culture as the backdrop for the story line. Covering a historical period from 1943 to the late '60s, the film dramatizes the story of Carl Brashear (Cuba Gooding, Jr.), the first African American to become a Navy master diver, and his relationship with Billy Sunday (Robert DeNiro), a Southern white Naval officer. With their Southern backgrounds, the racial hostilities run deep between Brashear, the son of a black sharecropper, and Sunday, the son of a poor white farmer displaced by black sharecroppers. Added to that personal resentment is the Navy's tradition of relegating black sailors to menial jobs and to limited advancement in rank.

The Brashear-Sunday conflict propels the story along, as it chronicles the commitment that Brashear makes to follow his father's mandate:

"Don't quit on me!" Consequently, Brashear's defiance of, challenge to, and achievement over the established system represents a personal accomplishment and a promise between a father and son. This father-son dynamic illustrates the manner in which lessons of manhood are passed down and given tangible manifestations. Brashear's father, Mac (Carl Lumbly), seen early in the film, continues to have a powerful presence throughout the story. As Brashear carries and cherishes a homemade radio fashioned by Mac, Brashear literally keeps the symbolic device of communication close by — inscribed with his father's words, "A son never forgets." When Sunday deliberately breaks the radio during a heated confrontation between the two protagonists, Brashear's anger is as much a response for an attack on his father as himself. At the end, after Sunday has reassembled the radio and left it for Brashear, both Brashear and the audience recognize the personal triumph of both the physical challenge and of the spirit that's attained for all three men — a trinity of masculine fulfillment.

Between the breaking and fixing of that radio, Brashear and Sunday endure their individual torments: Brashear loses a leg and possibly his wife and son, while Sunday loses his hard-earned military ranking of master chief and suffers from alcoholism. At the declivity of their lives, both men perceive their passion and manhood as inextricably linked to their careers as Navy divers. As Brashear, an amputee, and Sunday, a recovering alcoholic, train and work together to prepare the former to be reinstated as an active diver, the men have transcended their racial discord and bonded on another level of significance — living with honor and on their own terms. The Brashear-Sunday buddyship solidifies itself in the sequences covering the four-week preparation for a military hearing, and it claims victory over numerous obstacles when Brashear, coached by Sunday, passes the final physical hurdle for reinstatement. Brashear and Sunday share a common personal dream and ethos, which Brashear confesses aloud, like a rosary, at the military hearing. He states: "The Navy is not a business.... We have many traditions ... some good, some bad, and I've experienced most of them. However, I wouldn't be here today if it wasn't for our greatest tradition of all ... honor, sir!"

Brashear and Sunday belong to the military culture, which, a world unto itself, exists on codes that remain alien to the civilian world. This alienation surfaces in the marriages of the protagonists, as each man possesses affection for his wife, but maintains a fidelity to his career. Their metaphorical marriage to the Navy and its codes renders a secondary status to the women in their lives. Brashear's wife, Jo (Aunjanue Ellis), comprehends this fact due to her father's remote connection to her, and Sunday's wife, Gwen (Charlize Theron), attempts to deal with this fact with alcohol and public displays for attention. Both men treat their wives as resources for support and understanding, but their passions spring from their professions. The masculine need to find validation and purpose through work, rather than familial nesting, resonates strongly for the protagonists. As Michael Kimmel notes, "[T]he workplace has been seen as a masculine arena, where men could test and prove their manhood against other men ... a place where men created themselves as men."[3] Brashear and Sunday believe that their raison d'etre rests within assuming, or at the very least teaching, the esteemed role of a Navy diver.

In comparison with the dramatic and thematic achievements of a film such as *Men of Honor*, the movie *Pros and Cons* (2001) contains few admirable qualities. An alleged comedy, the movie attempts to combine elements of *Stir Crazy* (1980) with *The Shawshank Redemption* (1994) without the humor of the former or the depth of characterization of the latter. In two cases of innocent men being sent to prison, Ben Babbitt (Larry Miller), a timid, clumsy white accountant and Ron Carter (Tommy Davidson), a fast-talking black man, find themselves thrown into the jungle of felons. Combining Babbitt's accounting skills and his misinterpreted toughness with Carter's hustling skills, the two ingratiate themselves to Kyle (Delroy Lindo), the black inmate who runs the prison and organizes an escape.

Committed to one another in *Men of Honor*, Navy divers Billy Sunday (Robert DeNiro, left) and Carl Brashear (Cuba Gooding, Jr.) face one more challenge of courage.

The Babbitt-Carter union represents the ultimate situation of characters who have nothing in common. Before prison time, Babbitt's world of working at a high-powered investment firm receives more detail for the sake of later plot twists, while Carter's background remains vague. Their incarceration constantly reverberates with familiar racial and gender stereotypes without any fresh or inventive dialogue or depiction. When pressured by Kyle about his background and possible black ancestry, Babbitt responds: "Yes, we're crazy blacks.... I like jazz but only on the banjo.... When there's a riot, I steal my own TV."

In regard to gender, the issue of homosexual activity recurs throughout the movie as a source for gags. As Babbitt and Carter share a cell and become well-known on the block, the assumption about their romantic union spreads as highlighted in a scene where an effeminate white inmate discusses cell decorations with Carter. Carter, consequently, insists that his masculinity be affirmed and announced aloud by Babbitt, demanding: "Say I'm the man!" Later, when negotiating the escape with Kyle, Babbitt claims that he and Carter are indeed a romantic couple as a way of justifying that both be included in the breakout. Following that ruse, on the outside at a nightclub, Kyle arranges for two black women to show Babbitt some intimate attention because he is the "man," indicating that Carter is the "woman," which is the ultimate insult. This feminization of Carter carries a particularly harsh meaning to this black male attempting to posture himself with equanimity among other men. As Marlon Riggs observes, "Black macho prescribes an inflexible ideal: Strong black men ... don't flinch, don't weaken, don't take blame or shit, take charge, step-to when challenged, and defend themselves without pause for self-doubt."[4] Carter's assignment as gay undercuts both his masculine and racial identities, denying him inclusion into his desired communities.

The confirmation of the Babbitt-Carter heterosexuality extends from two convenient women characters: Babbitt's fiancée, Eileen (Julie Warner), and Carter's wife, Pam (Simaria Graham). In a similar rendering as their male partners, Eileen is shown in more detail, working a portable coffee kiosk in a business building while Pam exists in an amorphous, rootless world. Both women characters appear when their presence assists the Babbitt-Carter duo in their efforts to survive prison and, bizarrely, at the end when the women appear in black leather as two gun-waving tough girls trying to protect their men.

The Babbitt-Carter buddyship exists on the thinnest of premises, suggesting that a few months in jail erases, rather than intensifies, racial and class differences. Babbitt and Carter unexplainably bond and befriend one another without any discernible cause and effect. Their trust magically exists, and their contention revolves around the perception of the male-versus-female roles in their cell. At the film's conclusion, when the two, along with their women, are allowed to go free by the authorities, the suggestion is that their closeness will continue, but without a foundation for that union, the ending is not convincing. The framework and ingredients for a successful interracial buddy film are present, but the one-dimensional aspect of the characters and the shallowness of the story negate the possibilities.

In another Asian-Caucasian pairing, the film *Shanghai Noon* (2001) and its sequel, *Shanghai Knights* (2003), place the buddy duo in late-19th century America and London, respectively. Both films contain what film historian William H. Phillips calls a "combination of genres (kung fu and western with a lot of broad comedy)."[5] As hybridizations of genres, the films rely on the interracial buddy pattern to frame their stories, but the first film is superior in its overall effectiveness to the latter.

In the first film, as a royal guardsman to the Chinese emperor, Chon Wang (Jackie Chan) journeys to frontier Nevada to deliver gold as a ransom for the kidnapped Princess Pei Pei (Lucy Liu). In the wild West, he confronts and later joins the wisecracking white outlaw Roy O'Bannon (Owen Wilson) in completing the mission. During the early part of the film, Wang and O'Bannon are oppositional, following a clumsy train robbery that leaves both men stranded in the desert. On his part, Wang ventures into Indian territory, befriending a tribe of Sioux who reward him with a bride. Due to wearing his traditional, cultural clothing, Wang is called — a la *Dances with Wolves*— the "Man Who Fights in Dress," yet his masculinity remains unquestioned because of his combat skills. As for O'Bannon, he survives the desert and situates himself within the saloon, where he gambles and flirts with women — seemingly his masculine calling in life.

The Wang-O'Bannon connection grows stronger as they live a common destiny: jail time, exchanging fighting skills, being tortured by the villains, and facing the gallows. With each new wrinkle in the plan to retrieve the gold and save the princess, the protagonists must rely upon one another. Throughout their ordeals, they confront the same equal mistreatment from the villains, as they continually work to understand their cultural differences. Their closeness evolves from their mutual discovery of one another and their eventual acceptance of the pronounced, irritating cultural differences. When captured and tortured by the villains, O'Bannon asserts their mutual condition as the two are repeatedly beaten: "We're men! We're not piñatas!" And in the final showdown, Wang and O'Bannon ready their guns — a la *Butch Cassidy and the Sundance Kid—*

before rushing out of a church to face opposing gunfire. Wang says proudly: "We stick together. We are partners!"

Through the combined dialogue and plot situations, the buddyship of the two remains a focus in the film. Despite the historical events that gave evidence of the hostilities between Chinese and Caucasians in the old West, *Shanghai Noon* suggests that interracial conflicts merely needed the Wang-O'Bannon model to assuage tensions. At the end of the film, the two heroes are made the sheriffs of Carson City, Nevada, indicating the willingness of both the law and the system to accept the value of their buddyhood.

The acceptance of the Asian-Caucasian union owes a great deal to the screen persona developed by Jackie Chan. Proclaiming a warmth and vulnerability absent from other tough, aggressive Asian martial arts heroes, Chan evokes an accessible, non-threatening masculinity. As Yvonne Tasker suggests, "Jackie Chan's combination of action with slapstick comedy is quite distinct from the earnest and anxious suffering of the white stars, and from the dominating figure of Bruce Lee. His films are much more at ease with the hectic heroics of their male protagonists, heroics that are at once offered as spectacle and comically undercut."[6] When coupled with Owen Wilson, a white comic star whose slacker-surfer persona resonates with a younger audience, the popularity of the *Shanghai* films is not unexpected.

When the sequel appeared two years later, Wang was still Sheriff, but O'Bannon had traveled back to New York City to invest the gold that he and Wang recovered. And when correspondence arrives from China from Wang's sister, Chon Lin (Fann Wong), that their father has been murdered by an English aristocrat name Rathbone (Aidan Gillen), Wang travels to New York and gathers O'Bannon for a journey to London. Most of the story of *Shanghai Knights* unfolds in London, as both Wang (from the Far East) and O'Bannon (from America) are viewed as outsiders. Unfortunately, the filmmakers decided to integrate anachronistic dialogue and music (pop music from the 1960s and 1970s) and well-known fictional figures and actual people (Sherlock Holmes, Jack the Ripper, Sir Arthur Conan Doyle, Charlie Chaplin) into the storyline, transforming the film into an odd, postmodern experiment. Somewhere beneath the mixing of the *mise en scène*, cinematic tones, and contemporary language, the film returns to the buddy relationship to ground itself in some kind of familiarity. As before, the Wang-O'Bannon duo fight together for what O'Bannon identifies as "friendship, loyalty, honor."

One of the more interesting aspects of the film relates to the sexual attraction shared between O'Bannon and Chon Lin. In their instant lust

Buddies Chon Wang (Jackie Chan, left) and Roy O'Bannon (Owen Wilson) combine their efforts to rescue a princess and a coffer of gold in *Shanghai Noon.*

for one another, the characters spend much of the movie to find a way to develop a romance. At first, Wang defiantly objects, even sharing disparaging words to his sister about O'Bannon. Wang supports both his Chinese and the larger white perspective against interracial romance and sexuality, implying the preference for a purity of lineage. His position illustrates Richard Dyer's cultural observation that "[i]f races are conceptualized as pure ... then miscegenation threatens that purity."[7] Yet by the end, Wang's belief in and respect for his buddy wins over his ethnocentric view, as the door is opened for the relationship to develop after the movie ends. Yet, in connecting back to *The Corruptor*, this area of miscegenation receives a similar, albeit visually different, handling. Both films presented white male partners enamored with Asian women, and despite the verbal protest by Asian men, the sexual and/or romantic connection occurs. The accessibility of women of color to white males appears to be a given fact. Conversely, the Asian male partners in both films have neither the interest seemingly nor the opportunity to be involved with white women.

Moving forward in historical setting to a contemporary caper, *Ocean's Eleven* (2001) was anointed by one popular critic with terms such as "smooth," slick," and "cool"; he felt the film fulfilled the "well established" structure of the genre, including the "scary external shot of the impenetrable targets, the inside information, and voice-over as we see guards going about their work, the plan with split-second timing."[8] The movie revisits the story made popular in a previous generation by the infamous Rat Pack. In this new version, the masterminding comes from the titular character Danny Ocean (George Clooney), a thief just released from prison and out to take money from a Las Vegas casino owner who has also taken his ex-wife. Ocean's mirror image in experienced hustling is Rusty (Brad Pitt), a man who enjoys the thrill of pulling off an impossible heist. These two characters enjoy the most interesting screen moments as they represent a particular kind of male relationship rooted in the "cool pose." The two articulate in shorthand to one another through coded conversations, glares, and minimalized physical movement. They exemplify the attributes of cool identified by scholars Richard Majors and Janet Mancini Billson: "Cool pose is a ritualized form of masculinity that entails behaviors, scripts, physical posturing, impression management, and carefully crafted performances that deliver a single, critical message: pride, strength, and control."[9] In discussing the dimensions of the "cool pose," Majors and Billson apply their theories to black masculinity, but interestingly, in this film, the white masterminds possess those attributes while the three men of color display more verbal and physical expressions of masculinity.

In planning the casino heist, Ocean and Rusty recruit two blacks and one Asian to round out the crew. Frank (Bernie Mac), an American black, is a card dealer who reads and manipulates people; Basher (Don Cheadle), a British black, is an explosives expert; and Yen (Shaobo Qin), an Asian, is a circus contortionist. These three are significant to the completion of the job, and they function with the crew without any discernible friction concerning race. Their risks, preparation, and share in the multi-million-dollar prize are the same as their white comrades, and in the successful completion of the job, their faces glow with accomplishment in a final panning shot of the entire crew in front of the exterior water fountain show of the Vegas casino.

As a part of the con, Frank and fellow crew member Linus (Matt Damon) play the racial angle to divert the casino owner, Terry Benedict (Andy Garcia), from his regular schedule of rounds in the casino. With Linus masquerading as an agent of the Nevada Gaming Commission, Frank accuses him of racism in revealing his criminal past, as both feign a heated and physical scuffle. Busted for dealing blackjack, Frank states angrily: "Black man can't earn a decent wage in this state.... Want me to shine your shoes? Want me to smile at you? You definitely won't let me deal the cards. You might as well call it *white* jack." This racial theater permits the diversion necessary to get Linus inside the locked doors leading to the casino vault.

Basher, speaking with a heavy British accent, displays a wild, animated personality and a style of clothing that matches his fascination with blowing things apart. His racial identity is secondary to his nationality, as his expertise is proven in his technical jargon and his ability to render a blackout along the Vegas strip. With a single-minded pursuit of fulfilling his skills, Basher's obsession with the tools of his trade makes him compulsive. However, his conscious masculinity surfaces in a quick gesture of covering his groin area with one hand, while triggering an electromagnetic device with the other to create the power failure on the Vegas strip.

On his part, Yen's small physical stature and boyish looks give him the most innocent appearance among the men. Out of all the crew, his skill that's contributed to the heist — namely, somersaulting above the bank vault's sensored floors— is the most body-oriented and physically demanding. Ironically, however, his physique offers the most questionable masculine authenticity. With the wiry body of a young girl gymnast and a high feminine inflection in his voice, Yen reifies the conventional masculine toughness of the other men, while cushioning his effeminate qualities with comic relief.

The three men of color remain womanless— as do all the other men, except for Ocean, who reclaims his wife, Tess (Julia Roberts). In this company of men, masculinity is affirmed by the mere courage to attempt the danger-ridden heist. This courage is underscored by Benedict's reputation as a dangerous and ruthless mobster. Prison time serves as the least peril of the heist, since the wrath of Benedict would mean a painful death. As Reuben (Elliot Gould), the financier for the heist, reminds Ocean and Rusty: "With Benedict ... he'll kill you, and then he'll go to work on you.... You gotta be nuts!" Being "nuts" translates into audacity, brassiness, and boldness of manhood that defies the odds and embraces the danger of a life-or-death situation.

In a distinctive contrast, another caper film, *Heist*, appeared in the same year as *Ocean's Eleven*, bearing the appropriate elements of the genre, but rendered in a contrasting tone and style. In heist, the crew is smaller in number, and the connection between the white and black males has more depth and development. Without the connection between Joe Moore (Gene Hackman), a white con artist, and Bobby (Delroy Lindo), a black con artist, the story would lose its coherence. And in this David Mamet film, coherence is a key concern in a script written with numerous plot turns, character contours, and language that's mundane, provocative, profane, and repetitive all at once.

During a jewelry-store robbery that opens the film, Moore's face is caught on video security, and he decides the time is right to retire to a far-

Four caper buddies — Livingston Dell (Eddie Jemison, left), Basher Tarr (Don Cheadle), Saul Bloom (Carl Reiner), and Frank Catton (Bernie Mac) — keep their cool in *Ocean's Eleven*.

away island locale. But Bergman (Danny DeVito), the "fence" for the jewelry heist, attempts to manipulate Joe and his crew into doing one more heist — the "Swiss thing." After various permutations, the job is done as Moore and Bobby survive, going in separate ways with a future of wealth ahead of them. Moore and Bobby are experienced criminals, and both have an insight into the people whom they encounter. Importantly, they have an ability to improvise a situation and keep it under their control. Having a history together professionally has provided the two with an interpersonal understanding, knowing that "trust" in their business is a fragile commodity. Both men distrust Bergman and his crew, formulating their own con within the con to assure an alternate plan if events go wrong. Though both are deadly men, as illustrated in a final shootout with Bergman and his henchmen, neither Moore nor Bobby leans on violent, impulsive behavior as the first choice.

Their confidence and calm-under-stress demeanors become tested when Bergman insists that his nephew, Jimmy Silk (Sam Rockwell), joins in on the "Swiss thing." Cocky, rash, and trigger-happy, Silk resents Moore's and Bobby's authoritative attitudes; in particular, Silk measures the opportunity to take away Moore's younger wife, Fran (Rebecca Pidgeon). Moore and Bobby take Silk into the plan but never allow him inside their relationship. Their quick read of his volatile personality proves correct when they masquerade as county surveyors on the highway. As highway patrolmen stop to question Moore and Bobby's roadside activity, the two improvise a scenario that avoids a possible confrontation. Looking on from a nearby parked car with Pincus (Ricky Jay), another crew member, Silk draws his gun, ready to shoot the patrolmen. Misunderstanding Moore's improvised tirade, Silk questions Moore's rambling until Pincus reassures him that Moore's in control: "My motherfucker's so cool that when he goes to bed, sheep count him."

After the "Swiss thing," Moore and Bobby work together, melting down the stolen gold from the Swiss airliner and pouring it into molds that will allow Moore to complete one last con that alludes to an anticipated double-cross. Moore trusts Bobby completely to pull him in on the plan. At the end, Moore and Bobby comprehend that their partnership is over. With Moore's face exposed in the earlier jewel heist, he plans to buy reconstructive surgery to attain a new look. Sitting together at a diner, they don't mention the obvious parting of the ways, but they, in their cool, manly dispositions, share a final moment of laughter.

> Bobby: "Don't let him [plastic surgeon] put you all the way under. I know a cat ... went to get his face fixed ... woke up ... [with] a pair of tits."
> Moore: "That's ... bad ... no question."
> Bobby: "Nahhh, he landed back on the inside and never had to want for cigarettes."

These parting moments between the two corroborate Peter Lyman's viewpoints about the significance of joking among males. He writes, "[T]he emotional structure of the male bond is built upon a joking relationship that 'negotiates' the tension men feel about their relationship with each other."[10] Using their laughter as a signal to leave, Bobby passes a note to Moore indicating where his cut of the money should be wired — one final indication of trust that his buddy will send his share. Then Bobby leaves in a car with a black woman, who is presumably, from their brief dialogue, his wife.

Just as *Heist* is not the typical caper story with conventional dialogue, the bond between Moore and Bobby contains its singular qualities. The two males obviously know one another much better than the audience ever will, as they maneuver their world in a calculated manner, recognizing in one another a kindred mind and someone to respect and trust.

In a completely different genre, the war film *Windtalkers* (2002) looks at a distinct occurrence during World War II — the manner in which Indians participated as key personnel in the Pacific battles. The fact that the filmmakers chose to explore this event with the interracial buddy pattern emerges as both the film's strength and weakness.

With the battle scenes from the earlier *Saving Private Ryan* (1998),

Keeping control during a job, Pincus (Ricky Jay, left), Joe Moore (Gene Hackman), and Bobby (Delroy Lindo) survey the streets in *Heist*.

directed by Steven Spielberg, establishing a new standard for visualizing combat, *Windtalkers* duplicated the graphic gore. The movie's director, John Woo, captured the violent, chaotic loss of life, sanity, and body parts with an unflinching lens. The story roots itself in the experiences of Joe Enders (Nicolas Cage), a white Marine whose traumatic ordeal in a 1943 battle in the Solomon Islands leaves him physically and emotionally damaged, carrying the guilt of losing 15 fellow soldiers due to following orders. At the same time, as a method for circumventing the enemy's ability to break American communication signals, the military trains Navajo Indians to use their native language to send radio codes. Benny Yahzee (Adam Beach), a reservation Navajo with a wife and son, volunteers for the special training, later explaining to Enders: "It's my war, too, sergeant. I'm fighting for my country, for my land, and for my people." Yahzee's statement opens up one of the most fundamental questions of the film: Why does he feel this way about the war? However, the movie never gets deep into that political, psychological realm of the character, nor the reasons why Yahzee proudly announces that he named his son "George Washington." Instead, the growing union between Yahzee and Enders assumes a more prominent importance as the movie develops. Yahzee — a gentle, reflective man — wants to become a history professor in the future, while Enders — a bitter, compulsive loner — hopes for death to end a life haunted by his past actions.

Enders, a good marine, accepts his orders to protect Yahzee, or if need be, the additional order to kill him to prevent his capture and interrogation by the enemy. The latter order causes Enders to remain distant and stoic towards Yahzee's efforts to extend friendship. Additionally, when Yahzee hesitates to kill a Japanese soldier, Enders completes the job mechanically. Yahzee's respect for human life, even on the battlefield, conflicts with Enders's maniacal and heartless killing. However, as Enders observes Yahzee's cultural pride and skillful handling of racist statements from a white soldier named Chick (Noah Emmerich), Enders finds it difficult to resist opening up to Yahzee as a person rather than viewing him as a special assignment. Enders's admiration for Yahzee increases as the latter utilizes a racist comment made about Indians and Japanese looking the same. When pinned down between the enemy and friendly fire, Yahzee volunteers to put on the enemy's uniform and to walk into their camp to obtain a radio; Enders goes with him to masquerade as a prisoner of war. In the aftermath, a colonel arrives to camp and presents the Silver Star medal of valor to Enders, but Enders insists that Yahzee be recognized as well:

> Colonel: "Oh, the Indian."
> Enders: "Begging the colonel's pardon ... he's a Navajo, of the Bitter
> Water people, born from the Towering House Clan."

Here, Enders repeats the prideful statement that Yahzee made earlier in response to stereotypical quips from Chick. By doing so, Enders substantiates Yahzee's integrity as a Navajo and a soldier, dismissing the pejorative connotations of "Indian."

Later, while sipping rice wine together, Enders confesses the guilt to Yahzee for receiving his previous medal following the Solomon Islands trauma. When Enders passes out, Yahzee performs a ceremonial chant to protect Enders from harm. Enders and Yahzee slowly attain a common ground: talking of their mutual Catholic backgrounds, of Yahzee's son, of Enders's possible visitation to Arizona, and of Enders's Italian background. Soon, they relate as men, exchanging their insecurities and assorted memories.

Enders and Yahzee remain men also in their normalized relationships with the opposite sex. Yahzee's heterosexual drive is accounted for through his wife and son, while Enders's sexuality is connected casually to a veterans hospital nurse named Rita (Frances O'Connor), who cares for Enders and who writes affectionate letters that go unanswered. Abruptly, their peaceful connection breaks down after a battle in a small village where Enders kills another Navajo code-talker, Charlie Whitehorse (Roger Wyllie), who's being taken prisoner by the enemy.

As a parallel duo, Charlie Whitehorse and Sergeant Anderson (Christian Slater) are assigned to the same recon unit as the Enders-Yahzee duo. However, from the beginning Anderson extends himself to Whitehorse as a fellow soldier, questioning the secret order that he and Enders received. Anderson tells Enders: "We came here to kill Japs, not Marines." The Anderson-Whitehorse connection gains closeness during those short moments of rest as the two men play their harmonica and flute, respectively, blending their instruments in a metaphorical blending of their different cultures.

Despite the ensuing rift in the Enders-Yahzee buddyship, the two reclaim their comradeship during a final battle. Fighting the enemy side by side, both are wounded, but carrying Yahzee on his back, Enders commits one last act of bravery to save his friend. Back home with his wife and son on the reservation, Yahzee shows Enders's dog tags and instructs his son: "If you ever tell a story about him, George, say that he was my friend."

Yahzee claims ownership of Enders, immortalizing his white buddy's heroism by placing him into the Navajo storytelling tradition. The film constructs the Enders-Yahzee buddyship as a meeting of two brave men who find additional courage and meaning by their relationship with one another. Here, the interracial buddy motif confirms the power of male bonding to overcome racism and to underscore American valor.

Unfortunately, valor eluded consideration in the action-comedy *Showtime* (2002), which teamed up characters portrayed by Robert DeNiro and Eddie Murphy. This kind of action-comedy is typical fare for Murphy, but for DeNiro, his preferred roles appear to be more dramatic and edgier. Although one film historian writes that "DeNiro is famous for his rigorous preparations ... researching his roles exhaustively ... [preferring] to bury himself in a role,"[11] *Showtime* is the kind of film that can bury even a seasoned actor in mediocrity. Set in contemporary Los Angeles, this comedy attempts to lightheartedly critique the very buddy paradigm that it winds up embodying. The result is a movie that contains comedic moments that appear in abrupt and extreme tones when compared with its dramatic-action scenes.

A divorced loner, undercover detective Mitch Preston (DeNiro) is forced by his captain to participate in a reality television show by joining up with Trey Sellars (Murphy), an officer who aspires to be both a detective and an actor. Serious and impatient, Preston endures having his professional and personal life mutated by Sellars and Chase Renzi (Rene Russo), the fast-talking producer of the reality program.

The Preston-Sellars pairing brings diametrically opposed personalities into a partnering situation that remains tense throughout most of the film. Preston bristles at Sellars's camera-conscious police work that aims for the melodramatic, as he dismisses Sellars's claim to be a "real cop." It's not until the physical confrontation with a mob boss, Vargas (Pedro Damian), that Preston begins to gain respect for Sellars. As the Preston-Sellars duo fight, punch for punch, with the villains, Sellars earns a different status by displaying his toughness and showing his reliability. As Preston informs Sellars about partnering: "When we're out there on the job, you're the only person in the world that I can depend on ... just you." With a conservative approach to his work, and dealing with a divorce in his personal life, Preston abhors the media touches that try to modify who he is. In particular, he resists the "bonding" that Sellars offers to do for the many hidden cameras and bemoans the interior redecorating, including a dog, that Chase suggests is appropriate for "male buddies."

Despite his love for the cameras, Sellars shows his aggressively masculine side during a chase scene with the Vargas gang, ending with Sellars saving Preston's life from an exploding vehicle crash. Then, afterwards, as the captain rescinds the reality taping due to the destructive chase, Preston learns that Sellars defended him and took responsibility for the pubic damage. In his stoic, indirect male fashion, Preston phones Sellars to offer to help him pass his detective exam.

By this juncture, the Preston-Sellars duo have gelled, allowing them to mount one last stand against Vargas when he kidnaps Chase. As the duo hurry to rescue the girl, they wind up hanging, handcuffed together, from a high-rise office building. The final shot of the two dangling on a

precipice, chained together, functions as a visual metaphor for their inde-
structible union.

In an odd shaping of the story, Preston's personal life gets screen time
in an effort to create verbal humor and sight gags, while the personal life
of Sellars, the single buddy, remains vague. Living alone in his male-
decorated apartment, Preston has created a pottery shop, where he spins
disfigured items as part of his divorce therapy. The alleged "softness" of
working with pottery finds balance in Preston's rumpled appearance and
his unyielding grumpiness. However, Sellars's personal life surfaces only
in his efforts to audition for roles when off duty, or dropping in at Preston's apartment to talk and "bond." Preston doesn't have a romantic relationship or hobby or passion in his life; consequently, his new Corvette
functions as the symbol of his libido and passion.

The element that keeps this buddyship authentic is that their relationship serves as a prime factor in the story's plot. As the reality show's producer, Chase continually makes decisions based upon well-known buddy
films and television cop shows. In the sequences that work best as parody,
actor William Shatner portrays himself, a veteran from the *T.J. Hooker* television series. As a hired consultant to the reality show, he tries to coach
the behavior and mannerisms expected of television cops, i.e., real men.
His techniques for delivering tough lines, raising eyebrows, jumping onto
car hoods, and breaking through doors connect directly to the conventional
notions of buddy cops working together. In essence, his character punctuates those masculine elements—the fictions—created and maintained
by the media, even as the audience reciprocates its endorsement. Those
dissecting moments in the film are both clever and entertaining, but unfortunately too few to make *Showtime* a memorable commentary on masculinity in the media and the interracial buddy scenario.

In yet another buddy vehicle, Eddie Murphy appears again in the
same year in *I Spy* (2002). Resembling the original television series only
in its title, foreign settings, and names of lead characters, this big-screen
version boasts of high-tech gadgets and a ludicrous story. Special Agent
Alex Scott (Owen Wilson)—a whining white operative with limited
skills—teams up with Kelly Robinson (Murphy)—an egotistical, arrogant
black boxing champ—to locate a stealth jet with a cloaking device that
makes it invisible. The interracial buddy pair begin their mission with
opposing interests and loyalties. For Scott, his efforts focus on completing the assignment and seducing fellow agent Rachel Wright (Famke
Janssen), while Robinson focuses only upon his ego as he refers to himself in the third person throughout the film.

In an interesting set-up at the beginning, Robinson, the black man,

In the action-comedy *Showtime*, reluctant buddies Mitch Preston (Robert DeNiro, left) and Trey Sellars (Eddie Murphy) confront gun-running villains.

possesses more power through his celebrity status than Scott does through his agent status. In particular, Robinson's achievements as a black professional athlete elevate his significance in the public arena. Cultural critic Todd Boyd perceives that anointed position as "the way in which African American males, through sports, can create a space of resistance and free expression that announces a relative notion of empowerment."[12] This significance is illustrated when Robinson receives a personal phone call from the president of the United States, and their audible dialogue suggests that the latter, in a Bill Clinton-esque vocal style, speaks ebonics and asks Robinson to work the mission as a personal favor. Robinson, sitting among his entourage of black male bodyguards and beautiful women, brags about his White House connection and his importance to the country. In contrast, Scott suffers the indignity of being shackled with secondhand, inferior spy equipment and doubts about his skills from the staff and leaders of the Bureau of National Security.

The ensuing clash between Robinson and Scott revolves around each man's efforts to demonstrate who has charge of the mission. Robinson's loud-mouthed, high-decibel approach seems to win out over Scott's manipulative, paternalistic style at first. However, Scott exploits Robinson's masked fear during the jet ride to Budapest, and when on the ground through a fake abduction and interrogation. Pretending to be a sex-crazed boxing fan, Rachel lures Robinson into a mock situation, where she and several masked men threaten to castrate Robinson if he doesn't reveal information about the mission and his associates. Robinson pleads, "Please don't cut off Kelly Robinson's penis," before he begins to describe Scott in detail for his captors. Played for laughs, the scene follows previous sexually related boastings by Robinson, indicating that "perfume is for ladies and sissies" and that he plans to "wax that [Rachel's] ass" in his proficiency as a lover. In the mock interrogation, he's reduced to a babbling "sissy" until Scott breaks into the room to rescue him. Finally confessing the abduction as a test, Scott has now gained the power by demonstrating he has the ultimate control and knows how to destroy Robinson's bravado.

In another notable shaping of characters, the two male protagonists are given a distinction by race via their language and attitudes. Scott views Robinson as a "born jerk," and Robinson refers to Scott as a "blond-ass surfer boy" during an initial meeting. But as the film progresses, Robinson's ethnicity remains underscored through his own references to race *and* through his use of profanity. Scott, on his part, doesn't articulate the racial distinction, nor does he deliver profane language in the machine-gun fashion of Robinson. As an extension of the racial angle, Robinson's extensive sexual experience is articulated through his bragging and his assemblage of doting women in various scenes. Then, in one sequence, while using technology that allows Robinson and Scott to communicate aurally and visually simultaneously, the former coaches the latter in seducing Rachel. Taking the lyrics from Marvin Gaye's "Sexual Healing," Scott repeats the words dictated by Robinson, allowing Robinson and the audience to get a voyeuristic peek at Rachel in her panties and top.

At the same time, another male character of color, Carlos (Gary Cole), serves as a person of envy for Scott. Carlos reigns as the spy supreme *and* as the lover who makes women swoon. As film historian Clara E. Rodriguez acknowledges, "[S]tereotypes such as the Latin lover ... have persisted throughout all eras in film.... Moreover, the characters were usually morally or esthetically limited."[13] Carlos is the "cool," arrogant Latino lover whose accent, black leather clothing, silky hair, and Ferrari symbolize the proficiency in work and in bed that Scott desires. Sandwiched between the two men of color, Scott's whiteness assumes an accentuated morality (when compared with Robinson) and an unappreciated expertise (when compared with Carlos). Though subtly rendered, the effect is that the white male character possesses qualities that make him more likable and admirable than the two males of color with whom he interacts.

The crazed buddyship between pro boxer Kelly Robinson (Eddie Murphy) and secret agent Alex Scott (Owen Wilson) survives devious agents and saboteurs in *I Spy*.

In an appropriate number of chase scenes, explosions, and gun battles, the Robinson-Scott duo comprehend their common dilemmas. Robinson's frantic chatter and excited behavior during dangerous predicaments are juxtaposed with Scott's ululant but decisive action. As Scott creates escape routes and analyzes problems, Robinson utters masculine-driven statements, such as, "Kelly Robinson doesn't get on the back of the scooter like some bitch."

I Spy never quite achieves credibility as an action or comedic film, as it falls short of being fresh in shaping either genre. As an interracial buddy film, it contains the required elements of the paradigm, including a scene in a sewer where the Robinson-Scott buddies confess their personal backgrounds and weaknesses, but overall the dialogue and the characters remain flat and forgettable. In a more successful manner, in the caper film *The Italian Job* (2003), the dialogue and characters display contours that make the relationships and the movie an engaging experience. Similar to the remake of *Ocean's Eleven* released two years earlier, *The Italian Job* rallies a collection of young, hip con people in a fast-paced, slick story.

In Venice, Italy, a team of specialists carries out an elaborate theft of a guarded vault of gold — a scheme masterminded by Charlie Croker (Mark Wahlberg), the young protégé of the senior thief, John Bridger (Donald Sutherland). When the team is left for dead and Bridger is killed by Steve (Edward Norton), a deceitful, subversive crew member, Charlie leads the team to reclaim the gold and to get revenge. One year later, adding Stella Bridger (Charlize Theron), John's daughter, to the plan, the team initiates and gains its revenge when it locates Steve in Los Angeles.

Although Charlie had been crowned the mastermind in Venice by the elder Bridger, the unfolding plan in Los Angeles displays an equality of the crew, which is underscored by quick flashbacks about each member as the team is reassembled. The character named Left Ear (Mos Def), the team's one black member, is the demolition and explosives expert. And though Left Ear displays the same expertise as Basher, the black specialist in *Ocean's Eleven*, the similarities end there. Left Ear, an inner-city kid, began experimenting with explosives in school, when one prank caused him to lose hearing in his right ear. Quiet and methodical, Left Ear first appears in Venice chatting about his interest in DaVinci, architecture, and poetry. Then, following the successful heist, he announces that he'll be using his share of the gold to buy a dream house in the south of Spain that has a "library full of first editions, a room for my shoes." Left Ear, though as young as his buddies, possesses a mature outlook about his life, even as he shows a wide-eyed fascination about his work. When he and Charlie set explosives beneath Hollywood Boulevard to target an armored truck, Left Ear hesitates, as though in worship, before inserting the detonator. Left Ear reveres the power of the bombs and the deadly consequences of mishandling them. Knowing that the charges could erupt at any time, Left Ear tells Charlie, "I love you, man." And though played for humor, the

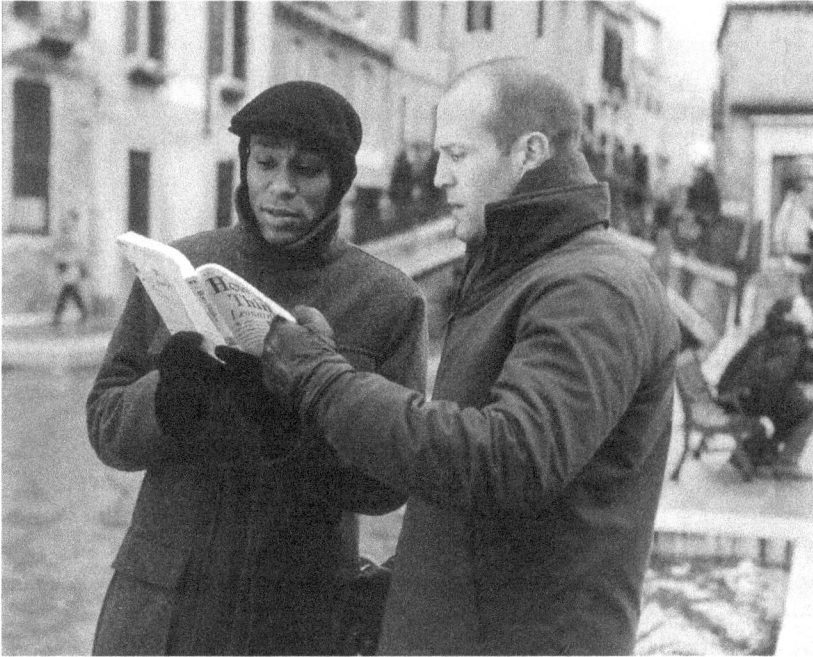

On the streets of Venice in *The Italian Job*, two heist buddies — Left Ear (Mos Def, left) and Handsome Rob (Jason Statham) share a reflective second with a book.

scene shows that Charlie respects Left Ear's expertise and comprehends the danger as well, as he responds, "I love you, too."

Resourceful and inventive, Left Ear works smoothly as well with his other white buddies— Lyle (Seth Green), the computer genius, and Handsome Rob (Jason Statham), the wheel man. Their shared screen moments display both amiability and a professional alliance. In that bond, the realization about their common victory or their common death is a palpable factor. They know that they can trust the others, and their lengthy relationship over the year emphasizes a pact that goes beyond money and individual wealth. *The Italian Job* tackles the objectives important to the genre, but in the pursuit of fulfilling the caper demands, the bond among the crew members exhibits both a personal and professional interlinking.

The Echo Patterns of the Early Millennium

The first three years of the millennium witnessed the continued use of interracial male characters interacting in varying semblances of buddyship. As in earlier decades, some films merely developed partial elements of the authentic interracial buddy pattern to market a film, to provide plot points, or to supply a dramatic denouement. A number of films, such as *Under Suspicion* (2000), *Changing Lanes* (2002), *Training Day* (2002), *The Sum of All Fears* (2002), *John Q* (2003), *Bulletproof Monk* (2003), *S.W.A.T.* (2003), *Basic* (2003), and *Out of Time* (2003) reflected male interaction across racial lines where characters were inextricably connected and/or reliant upon one another. However, in those movies, the interracial buddy scenario was not the substantial focus of the story. During those years, three films in particular illustrate the attributes of the interracial buddy pattern that served portions of the film rather than the complete story.

Somewhere between the future and confusion, *Rollerball* (2002) offers up a tepid commentary on the connection between media ratings and greed. In its stylistic vision of a professional extreme sport that merges rollerskating, motorcycle racing, and rugby, the story does integrate the friendship between Jonathan Cross (Chris Klein), the white athletic star of the sport, and Marcus Ridley (LL Cool J), the black star of the same sport. Basically, Ridley saves Cross from the police and offers his daredevil friend the opportunity to join the rollerball league, organized and played in Russian countries, to make big money and glory.

From the dialogue, Cross and Ridley have known one another since high school, and once together on the same professional team they're inseparable publicly. Cross has an on-screen romance with a woman athlete named Aurora (Rebecca Romijn-Stamos), while Ridley's wife and kids are discussed but remain off-screen. And though Ridley has been playing in the league longer than Cross, somehow the latter enters the league and in four months becomes the premier player. Cross, consequently, remains the focus character of the film, and his link to Ridley receives attention when the protagonist needs counseling from his black friend and when the two plan to secretly escape Russia to avoid the deliberate violence inserted into the games by sadistic league owner Petrovich (Jean Reno).

Rollerball presents a black-white friendship of plot convenience, one that's set up to enhance the white protagonist. Even at the end, when trapped at the border, Cross encourages Ridley to go ahead without him in order to make a motorcycle jump across the border's bridge that can only be done with one rider. The gesture by the white protagonist rings with noble sacrifice, but when Ridley is killed, his death provides the additional emotional fuel for Cross's vengeance.

Similar to *Pure Luck* (1991), *National Security* (2003) is one of those films that's painful to watch. It invests so much energy and screen time in being silly that a cogent story with well-defined characters never develops. The relationship between Earl Montgomery (Martin Lawrence), a black want-to-be cop, and Hank Rafferty (Steve Zahn), a white ex-cop, runs on animosity and discord until the final act of the story. Montgomery, kicked out of the police training program, and Rafferty, doing six months of jail time after being convicted of police brutality and assault against Montgomery, eventually find themselves working as security guards who stumble onto the same crime. In those closing sequences, while fighting a life-or-death struggle against a villainous gang, Montgomery and Rafferty find a sustained amiability.

This film typifies the way in which marketing the interracial buddy formula serves as a ploy to reach a wide crossover audience. The trailers for the film suggested the traditional buddy cop story filled with laughs and action, but instead the story exploited racial profiling, Afrocentrism, interracial romance, and community action. Montgomery whines about his mistreatment due to his black identity, while Rafferty's dilemmas due to his white identity are the fodder for alleged jokes. The eventual buddyship that is suggested appears to be more of a convenience to end the film, rather than any situations and character development on the screen.

In a more memorable vehicle, *Tears of the Sun* (2003) explored the pain and gritty reality of a country torn apart by rebellion and ethnic cleansing. In a Nigerian jungle, several white American nationals must be evacuated, and Lieutenant A. K. Waters (Bruce Willis) leads his Navy Seals squad of seven, including two blacks, to carry out the mission. Battling the strong-willed Dr. Lena Hendricks (Monica Belluci), a white woman committed to the black Africans in her care, Waters has to choose between following orders and following his conscience. Waters and his men, particularly Zee (Eamonn Walker), a stern black soldier, understand the direct orders to gather the whites, but they are fully aware that the black indigenous people will be slaughtered if left behind. Unable to airlift the people, Waters and his men must hike some 28 civilians to the contiguous Cameroon border while being chased by rebel troops.

Although Waters is clearly in command as the squad follows orders, he treats the men equally when breaking the orders and the rules of engagement about interfering with domestic activities. He confesses to his men: "I broke my own rule. I started to give a fuck." And though his men have mixed emotions about deviating from their mission, they all begin to see the black indigenous people as human beings who need their help. In particular, after fighting guerrillas who are slaughtering a village of unarmed people from a different ethnic group, Zee confesses to Waters: "Those Africans are my people, too. For all the years that we've been told to stand down and to stand by, you're doing the right thing."

Their effort to help becomes complicated as one of the black refugees, Arthur Azuka (Sammi Rotibi), turns out to be the only survivor of the executed royal family. In the aftermath of a bloody battle, Arthur falls apart emotionally. In the quintessential masculine statement by Waters, he tells Arthur: "Now cowboy the fuck up!" Waters speaks both as an American and as a white male to the black African male. The image of the "cowboy" adhered to the male-oriented profanity asserts the ultimate masculine symbol of toughness, leadership, and courage. And though the rugged language suits an experienced combat soldier attempting to motivate a civilian, the fact that a white male character barks the line to a black male character also resonates with perhaps an unintended, but visible, meaning. The white male must instruct the black male on how to behave and assume the attitude of being a man.

However, that racially charged scene does not represent the dominant implications of the film that underscore the human thread that connects despite racial differences. In a final burst for the freedom of the refugee village at the Cameroon border, several soldiers and black indigenous people are killed. And as Waters and Zee survive, leaning upon one another, the impact of the interracial dependence and bonding is reinforced.

*   *   *

Both the authentic interracial buddy films and the echo films during the past few years testify to the continuing appeal of the formula to filmmakers and to audiences. Collectively, the cinematic partnerships between men easily simplify the critical questions and concerns that face men in American society. Additionally, too often the screen depictions of male harmony across racial and cultural chasms deliberately avoid the particular dynamics encountered by men of color. In short, the interracial buddy scenario testifies to the ideal at the expense of the real; the paradigm fosters the status quo while alluding to the radical. In a trickster fashion, those cinematic images can perform a cultural and political sleight-of-hand that exploits stereotypes, myths, and conjectures. For better or worse, the interracial buddy riff will educate audiences one way or the other. But taken at its best, the interracial buddy pattern forces viewers to be cognizant of — and hopefully critical thinkers about — the crucial interplay between visual messages and the manner in which viewers interpret, acquire, and nurture perspectives about masculinity and racial interactions.

Notes

The abbreviation MHL/MPA indicates materials researched
in the Archival Files, Margaret Herrick Library, The
Motion Picture Academy, Beverly Hills, California.

Introduction

1. Deborah Blum, "The Gender Blur: Where Does Biology End and Society Take Over?" in *Signs of Life in the USA: Readings on Popular Culture for Writers*, 3rd edition, edited by Sonia Maasik and Jack Solomon (Boston: Bedford Books, 2000), p. 455.

2. Michael Kimmel, *The Gendered Society*, 2nd edition (New York: Oxford University Press, 2004), p. 3.

3. Cooper Thompson, "A New Visions of Masculinity," in *Race, Class, and Gender in the United States*, 5th edition, edited by Paula S. Rothenberg (New York: Worth Publishers, 2001), p. 631.

4. Lee Clark Mitchell, *Westerns: Making the Man in Fiction and Film* (Chicago: The University of Chicago Press, 1996), p. 154.

5. Carmen Vazquez, "Appearances," in *Rereading America*, 5th edition, edited by Gary Colombo, Bonnie Lisle, and Robert Cullen (Boston: Bedford Books, 2001), p. 498.

6. W. E. B. DuBois, *The Souls of Black Folks*, edited by Henry Louis Gates, Jr., and Terri Hume Oliver (New York: Norton, 1999), p. 5.

7. Stuart Hall, "What Is the 'Black' in Black Popular Culture?" in *The Black Studies Reader*, edited by Jacqueline Bobo, Cynthia Hudley, and Claudine Michel (New York: Routledge, 2004), p. 256.

8. Steve Neale, *Genre and Hollywood* (London: Routledge, 2000), p. 10.

9. Wes D. Gehring, editor, *Handbook of American Film Genres* (Westport, Connecticut: Greenwood Press, 1988), pp. 1–2.

10. Quoted in Neale, p. 12.

11. Jeanine Basinger, *American Cinema: One Hundred Years of Filmmaking* (New York: Rizzoli Int'l Publications, 1994), p. 108.

12. S. Craig Watkins, "Ghetto Reelness: Hollywood Film Production, Black Popular Culture and the Ghetto Action Film Cycle," in *Genre and Contemporary Hollywood*, edited by Steve Neale (London: British Film Institute, 2002), p. 243.

13. Stuart M. Kaminsky, *American Film Genre: Approaches to a Critical Theory of Popular Film* (New York: Dell, 1977), p. 18.

14. Robert A. Strikwerda and Larry May, "Male Friendship and Intimacy," in *Rethink-*

ing Masculinity: Philosophical Explorations in Light of Feminism, 2nd edition, edited by Larry May, Robert A. Strikwerda, and Patrick D. Hopkins (Lanham, Maryland: Rowman & Littlefield, 1996), pp. 81–83.

Chapter One

1. John Belton, *American Cinema/American Culture* (New York: McGraw-Hill, 1992) pp. 14–15.
2. Ed Guerrero, *Framing Blackness: The African American Image in Film* (Philadelphia: Temple University Press, 1993), p.19.
3. Donald Bogle, *Toms, Coons, Mulattoes, Mammies, and Bucks: An Interpretive History of Blacks in American Films* (New York: Continuum, 1990), p. 36.
4. *Ibid.*, p. 39.
5. *Ibid.*, p. 42.
6. "David Harum," *Variety* (March 6, 1934).
7. "Fox's 'David Harum' a 'Dud,'" *Hollywood Reporter* (February 15, 1934), MHL/MPA.
8. Beverly Hills, "Harum, Scare 'Em, Hepburn," *Liberty*, MHL/MPA.
9. "David Priest," *Variety* (October 16, 1934).
10. John Baxter, "John Ford," *The St. James Film Directors Encyclopedia*, edited by Andrew Sarris (Detroit: Visible Ink Press, 1998), p. 174.
11. P. S. Harrison, editor, "'Steamboat Round the Bend' with Will Rogers," *Harrison Reports* (September 7, 1935), p. 142.
12. *Buck Benny Rides Again*, Press Booklet, Paramount Pictures, MHL/MPA.
13. *Ibid.*
14. Michael Kimmel, *Manhood in America: A Cultural History* (New York: The Free Press, 1996), p. 233.
15. Mark A. Reid, *Redefining Black Film* (Berkeley: University of California Press, 1993), p. 13.
16. P. S. Harrison, editor, "Home of the Brave," *Harrison's Reports* (May 7, 1949), p.74.
17. Bosley Crowther, "Home of the Brave," *The New York Times Film Reviews* (May 13, 1949), 29:1.

Chapter Two

1. Lerone Bennett, Jr., *Before The Mayflower: A History of Black America*, 6th edition, (New York: Penguin Books, 1988), p. 365.
2. Robert Kolker, *Film, Form, and Culture* (New York: McGraw-Hill, 2002), p. 82.
3. Harry M. Benshoff and Sean Griffin, *America on Film: Representing Race, Class, Gender, and Sexuality at the Movies* (Malden, Massachusetts: Blackwell Publishing, 2004), p.104.
4. *Ibid.*, p. 105.
5. Sidney Poitier, *The Measure of a Man* (San Francisco: HarperCollins, 2000), pp. 100–101.
6. Bennett, p. 546.
7. Mark A. Reid, *Redefining Black Film* (Berkeley: University of California Press, 1993), p. 78.
8. Ed Guerrero, *Framing Blackness: The African American Image in Film* (Philadelphia: Temple University Press, 1993), pp. 72–73.
9. Hernan Vera and Andrew M. Gordon, *Screen Saviors: Hollywood Fictions of Whiteness* (Lanham, Maryland: Rowman & Littlefield, 2003), p. 160.
10. Benshoff and Griffin, p. 102.
11. This translation was given in the notes of the DVD special features that accompany *The Lone Ranger and the Lost City of Gold*. The DVD packet is dated 2001.

12. Leslie Halliwell, *Halliwell's Film Guide*, 7th edition (New York: Harper and Row, 1989), p. 610.
13. Michael Kimmel, *Manhood in America* (New York: The Free Press, 1997), p. 252.
14. Benshoff and Griffin, p. 102.
15. James Robert Parish and George H. Hill, *Black Action Films* (Jefferson, North Carolina: McFarland, 1989), p. 246.
16. *Ibid.*, p. 247.
17. Donald Bogle, *Toms, Coons, Mulattoes, Mammies, and Bucks* (New York: Continuum, 1990), p. 215.
18. Parish and Hill, p. 227.
19. Robert Bly, "What Men Really Want," in *To Be a Man*, edited by Keith Thompson (Los Angeles: Tarcher, 1991), p. 17.

Chapter Three

1. Gary Nash, editor, *The American People: Creating a New Nation and a Society*, Volume II, 4th edition (New York: Longman, 1998) pp. 1018–1066.
2. David A. Cook, *Lost Illusions: American Cinema in the Shadow of Watergate and Vietnam, 1970–1979*, Volume 9, in The History of the American Cinema Series (New York: Charles Scribner's Sons, 2000), pp. 26–27.
3. David Denby, "Movies Americana," *The Atlantic*, March 1971, p. 106.
4. Stanley Kaufmann, "Arts and Lives," *The New Republic*, September 20, 1977, p. 24.
5. Paul Zimmerman, "Kung Foolish," *Newsweek*, April 7, 1975, p. 82.
6. Pauline Kael, "The Current Cinema," *The New Yorker*, January 17, 1977, pp. 98–99.
7. Peter Biskind, *Easy Rider, Raging Bulls* (New York: Touchstone, 1999), p. 348.
8. *Ibid.*, p. 349.
9. Al Auster and Leonard Quart, "The Working Class Goes to Hollywood: 'F.I.S.T.' and 'Blue Collar,'" *Cineaste*, Fall 1978, Volume IX, Number 1, p. 6.
10. *Ibid.*, pp. 6–7.
11. Tim Miller, "Suck, Spit, Chew, Swallow: A Performative Exploration of Men's Bodies," in *Masculinity: Bodies, Movies, Culture*, edited by Peter Lehman (New York: Routledge, 2001), p. 282.
12. Ruth L. Hirayama, "Rocky II," in *Magill's Survey of Cinema*, Second Series, Volume 5, edited by Frank N. Magill (Englewood Cliffs, New Jersey: Salem Press, 1981), p. 2043.
13. Donald Bogle, *Toms, Coons, Mulattoes, Mammies, and Bucks* (New York: Continuum, 1990), pp. 258–259.

Chapter Four

1. John Belton, *American Cinema/American Culture* (New York: McGraw–Hill, 1994), p. 316.
2. *Ibid.*
3. Ed Guerrero, *Framing Blackness: The African American Image in Film* (Philadelphia: Temple University, 1993), p. 128.
4. *Ibid.*
5. Melvin Donalson, *Black Directors in Hollywood* (Austin: The University of Texas Press, 2003), p. 40.
6. *Ibid.*
7. Ed Guerrero, "The Black Image in Protective Custody: Hollywood's Biracial Buddy Films of the Eighties," in *Black American Cinema*, edited by Manthia Diawara (New York: Routledge, 1993), p. 243.
8. *Ibid.*
9. Herman Beavers, "The Cool Pose: Intersectionality, Masculinity, and Quiescence in

the Comedy and Films of Richard Pryor and Eddie Murphy," in *Race and the Subject of Masculinities*, edited by Harry Stecopoulos and Michael Uebel (Durham, North Carolina: Duke University Press, 1997), p. 271.

10. "The Empire Strikes Back," Salon.com (May 13, 1999).

11. Donald Bogle, *Toms, Coons, Mulattoes, Mammies, and Bucks* (New York: Continuum, 1990), p. 271.

12. Christopher Null, "Police Academy," FilmCritic.com (August 5, 2004).

13. *Ibid.*

14. John Ulmer, "Police Academy," www.movie-vault.com (August 5, 2004).

15. Barbara Bate and Judy Bowker, *Communication and the Sexes*, 2nd edition (Prospect Heights, Illinois: Waveland Press, 1997), p. 167.

16. Roger Ebert, "Lethal Weapon," *Chicago Sun-Times* (March 6, 1987), www.suntimes.com.

17. Robyn Wiegman, "Bonds of (in)Difference," in *The Masculinity Studies Reader*, edited by Rachel Adams and David Savran (Malden, Massachusetts: Blackwell, 2002), p. 217.

18. Sharon Willis, *High Contrast: Race and Gender in Contemporary Hollywood Film* (Durham, North Carolina: Duke University Press, 1997), p. 36.

19. Hernan Vera and Andrew M. Gordon, *Screen Saviors: Hollywood Fictions of Whiteness* (Lanham, Maryland: Rowman & Littlefield, 2003), p. 158.

20. *Ibid.*, p. 7.

21. Cynthia J. Fuchs, "The Buddy Politic," in *Screening the Male: Explorations of Masculinities in Hollywood Cinema*, edited by Steven Cohan and Ina Rae Hark (New York: Routledge, 1993), p. 197.

22. Brandon Curtis, "Hamburger Hill," *Washington Post* (May 30, 2002).

23. *Ibid.*

24. Rita Kempley, "Bat 21," *Washington Post* (October 21, 1988).

25. *Ibid.*

26. Rolbert Kolker, *Film, Form, and Culture*, 2nd edition, (New York: McGraw-Hill, 2002), p. 147.

Chapter Five

1. Ron Takaki, "A Different Mirror," in *Rereading America*, 4th edition, edited by Gary Columbo, Robert Cullen, and Bonnie Lisle (Boston: Bedford, 1998), p. 555.

2. Douglas Kellner, "Cultural Studies, Multiculturalism and Media Culture," in *Gender, Race, and Class in Media*, edited by Gail Dines and Jean M. Humez (Thousand Oaks, California: Sage Publications, 1995), p. 8.

3. Laura Mulvey, "Visual Pleasure and Narrative Cinema," in *Film and Theory: An Anthology*, edited by Robert Stam and Toby Miller (Malden, Massachusetts: Blackwell Publishers, 2000), p. 486.

4. Joseph M. Boggs and Dennis W. Petrie, *The Art of Watching Films* (Boston: McGraw-Hill, 2004), p. 440.

5. Rita Kempley, "Hangin' with the Homeboys," *Washington Post* (September 27, 1991), www.washingtonpost.com.

6. Roger Ebert, "Hangin' with the Homeboys," *Chicago Sun-Times* (September 27, 1991), www.suntimes.com.

7. Sharon Willis, *High Contrast: Race and Gender in Contemporary Hollywood Films* (Durham: Duke University Press, 1997), p. 56.

8. Chuck Berg, quoted in Boggs and Petrie, p. 441.

9. Richard Majors and Janet Mancini Billson, *Cool Pose: The Dilemmas of Black Manhood in America* (New York: Touchstone, 1992), p. 92.

10. Robert A. Strikwerda and Larry May, "Male Friendship and Intimacy," in *Rethinking Masculinity*, 2nd edition, edited by Larry May, Robert A. Strikwerda, and Patrick D. Hopkins (Lanham, Maryland: Rowman & Littlefield, 1996), pp. 81–82.

11. Krin Gabbard, "Someone Is Going to Pay: Resurgent White Masculinity in *Ransom*," in *Masculinity: Bodies, Movies, Culture*, edited by Peter Lehman (New York: Routledge, 2001), p. 15.

12. Melvin Donalson, *Black Directors in Hollywood* (Austin: University of Texas Press, 2003), p. 141.

13. Harry M. Benshoff and Sean Griffin, *America on Film: Representing Race, Class, Gender, and Sexuality at the Movies* (Malden, Massachusetts: Blackwell Publishing, 2004), p. 237.

14. Michael Eric Dyson, *Holler If You Hear Me: Searching for Tupac Shakur* (New York: Basic Civitas, 2001), p. 62.

15. Hernan Vera and Andrew M. Gordon, *Screen Saviors: Hollywood Fictions of Whiteness* (Lanham, Maryland: Rowman & Littlefield, 2003), p. 180.

16. Cyrus Purnell, "*Money Talks* Cashes in on Buddy Genre," *The Daily Beacon* (September 5, 1997), www.dailybeacon.utk.edu.

17. Willis, pp. 41–42.

18. Marsha Kinder, "Violence American Style: The Narrative Orchestration of Violent Attractions," in *Violence and American Cinema*, edited by J. David Slocum (New York: Routledge, 2001), p. 179.

19. Andrew Kimbrell, *The Masculine Mystique: The Politics of Masculinity* (New York: Ballantine Books, 1995), p. 74.

20. bell hooks, *Black Looks: Race and Representation* (Boston, Massachusetts: South End Press, 1992), p. 90.

21. Peter X Feng, *Identities in Motion: Asian American Film and Video* (Durham, North Carolina: Duke University Press, 2002), p. 154.

22. Lillian B. Rubin, "The Approach-Avoidance Dance: Men, Women, and Intimacy," in *Men's Lives*, 5th edition, edited by Michael S. Kimmel and Michael A. Messner (Boston: Allyn and Bacon, 2001), p. 357.

23. Gina Marchetti, "They Worship Money and Prejudice," in *Classic Hollywood, Classic Whiteness*, edited by Daniel Bernardi (Minneapolis: University of Minnesota Press, 2001), p. 76.

24. Donalson, p. 308.

25. Jerome Hillman, "Love in Male Friendship," in *To Be a Man*, edited by Keith Thompson (Los Angeles: Tarcher, 1991), p. 228.

26. Wensley Clarkson, *John Travolta: Back in Character* (Woodstock, New York: Overlook Press, 1997), pp. 233–234.

Chapter Six

1. Peter Lehman, *Running Scared: Masculinity and the Representation of the Male Body* (Philadelphia: Temple University Press, 1993), p. 71.

2. Cornel West, "Black Sexuality: The Taboo Subject," in *Traps: African American Men on Gender and Sexuality*, edited by Rudolph P. Byrd (Bloomington: Indiana University Press, 2001), p. 304.

3. Michael S. Kimmel, *Gendered Society*, 2nd edition (New York: Oxford University Press, 2004), p. 184.

4. Marlon Riggs, "Black Macho Revisited," in *Traps: African American Men on Gender and Sexuality*, edited by Rudolph P. Byrd and Beverly Guy-Sheftall(Bloomington: Indiana University Press, 2001), p. 296.

5. William H. Phillips, *Film: An Introduction*, 2nd edition (Boston: Bedford, 2002), p. 235.

6. Yvonne Tasker, "Fists of Fury: Discourses of Race and Masculinity in the Martial Arts Cinema," in *Race and the Subject of Masculinities* (Durham, North Carolina: Duke University Press, 1997), p. 331.

7. Richard Dyer, *White* (London: Routledge, 1997), p. 25.

8. Roger Ebert, *Roger Ebert's Movie Yearbook 2003* (Kansas City: Andrews McMeel Publishing, 2003), pp. 443–444.

9. Richard Majors and Janet Mancini Billson, *Cool Pose: The Dilemmas of Black Manhood in America* (New York: Touchstone, 1992), p. 4.

10. Peter Lyman, "The Fraternal Bond as a Joking Relationship: A Case of the Role of Sexist Jokes in Male Group Bonding," in *Men's Lives*, 5th edition, edited by Michael S. Kimmel and Michael A. Messner (Boston: Allyn and Bacon, 2001), p. 158.

11. Louis Gianetti, *Understanding Movies*, 10th edition (Upper Saddle River, New Jersey: Pearson/Prentice Hall, 2005), p. 271.

12. Todd Boyd, "The Day the Niggaz Took Over: Basketball, Commodity Culture, and Black Masculinity," in *Out of Bounds: Sports, Media, and the Politics of Identity*, edited by Aaron Baker and Todd Boyd (Bloomington: Indiana University Press, 1997), p. 133.

13. Clara E. Rodriguez, *Heroes, Lovers, and Others: The Story of Latinos in Hollywood* (Washington: Smithsonian Books, 2004), pp. 2–3.

Bibliography

*The abbreviation MHL/MPA indicates materials researched
in the Archival Files, Margaret Herrick Library, The
Motion Picture Academy, Beverly Hills, California.*

Auster, Al, and Leonard Quart. "The Working Class Goes to Hollywood: 'F.I.S.T.' and 'Blue Collar.'" *Cineaste*, Volume IX, Number 1 (Fall 1978): 4–7.

Basinger, Jeanine. *American Cinema: One Hundred Years of Filmmaking.* New York: Rizzoli Int'l Publications, 1994.

Bate, Barbara, and Judy Bowker. *Communication and the Sexes.* 2nd edition. Prospect Heights, Illinois: Waveland Press, 1997.

Baxter, John. "John Ford." *The St. James Film Directors Encyclopedia.* Edited by Andrew Sarris, 172–176. Detroit: Visible Ink Press, 1998.

Beavers, Herman. "The Cool Pose: Intersectionality, Masculinity, and Quiescence in the Comedy and Films of Richard Pryor and Eddie Murphy." *Race and the Subject of Masculinities.* Edited by Harry Stecopoulos and Michael Uebel, 253–285. Durham, North Carolina: Duke University Press, 1997.

Belton, John. *American Cinema/American Culture.* New York: McGraw-Hill, 1992.

Bennett, Lerone, Jr. *Before the Mayflower: A History of Black America.* 6th edition. New York: Penguin Books, 1988.

Benshoff, Harry M., and Sean Griffin. *America on Film: Representing Race, Class, Gender, and Sexuality at the Movies.* Malden, Massachusetts: Blackwell Publishing, 2004.

Bingham, Dennis. *Acting Masculine: Masculinities in the Films of James Stewart, Jack Nicholson, and Clint Eastwood.* New Brunswick, New Jersey: Rutgers University Press, 1994.

Biskind, Peter. *Easy Rider, Raging Bulls.* New York: Touchstone, 1999.

Blum, Deborah. "The Gender Blur: Where Does Biology End and Society Take Over?" *Signs of Life in the USA: Readings on Popular Culture for Writers.* 3rd edition. Edited by Sonia Maasik and Jack Solomon, 453–459. Boston: Bedford Books, 2000.

Bly, Robert. "What Men Really Want." *To Be a Man.* Edited by Keith Thompson, 16–23. Los Angeles: Tarcher, 1991.

Boggs, James M., and Dennis W. Petrie. *The Art of Watching Films.* Boston: McGraw-Hill, 2004.

Bogle, Donald. *Toms, Coons, Mulattoes, Mammies, and Bucks.* New York: Continuum, 1990.

Boyd, Todd. "The Day the Niggaz Took Over: Basketball, Commodity Culture, and Black

Masculinity." *Out of Bounds: Sports, Media, and the Politics of Identity.* Edited by Aaron Baker and Todd Boyd, 123–142. Bloomington: Indiana University Press, 1997.

Browne, Nick, editor. *Refiguring American Film Genres: History and Theory.* Berkeley: University of California Press, 1998.

Buck Benny Rides Again. Press Booklet. Paramount Pictures MHL/MPA.

Clarkson, Wensley. *John Travolta: Back in Character.* Woodstock, New York: Overlook Press, 1997.

Cohan, Steven. *Masked Men: Masculinity and the Movies in the Fifties.* Bloomington: Indiana University Press, 1997.

Cook, David A. *Lost Illusions: American Cinema in the Shadow of Watergate and Vietnam, 1970–1979.* Volume 9. The History of the American Cinema Series. New York: Charles Scribner's Sons, 2000.

Crowther, Bosley. "Home of the Brave." *The New York Times Film Reviews.* May 13, 1949, 29:1.

Curtis, Brandon. "Hamburger Hill." *Washington Post*, May 30, 2002.

"David Harum." *Variety*, March 6, 1934, MHL/MPA.

"David Priest." *Variety*, October 16, 1934, MHL/MPA.

Denby, David. "Movies Americana." *The Atlantic*, March 1971, 106–108.

Donalson, Melvin. *Black Directors in Hollywood.* Austin: The University of Texas Press, 2003.

DuBois, W. E. B. *The Souls of Black Folks.* Edited by Henry Louis Gates Jr. and Terri Hume Oliver. New York: Norton, 1999.

Dyer, Richard. *White.* London: Routledge, 1997.

Dyson, Michael Eric. *Holler If You Hear Me: Searching for Tupac Shakur.* New York: Basic Civitas, 2001.

Ebert, Robert. "Hangin' with the Homeboys." *Chicago Sun-Times*, www.suntimes.com, September 27, 1991.

_____. "Lethal Weapon." *Chicago Sun-Times*, www.suntimes.com, March 6, 1987.

_____. *Roger Ebert's Movie Yearbook 2003.* Kansas City: Andrews McMeel Publishing, 2003.

"The Empire Strikes Back." Salon.com, May 13, 1999.

Feng, Peter X. *Identities in Motion: Asian American Film and Video.* Durham, North Carolina: Duke University Press, 2002.

"Fox's 'David Harum' a 'Dud.'" *Hollywood Reporter,* February 15, 1934, MHL/MPA.

Fuchs, Cynthia J. "The Buddy Politic." *Screening the Male: Explorations of Masculinities in Hollywood Cinema.* Edited by Steven Cohan and Ina Rae Hark, 194–210. New York: Routledge, 1993.

Gabbard, Krin. "Someone Is Going to Pay: Resurent White Masculinity in *Ransom.*" *Masculinity: Bodies, Movies, Culture.* Edited by Peter Lehman, 7–23. New York: Routledge, 2001.

Gehring, Wes D., editor. *Handbook of American Film Genres.* Westport, Connecticut: Greenwood Press, 1988.

Gianetti, Louis. *Understanding Movies.* 10th edition. Upper Saddle River, New Jersey: Pearson/Prentice Hall, 2005.

Guerrero, Ed. "The Black Image in Protective Custody: Hollywood's Biracial Buddy Films of the Eighties." *Black American Cinema.* Edited by Manthia Diawara, 237–246. New York: Routledge, 1993.

_____. *Framing Blackness: The African American Image in Film.* Philadelphia: Temple University Press, 1993.

Hall, Stuart. "What Is the 'Black' in Black Popular Culture?" *The Black Studies Reader.* Edited by Jacqueline Bobo, Cynthia Hudley, and Claudine Michel, 255–263. New York: Routledge, 2004.

Halliwell, Leslie. *Halliwell's Film Guide*, 7th edition. New York: Harper and Row, 1989.

Harrison, P. S., editor. "Home of the Brave." *Harrison's Reports*, May 7, 1949.

_____, editor. "'Steamboat Round the Bend' with Will Rogers." *Harrison Reports*, September 7, 1935.

Hillman, Jerome. "Love in Male Friendship." *To Be a Man*. Edited by Keith Thompson, 228–230. Los Angeles: Tarcher, 1991.

Hills, Beverly. "Harum, Scare 'Em, Hepburn." *Liberty*, MHL/MPA.

Hirayama, Ruth L. "Rocky II." *Magill's Survey of Cinema*, Second Series, Volume 5, edited by Frank N. Magill. Englewood Cliffs, New Jersey: Salem Press, 1981: 2041–2043.

hooks, bell. *Black Looks: Race and Representation*. Boston, Massachusetts: South End Press, 1992.

Kael, Pauline. "The Current Cinema." *The New Yorker*, January 17, 1977, 98–100.

Kaminsky, Stuart M. *American Film Genre: Approaches to a Critical Theory of Popular Film*. New York: Dell, 1977.

Kaufmann, Stanley. "Arts and Lives." *The New Republic*, September 20, 1977, 24–25.

Kellner, Douglas. "Cultural Studies, Multiculturalism and Media Culture." *Gender, Race, and Class in Media*. Edited by Gail Dines and Jean M. Humez, 5–17. Thousand Oaks, California: Sage Publications, 1995.

Kempley, Rita. "Bat 21." *Washington Post*, October 21, 1988.

_____. "Hangin' with the Homeboys." *Washington Post*, www.washingtonpost.com, September 27, 1991.

Kimbrell, Andrew. *The Masculine Mystique: The Politics of Masculinity*. New York: Ballantine Books, 1995.

Kimmel, Michael. *The Gendered Society*. 2nd edition. New York: Oxford University Press, 2004.

_____. *Manhood in America: A Cultural History*. New York: The Free Press, 1996.

Kinder, Marsha. "Violence American Style: The Narrative Orchestration of Violent Attractions." *Violence and American Cinema*. Edited by J. David Slocum, 63–100. New York: Routledge, 2001.

Kolker, Robert. *Film, Form, and Culture*. New York: McGraw-Hill, 2002.

Lehman, Peter. *Running Scared: Masculinity and the Representation of the Male Body*. Philadelphia: Temple University Press, 1993.

Lyman, Peter. "The Fraternal Bond as a Joking Relationship: A Case of the Role of Sexist Jokes in Male Group Bonding." *Men's Lives*. 5th edition. Edited by Michael S. Kimmel and Michael A. Messner, 157–166. Boston: Allyn and Bacon, 2001.

Majors, Richard, and Janet Mancini Billson. *Cool Pose: The Dilemmas of Black Manhood in America*. New York: Touchstone, 1992.

Marchetti, Gina. "They Worship Money and Prejudice." *Classic Hollywood, Classic Whiteness*. Edited by Daniel Bernardi, 72–91. Minneapolis: University of Minnesota Press, 2001.

Miller, Tim. "Suck, Spit, Chew, Swallow: A Performative Exploration of Men's Bodies." *Masculinity: Bodies, Movies, Culture*. Edited by Peter Lehman. New York: Routledge, 2001: 279–299.

Mitchell, Lee Clark. *Westerns: Making the Man in Fiction and Film*. Chicago: The University of Chicago Press, 1996.

Mulvey, Laura. "Visual Pleasure and Narrative Cinema." *Film and Theory: An Anthology*. Edited by Robert Stam and Toby Miller, 483–489. Malden, Massachusetts: Blackwell Publishers, 2000.

Nash, Gary, editor. *The American People: Creating a New Nation and a Society*, Volume II. 4th Edition. New York: Longman, 1998.

Neale, Steve. *Genre and Hollywood*. London: Routledge, 2000.

Null, Christopher. "Police Academy." FilmCritic.com, August 5, 2004.

Parish, James Robert, and George H. Hill. *Black Action Films*. Jefferson, North Carolina: McFarland, 1989.

Phillips, William H. *Film: An Introduction*. 2nd edition. Boston: Bedford, 2002.

Poitier, Sidney. *The Measure of a Man*. San Francisco: HarperCollins, 2000.

Purnell, Cyrus. "*Money Talks* Cashes in on Buddy Genre." *The Daily Beacon*, www.dailybeacon.utk.edu, September 5, 1997.

Reid, Mark A. *Redefining Black Film*. Berkeley: University of California Press, 1993.

Riggs, Marlon. "Black Macho Revisited." *Traps: African American Men on Gender and Sexuality*. Edited by Rudolph P. Byrd and Beverly Guy-Sheftall, 292–296. Bloomington: Indiana University Press, 2001.

Rodriguez, Clara E. *Heroes, Lovers, and Others: The Story of Latinos in Hollywood*. Washington: Smithsonian Books, 2004.

Rubin, Lillian B. "The Approach-Avoidance Dance: Men, Women, and Intimacy." *Men's Lives*. 5th edition. Edited by Michael S. Kimmel and Michael A. Messner, 353–358. Boston: Allyn and Bacon, 2001.

Strikwerda, Robert A., and Larry May. "Male Friendship and Intimacy." *Rethinking Masculinity: Philosophical Explorations in Light of Feminism*. 2nd edition. Edited by Larry May, Robert A. Strikwerda, and Patrick D. Hopkins, 79–94. Lanham, Maryland: Rowman & Littlefield, 1996.

Studlar, Gaylyn. *This Mad Masquerade: Stardom and Masculinity in the Jazz Age*. New York: Columbia University Press, 1996.

Takaki, Ron. "A Different Mirror." *Rereading America*. 4th edition. Edited by Gary Columbo, Robert Cullen, and Bonnie Lisle, 538–555. Boston: Bedford, 1998.

Tasker, Yvonne. "Fists of Fury: Discourses of Race and Masculinity in the Martial Arts Cinema." *Race and the Subject of Masculinities*. Durham, North Carolina: Duke University Press, 1997.

Thompson, Cooper. "A New Visions of Masculinity." *Race, Class, and Gender in the United States*. 5th edition. Edited by Paula S. Rothenberg, 630–636. New York: Worth Publishers, 2001.

Ulmer, John. "Police Academy." www.movie-vault.com, August 5, 2004.

Vazquez, Carmen. "Appearances." *Rereading America*. 5th edition. Edited by Gary Columbo, Bonnie Lisle, and Robert Cullen, 492–499. Boston: Bedford Books, 2001.

Vera, Hernan, and Andrew M. Gordon. *Screen Saviors: Hollywood Fictions of Whiteness*. Lanham, Maryland: Rowman & Littlefield, 2003.

Watkins, S. Craig. "Ghetto Reelness: Hollywood Film Production, Black Popular Culture and the Ghetto Action Film Cycle." *Genre and Contemporary Hollywood*. Edited by Steve Neale, 236–250. London: British Film Institute, 2002.

Wiegman, Robyn. "Bonds of (in)Difference." *The Masculinity Studies Reader*. Edited by Rachel Adams and David Savran, 201–225. Malden, Massachusetts: Blackwell, 2002.

West, Cornel. "Black Sexuality: The Taboo Subject." *Traps: African American Men on Gender and Sexuality*. Edited by Rudolph P. Byrd and Beverly Guy-Sheftall, 301–307. Bloomington: Indiana University Press, 2001.

Willis, Sharon. *High Contrast: Race and Gender in Contemporary Hollywood Film*. Durham, North Carolina: Duke University Press, 1997.

Zimmerman, Paul. "Kung Foolish." *Newsweek*, April 7, 1975, 82–83.

Index

Numbers in **bold italics** indicate photographs